SPECTACULAR
SISTERHOOD
OF
SUPERWOMEN

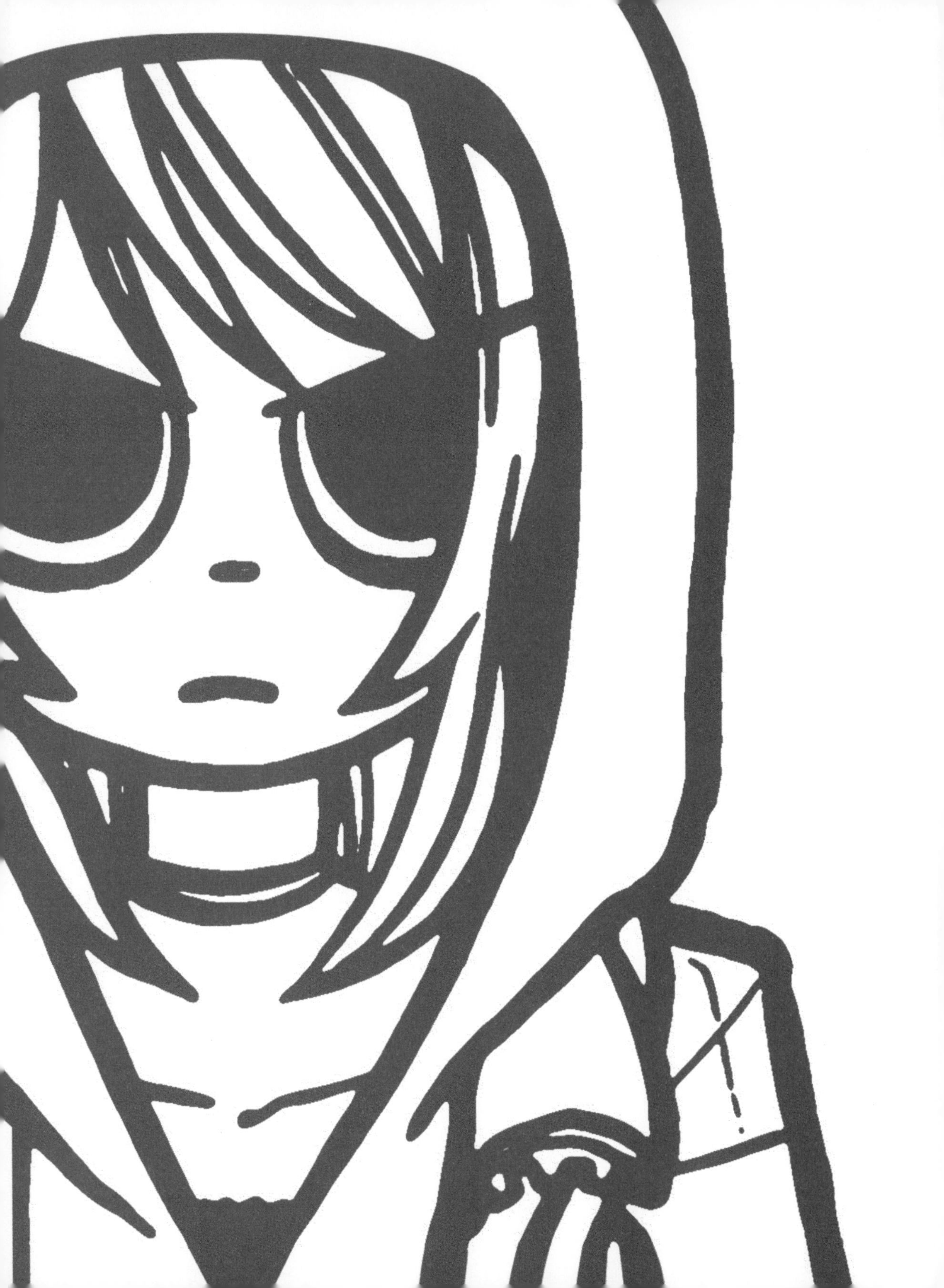

SPECTACULAR SISTERHOOD OF SUPERWOMEN

AWESOME FEMALE CHARACTERS FROM COMIC BOOK HISTORY

HOPE NICHOLSON

QUIRK BOOKS

PHILADELPHIA

Library of Congress Cataloging in Publication
Number: 2016946306

ISBN: 978-1-59474-948-3

Printed in China
Typeset in ARB 66 Neon Block, Avenir, and Garamond
Designed by Timothy O'Donnell
Production management by John J. McGurk

Quirk Books
215 Church Street
Philadelphia, PA 19106
quirkbooks.com

10 9 8 7 6 5 4 3 2 1

TO MY PARENTS,
JIM AND KAREN NICHOLSON,
WHO OPENED THEIR HOME TO ME
SO I COULD MAKE THIS BOOK

TABLE OF CONTENTS

Introduction 8

1

The 1930s: Birth of an Industry **12**

The Magician from Mars 14
Olga Mesmer 15
Sally the Sleuth 17
Torchy Brown 20
Icon of the Decade: Little Lulu 22

2

The 1940s: The Golden Age **26**

Black Cat 28
Gail Porter: Girl Photographer 30
Gale Allen and the Girl Squadron 31
Katy Keene 33
Madame Strange 34
Maureen Marine 36
Miss Fury 37
Señorita Rio 39
Starr Flag, Undercover Girl 40
Ultra Violet 43
The Wing 44
Icon of the Decade: Wonder Woman 46

3

The 1950s: Comics Code Crackdown **50**

Black Phantom 52
G.I. Jane 54
Gail Ford, Girl Friday 55
Jetta Raye 57
Lucy the Real Gone Gal 58
Man Huntin' Minnie of Delta Pu 59
Nurse Helen Grant 62
The Old Witch 63
Starlight 65
Tomboy 67
Wendy the Good Little Witch 68
Icon of the Decade: Supergirl 70

4

The 1960s: Superheroes Return **74**

Angel O'Day 76
Barbarella 77
Bikini Luv 79
Bunny Ball 81
Mystra and Dragonella 83
Nurse Betsy Crane 85
Pussycat 86
'Scot 88
Sue and Sally Smith, Flying Nurses 89
Tiffany Sinn 90
Vampirella 92
Icon of the Decade: Batgirl 96

5

The 1970s: Underground Comix Rise **100**

Friday Foster 102
Frieda Phelps 104
Laura Chandler 105
Leetah 107
Page Peterson 109
Pauline Peril 110
Pudge, Girl Blimp 113
Starfire 116
Superbitch 118
Survivalwoman 119
Zelda the Witch 121
Icon of the Decade: Ms. Marvel (Carol Danvers) . . . 124

6

The 1980s: Black-and-White Boom (and Bust) **128**

Amanda Waller 130
Cutey Bunny 132
Dakota North 133
Dazzler 135
Fashion in Action 138
Ginger Fox 139
Maggie Chascarrillo 141
Ms. Tree 143
Sindi Shade 145
Sunflower 147
Vanity 149
Icon of the Decade: Silk Spectre 152

7

The 1990s: "Comics Aren't Just for Kids" **156**

American Woman 158
Bitchy Bitch (and Bitchy Butch) 160
The Girl 161
The Jaguar 163
Jain 164
Jink 166
Liliane 169
Martha Washington 170
Scary Godmother 173
Simone Cundy 174
Squirrel Girl 175
Icon of the Decade: Witchblade 178

8

The 2000s: Webcomics and Comic-Cons **182**

Annabelle 184
Didi (Désirée Chastel) 185
Empowered 186
Jalisco 188
Jamie McJack 190
Jessica Jones 191
Nibbil 195
Rose Harvestar 197
The Saucy Mermaid 198
Street Angel 200
Xavin 202
Icon of the Decade: Ramona Flowers 204

9

The 2010s: Digital and Diverse **208**

Bandette 210
Beth Ross 212
Blaze 214
Bold Riley 216
Callie 218
Deathface Ginny 219
Gwen Dylan 221
Kath, Raven, and Angie 223
Keegan 224
Maika Halfwolf 225
Penny Rolle 228
Icon of the Decade: Ms. Marvel (Kamala Khan) . . . 230

Index 232
Art Credits 238
Acknowledgments 240

INTRODUCTION

Hello, and welcome to the definitive guide to female representation in comics!

Wait, that's not right . . .

Hello, and welcome to the most popular female characters in American and Canadian comics!

Hmm . . . still not quite it.

Hello, and welcome to the best female characters in comics?

Oh no, absolutely not.

Hello, and welcome to the weirdest, coolest, most of-their-time female characters in comics—for better or for worse.

Yes, now *that's* it!

Female protagonists in the world of comics sure have come a long way. And not always in the direction you'd expect. We went from stories featuring Lois Lane, a capable female reporter who cared more about a sense of duty than determining the kissing skills of a dude who wore underwear over his tights to tales of Lois, now starry eyed, marrying said dude decades later. We went from an Amazon princess teaching our world about the power of peaceful resolution and feminist sisterhood to a solitary warrior who makes out with Superman. (What? It's okay. He wasn't married to Lois Lane anymore.)

Yet this is not a book telling you that things were better back then . . .

We have come a long way. We've gone from having 90 percent of comics created by white men to a thriving industry of comics in all sorts of formats created by all sorts of people. And that's changing the characters we grow up with and love dearly—for the better. Today we don't just have comics about romance, or adventures, or superheroes, but also comics about the absurdities of daily life, the politics of surviving, and the vast diversity of people who are more representative of the world we live in than ever before. All of these changes are necessary and noteworthy.

We've also gone from being able to find comics only on racks in drugstores to venturing into a wide range of weird and wonderful shops and conventions to score our monthly installments. Graphic novels now take their rightful place in bookstores, and webcomics are accessible to anyone with an internet connection. And through the beauty of crowdfunding platforms, the power of publishing has migrated directly into the hands of comics creators of all kinds.

But along with all these advances, I fear we may be forgetting our history. We often fail to mention and honor all the amazing comics that have been made, comics that fought the status quo. We forget the history of subversive comics from decades past. We forget the trends in comics that defined each decade and entertained our parents, our grandparents, and, for some of you young'uns, your great-grandparents. We forget the long history of passionate female fans who have been fighting for respect since the beginning of the medium. We forget the female creators who gritted their teeth and rolled their eyes while playing in the boys' club; refusing to give up, they pushed up their sleeves and went to work all the same.

This book is a history of comics, though it's not a definitive one. It's told through female characters not only because they're easily lost to the sands of time, but also because they're usually much more interesting than their male counterparts. In no other comics history book will you find characters like Maureen Marine, an underwater preteen princess; Starlight the brave Huron warrior; Pudge, Girl Blimp, fighting to find her identity in 1960s San Francisco; Sindi Shade, a punk-rock rebel in a dystopian future; or Bitchy Bitch, a straw feminist parody. But you'll find them here.

These characters represent the many and varied changes the industry has gone through since the rise of the comic book in the 1940s. In these pages you'll find superpowered heroes in tights, plucky girl reporters, scantily clad bad girls, polyamorous florists, sexy horror hosts, and many more. You'll read about characters whose stories highlight the trends of their times, with special attention to those most likely to be forgotten, along with spotlights on a few who fought tooth and nail to remain well known.

These characters are here to guide you through the past eight decades of confusing, maddening, and entertaining comics history.

So come, let's start at the very beginning . . .

CHAPTER

1

the

19

30s

BIRTH OF AN INDUSTRY

$\longrightarrow$

THE 1930s

Sequential visual storytelling has existed for centuries, so the birth of comics cannot be traced back to a specific event. The line between illustrated stories and comic books is blurry, with comics gradually becoming a distinct storytelling format over a decades-long process. Comic books—that is, bundled pages of sequential art—date back to at least the mid-1800s. But it was in the 1930s that Superman debuted, and with that appearance came a raging excitement for comic books that solidified both the comics medium and the superhero genre (the two are inextricably intertwined).

Many of the first comic books were born from newspaper comic strips. Little Lulu was one, and her adventures were simple yet profound: she was a spunky forthright girl who took no flak from anyone. Other comics characters came from the opposite end of the medium—instead of being drawn from all-ages family-friendly comic strips, they started in the seedy underbelly of pulp anthologies. Action-adventure, science-fiction, Western, and crime comics all sprang from the pages of pulp magazines and later became staple genres of comic books produced by publishers like Marvel and DC. In the pulps you could read prose stories next to strips starring such characters as Olga Mesmer, Sally the Sleuth, Diana Daw, Polly of the Plains, and Betty Blake. Few of these characters made the transition to full-blown comics. (The exception was Sally the Sleuth, and it took her almost twenty years to do so.) The sources may have been salacious, but surprisingly they did have a moral code. Artists were not allowed to depict fully nude women or men, but naked female corpses were okay (hey, we're not saying it was a good moral code).

On the even seedier side of that spectrum were the crudely drawn "Tijuana bibles" passed around in men's clubs. These featured favorite comic characters, everybody from Blondie to Dick Tracy, involved in detailed sexual activities. This was the NC-17 fanfiction, if you will, of the 1930s.

After the premiere of Superman in *Action Comics* #1, in 1938, the single-issue comics format (previously relegated to detective stories, wholesome adventure comics, and newspaper reprints) exploded in popularity. Soon comic books of all genres were available on newsstands. Each issue typically featured a varied selection of adventures, evidence that every publisher was looking for that magical character that kids would cling to. And yes, many of these characters were women. In *Amazing Man*, we meet Super Ann, endowed with the power of ten men! Other comics had heroes like Neptina, a sometimes cruel undersea queen! Flyin' Jenny, aerial ace! And of course Sheena, Queen of the Jungle! In the 1930s, before comics had a chance to cement themselves into genres, female characters enjoyed a variety of careers and roles.

About the women who worked in comics during this decade, little is known. However, we do know that some creators, such as Jackie Ormes, the creator of Torchy Brown (page 20), were getting their start.

The 1930s also saw the beginnings of fan conventions, which were not yet comics focused but were connected mostly to science fiction. Women were active in this community, as organizers, essay writers, and fans. Myrtle Douglas, aka Morojo, was a well-known fanzine editor and designer of some of the first costumes for fan conventions. She's sometimes called "the mother of cosplay" for her role in encouraging and promoting fan culture and engagement.

Bottom line: although comics had been around for a while, the 1930s saw the birth of the industry in a chaotic and varied form. And women as creators, fans, and characters were there right from the start. ⚡

THE MAGICIAN FROM MARS	Half-Martian visitor whose whims become reality	**❝I can destroy time and space!❞**
		Created by: John Giunta and Malcolm Kildale
		First appearance: *Amazing-Man Comics #7* (Centaur Comics, 1939)

Predating Miss Fury, Fantomah, Wonder Woman, and most better-known superheroines, Jane 6EM35 is a sci-fi hero in the far future. Born to a human mother and a Martian father, she might have been just like any other half-Martian child were it not for an incident that occurred shortly after her birth. A nurse exposed the infant to cathode rays, causing Jane's genes to mutate and granting her special powers: anything she wishes for appears out of thin air.

In addition to wishing stuff into existence, Jane also possesses incredible strength, fantastic intelligence, immortality, and (of course) eternal youth and beauty. Though she can have anything in the world, her greatest desire—to visit her mother's homeland of Earth—remains out of reach. Her aunt forbids it and Jane can't bring herself to disobey her dear, sweet, elderly aunt . . . until her aunt locks her in a steel room. Then Jane says, "Well, I guess that's enough of that," steals a rocket ship, and gets the heck out of Martian-Dodge.

In her first adventure, Jane saves an entire spaceship, steals all its gold, and sends the haul to Earth, specifically to aid a renowned pediatrician and his quest to cure infant paralysis. (Though truth be told she keeps a little gold for herself so she can live comfortably. I mean, she's not Superman; she doesn't want to *work* for a living.) Exploring her new world, Jane helps the less fortunate, catches suicide jumpers in midair, halts air-trains from derailing, stops runaway bulls, and gives lectures to unethical criminals everywhere. She knows the difference between a desperate man driven to rob (and turns his life around with a gift of money) and a corrupt politician exploiting the working class (whose only gift from Jane is a sock in the kisser). But at times she still acts pettily: when an irate hotel guest demands ink for his pen, an annoyed Jane fills the lobby with ink.

When the Magician from Mars was created, standards for comic book superheroes had not yet been established. If these characters were a form of wish fulfillment, why not have a hero who possesses every possible superpower? These were, after all, the days before Superman had his kryptonite weakness. Of course, even Superman didn't have the godlike powers of Jane 6EM35. She soon found herself fighting increasingly powerful enemies; in one tale Jane conquers the literal embodiment of fear with the power of song. When Earth can no longer contain enough adventures, Jane sets off into space in pursuit of the scientific genius villain named the Hood, the one person powerful enough to defeat Jane. Who is revealed to be . . . her own elderly aunt!

The Magician from Mars was crudely drawn and scripted, but as a series it holds a great deal of charm and wish fulfillment. This action-packed comic is absolutely ridiculous, and awfully fun.

ESSENTIAL READING: You can follow Jane's final adventure in the reprint collection *Divas, Dames & Daredevils* (Exterminating Angel Press, 2013).

OLGA MESMER	A super-strong and feisty half-Venusian adventuress . . . and just maybe the first superheroine in comics	**"**Powers which were dormant throughout her childhood burst into light once she is aroused!**"**
		Created by: Watt Dell
		First appearance: *Spicy Mystery Stories* (Culture Publications, September 1937)

Who was the first female superhero? The answer is muddied because the superhero genre didn't come into being all at once (though after his appearance, Superman definitely became the standard for superhero comics). Superheroes might have capes and masks, but they might not. Is wearing a costume necessary to be a superhero? What about having powers? Is Batman a superhero, or is he just a masked adventurer? Do superheroes need to be dedicated to fighting crime? Until the tropes we know today were cemented, early superhero stories blurred the line between adventure, fantasy, and science fiction. Which is why Olga Mesmer is sometimes called the first superhero in comics, though she doesn't really fight crime at all.

THE ASTOUNDING ADVENTURES OF
OLGA MESMER

OLGA, ROD and SHAG run abruptly from the scene of the revolt of the Sitnaltans in an effort to find a long-hidden electric gun.

Her X-ray eyes enable OLGA to find the crypt in which it has been stored, and they find the outfit complete, except for a necessary ground cable. Shag offers to use his body for the contact.

VILE OMBO TAKE QUEEN AWAY?

NO, SHE'S STILL SAFE, THANK GOD!

But while these three assemble the ray-gun, Ombo and his rebels are gaining ground.

YOU MARGOT! SPEAK NOW! SAY OMBO YOUR KING!

NO? THEN YOU BE SLAVE!

... an eerie silence sweeps the ranks of Ombo's men: "Quietus!"—

KWA EE-TOOS!

KWA EE TOOS!

THE LONG-SLEEP GUN!

50

Olga Mesmer was the daughter of an immortal Venusian named Margot and a mortal human scientist, Dr. Hugo Mesmer. Olga's mother abandoned her, faking her own death after killing Olga's father upon discovering his infidelity with the X-ray vision he gave her. Raised by her guardian Hugh Rankin, Olga possesses supernatural strength, hypnotic powers, and X-ray vision. When Rankin reveals that he wants her to sleep with him, Olga sets out on her own. She gains a sidekick in the form of Rodney Prescott, to whom she grants some of her powers via a blood transfusion.

Olga has no costume, and no desire to fight crime, but is thrown into fantastical adventures one after the other. Is she a superhero if her adventures occur by happenstance? If so, Olga predates even Superman as an early comics hero. If not, she's still a powerful example of an ambitious female character.

In reality, Olga was never meant to be an inspirational figure. Her story appeared in a saucy men's pulp magazine (a sibling publication to Sally the Sleuth's *Spicy Detective Stories*, below). The content was designed primarily to titillate, rather than to represent a fully rounded woman. Well, Olga was round in certain ways, that's for sure, and often her adventures led to her outfits being ripped enough to see just how much.

Nevertheless, Olga was in charge of her world, and she wasn't at the mercy of male counterparts. We could do a lot worse for the first superheroine (though we could do a bit better too).

ESSENTIAL READING: No collection of Olga Mesmer strips has been published, but two have appeared in the Adventure House reprints *Spicy Mystery Stories 10/37* and *Spicy Mystery Stories 2/38*.

SALLY THE SLEUTH	Saucy sex symbol turned hard-boiled detective	"Gee Chief, I've heard of some girls liking to be whipped, but I'll take vanilla!"
		Created by: Adolphe Barreaux
		First appearance: *Spicy Detective Stories* (Culture Publications, Nov. 1934)

Arguably the first female detective in comics, Sally the Sleuth has a strange history, evolving from a nudie girl in distress to a business-suit-wearing power detective a decade later.

Like Olga Mesmer (page 15), Sally premiered in a scandalous pulp series published by Culture Publications, which offered a mix of comics and prose fiction. In strictly formatted two-page, twelve-panel adventures, Sally would be pitted against dangerous criminals on the orders of her private detective boss.

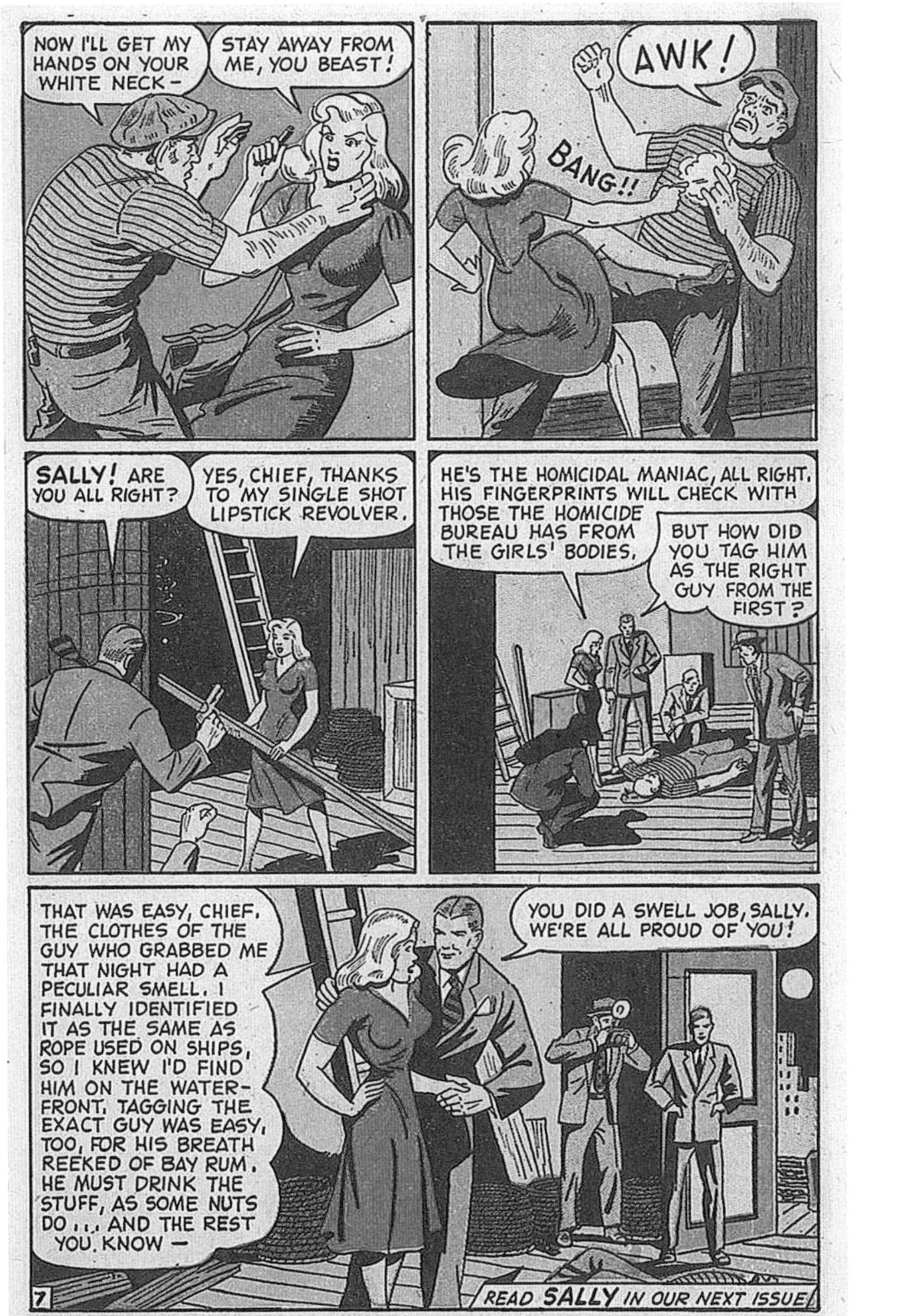
NOW I'LL GET MY HANDS ON YOUR WHITE NECK –
STAY AWAY FROM ME, YOU BEAST!
AWK!
BANG!!
SALLY! ARE YOU ALL RIGHT?
YES, CHIEF, THANKS TO MY SINGLE SHOT LIPSTICK REVOLVER.
HE'S THE HOMICIDAL MANIAC, ALL RIGHT. HIS FINGERPRINTS WILL CHECK WITH THOSE THE HOMICIDE BUREAU HAS FROM THE GIRLS' BODIES.
BUT HOW DID YOU TAG HIM AS THE RIGHT GUY FROM THE FIRST?
THAT WAS EASY, CHIEF. THE CLOTHES OF THE GUY WHO GRABBED ME THAT NIGHT HAD A PECULIAR SMELL. I FINALLY IDENTIFIED IT AS THE SAME AS ROPE USED ON SHIPS, SO I KNEW I'D FIND HIM ON THE WATER-FRONT. TAGGING THE EXACT GUY WAS EASY, TOO, FOR HIS BREATH REEKED OF BAY RUM. HE MUST DRINK THE STUFF, AS SOME NUTS DO ... AND THE REST YOU KNOW –
YOU DID A SWELL JOB, SALLY. WE'RE ALL PROUD OF YOU!
7
READ SALLY IN OUR NEXT ISSUE

Sometimes she operated with the aid of a strange little boy called Peanuts, who had a crush on her.

(Interesting side note: Culture Publications owner Harry Donenfield later bought the small publishing company DC Comics from Major Malcolm Wheeler-Nicholson after suing him. Comics were pretty cutthroat in the 1930s!)

Sally was an incredibly good detective, with a keen mind for quick and fast deductions based on the most minimal of clues. She frequently went undercover (usually as a showgirl or a professional flirt) and would do anything to crack a case. That almost always meant that she ended up dressed in a sheer negligee, or was completely naked. Despite a lack of clothing, Sally usually managed to conceal a gun on her person, and she saved herself about as often as she needed to be rescued.

While these stories were fun enough, and usually only a little bit racy (though we all could do without the rape references that show up in a few panels), Sally's tales don't end with the era of pre-comic-book pulps. She was brought back in the 1950s in *Crime Smashers*, a rough-and-tumble crime comic anthology series published by Culture's sister company, Trojan. New creators handled her adventures, now in bold, full color. In this series, Sally is still often used as a decoy to trap criminals in the act, and she carries a single-shot lipstick revolver (yes, I understand that revolvers by definition cannot be single shot, but that's what they called it). Even without her gun, Sally still manages to stay safe, being an expert at judo as well. This later version of Sally plays things a bit more by the book, using superior crime-solving skills to bust criminals, blackmailers, and murderers. And she doesn't even have to strip down to her bits to do so!

Sally the Sleuth is one of the original female heroines in comics, and she should be celebrated accordingly. However, that doesn't mean she's a perfect role model; because of her roots as a fetish detective heroine, hers might be one part of history you don't want your kids to read, even if it was your grandparents who created her.

ESSENTIAL READING: Look through old dirty books to see if you can find a copy of the *Spicy Detective* stories, or hunt through back-issue bins. Some of Sally's adventures have been reprinted by Malibu Graphics (*Spicy Tales Collection*, 1989) and Pulpville Press (*The Best of Sally the Sleuth*, 2013).

TORCHY BROWN	A Southern girl in the big city	66Together, with love in our hearts, we can lick anything!99
		Created by: Jackie Ormes
		First appearance: The Pittsburgh Courier, 1937

A plucky young black woman named Torchy Brown moves from the Deep South to New York City . . . Sounds like a scenario ripe with comedy, right? But though the tone of the initial strips was mostly humorous, the storylines quickly turned melodramatic. Torchy's naiveté and positive attitude helped guide her through misadventures that dealt with issues not commonly addressed in comics, including racial attacks, rape threats, and environmental pollution. Creator Jackie Ormes, who started her career as a journalist, was aggravated that topics talked about in the news never made it into comics. Put off by romance strips in which the main characters were weak, Ormes described her creation this way: "Torchy was no moonstruck crybaby, that and she wouldn't perish between heartbreaks."

Starting off as "Torchy Brown: From Dixie to Harlem" in the *Pittsburgh Courier* in 1937, the comic strip lasted only a year. But in 1950 it was revived, again by Ormes, as a full-page comic supplement called *Torchy in Heartbeats*. In this series, published in full color, Torchy's adventures became more serious, and humor took a backseat to drama. In addition to the comic, Torchy was a popular cutout paper doll, available in a supplement called *Torchy's Togs* that also ran in newspapers. Her outfits were inspired by Ormes's work producing fashion shows in Chicago and featured cutting-edge designs.

As a comic strip created by a black woman and featuring black characters, *Torchy Brown* faced obstacles that *Miss Fury*, *Brenda Starr*, and other strips with white heroines didn't showcase. Limited to African American newspapers, Ormes's creation never reached the wider distribution that it deserved. Still, Torchy's adventures hold their own as exciting, romantic, and well-drawn comics.

ESSENTIAL READING: *Jackie Ormes* by Nancy Golstein (University of Michigan Press, 2008) is a biography of the creator, with a large selection of Torchy Brown comic strips included.

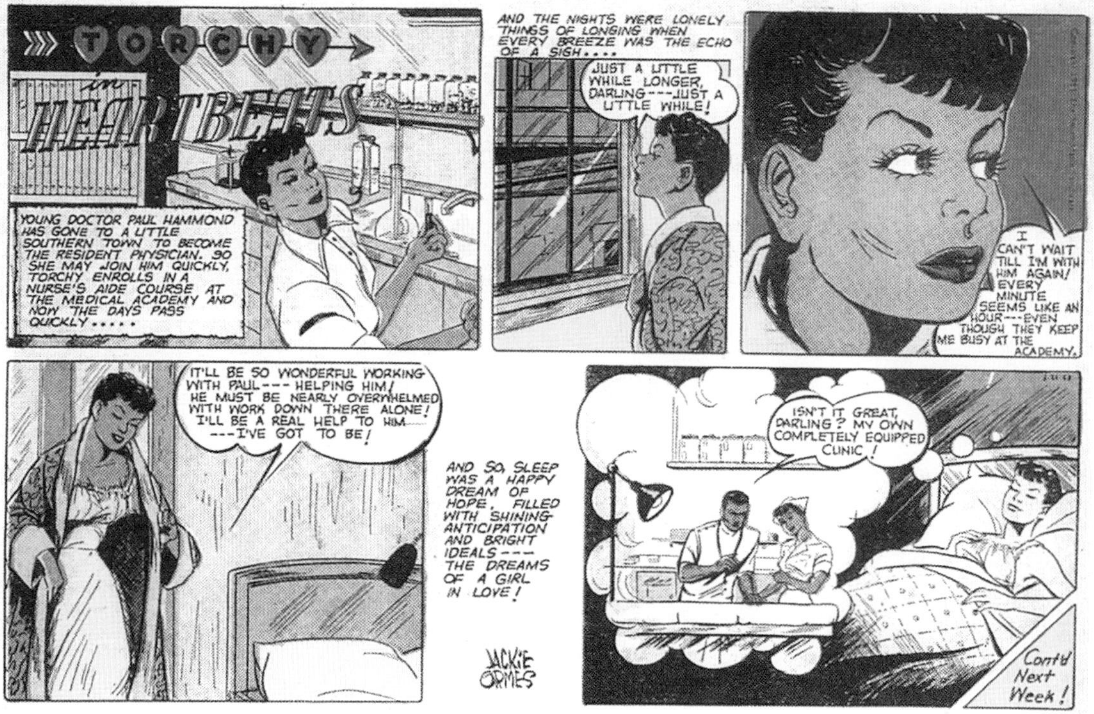
TORCHY
in HEARTBEATS
YOUNG DOCTOR PAUL HAMMOND HAS GONE TO A LITTLE SOUTHERN TOWN TO BECOME THE RESIDENT PHYSICIAN. SO SHE MAY JOIN HIM QUICKLY, TORCHY ENROLLS IN A NURSE'S AIDE COURSE AT THE MEDICAL ACADEMY AND NOW THE DAYS PASS QUICKLY.....
AND THE NIGHTS WERE LONELY THINGS OF LONGING WHEN EVERY BREEZE WAS THE ECHO OF A SIGH....
JUST A LITTLE WHILE LONGER, DARLING---JUST A LITTLE WHILE!
I CAN'T WAIT TILL I'M WITH HIM AGAIN! EVERY MINUTE SEEMS LIKE AN HOUR---EVEN THOUGH THEY KEEP ME BUSY AT THE ACADEMY.
IT'LL BE SO WONDERFUL WORKING WITH PAUL--- HELPING HIM! HE MUST BE NEARLY OVERWHELMED WITH WORK DOWN THERE ALONE! I'LL BE A REAL HELP TO HIM ---I'VE GOT TO BE!
AND SO, SLEEP WAS A HAPPY DREAM OF HOPE, FILLED WITH SHINING ANTICIPATION AND BRIGHT IDEALS--- THE DREAMS OF A GIRL IN LOVE!
ISN'T IT GREAT, DARLING? MY OWN COMPLETELY EQUIPPED CLINIC!
JACKIE ORMES
Cont'd Next Week!

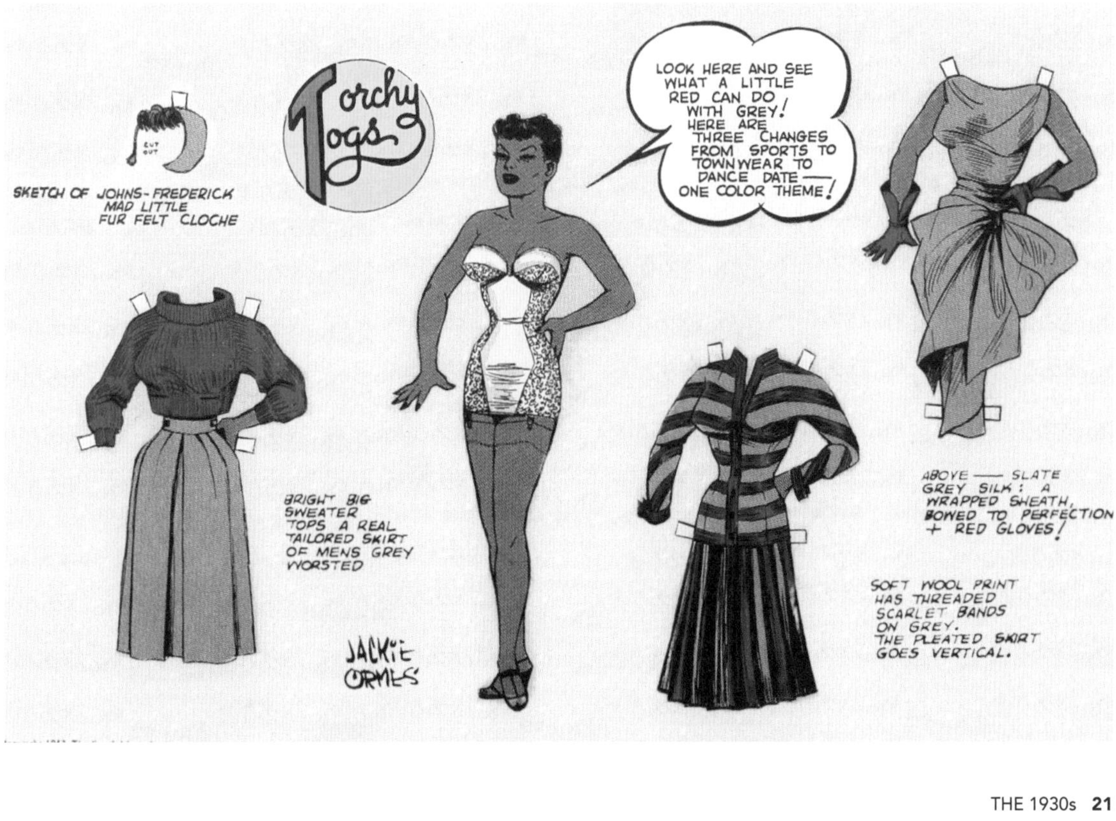
Torchy Togs
SKETCH OF JOHNS-FREDERICK MAD LITTLE FUR FELT CLOCHE
LOOK HERE AND SEE WHAT A LITTLE RED CAN DO WITH GREY! HERE ARE THREE CHANGES FROM SPORTS TO TOWNWEAR TO DANCE DATE — ONE COLOR THEME!
BRIGHT BIG SWEATER TOPS A REAL TAILORED SKIRT OF MENS GREY WORSTED
ABOVE — SLATE GREY SILK: A WRAPPED SHEATH, BOWED TO PERFECTION + RED GLOVES!
SOFT WOOL PRINT HAS THREADED SCARLET BANDS ON GREY. THE PLEATED SKIRT GOES VERTICAL.
JACKIE ORMES

LITTLE LULU	A feisty troublemaker who inspired generations of women	"I think I'll be president of the United States."
		Created by: Marjorie Henderson Buell
		First appearance: *Saturday Evening Post* (King Features, 1935)

Initially appearing in newspapers in the 1930s, Little Lulu (full name Lulu Moppet) was a welcome and fresh addition to the comics page. Created by Marjorie Buell, aka "Marge," Little Lulu was a cheery, curly-haired little girl prone to getting into trouble and indulging in shenanigans. She was created with the idea that little girls causing a bother are more charming to watch than little boys (and she may have been right; I've always found Dennis the Menace to be more irritating than charming).

Lulu's adventures weren't terribly epic: she'd steal food, get into fights, be a smart aleck, and try to get her way in every situation. But that's what made her so undeniably real. A tough 'n' tiny tot who knew what she wanted and dared to go after it, Lulu was also, perhaps inadvertently, an icon of strength and drive to girls and women alike. Many credit her adventures as their first experience with feminism. As the comics historian Maggie Thompson once observed: "I knew that the relationships were real, the adventures were real, and the fun was real. And I knew that, like Lulu, I could do whatever I had the wit to do." When other girl characters were being picked on by boys in comic strips, Little Lulu gave back as good as she got. Thompson writes: "She was tough to the point of occasional nastiness. Her ingenuity produced unsettling results. Her curiosity was untempered by caution . . . she was a different heroine for children. . . . Gag after gag was devoted to the fact that girls were not some sort of inferior breed."

Little Lulu should also be celebrated for her creator, Marjorie Buell, one of the most successful female cartoonists of the golden age. Keeping the rights to her character as she did was a rarity back in the '30s. And as Little Lulu blew up, Marge managed to use her creation's popularity to great success with merchandise and advertising deals. From her newspaper strip, Lulu branched off into animated cartoons (which ran into the 1990s) and full-length comic books. Lulu was also the mascot of an ad campaign for Kleenex tissues that ran for sixteen years. Little Lulu was a true star.

Buell's Little Lulu has cast a long shadow. In the 1990s, some of the most prominent women in the comics industry formed the group "Friends of Lulu," which promoted representation of female creators in comics for nearly two decades.

CHAPTER
2

The

19

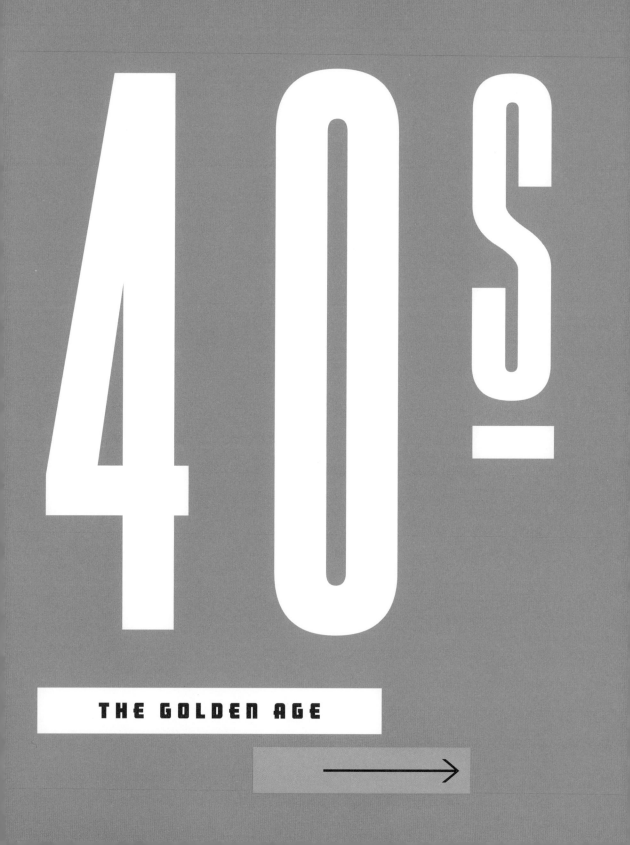

40s

THE GOLDEN AGE

THE 1940s

I f the comic book industry began in the 1930s, the decade that followed was definitely the boom years. Called the "golden age" for good reason, the 1940s saw comics published in increasingly large numbers, and in every conceivable genre, by a wide array of publishers. The most popular character during this decade? Well, although both Batman and Superman were going strong (it's unclear just how many issues were sold, but estimates place each at around 100,000 copies per monthly issue), it was Sheena, Queen of the Jungle, who released the most issues. Appearing in two of the top five most prolific comics (*Jumbo Comics* as well as her own title) Sheena was also Queen of the Comics.

The publisher of Sheena, Fiction House, was a fascinating company. Because of a shortage of male creatives caused by World War II, Fiction House hired women for all creative roles. Artist Murphy Anderson (Superman, Hawkman), who worked for Fiction House as a teenager, remembered that only a few men were present in the office. Notable artists in the company's bullpen include Lily Renée, who had escaped from Nazi-occupied Austria, and Marcia Snyder, a queer artist who lived with her girlfriend in Greenwich Village. Perhaps hiring so many women explains why Fiction House produced an abundance of female-centric stories.

Sales of comics in general increased dramatically in the mid-forties, with DC Comics (whose official name was Detective Comics, Inc., later National Comics Publications), Dell Comics, and Fawcett Comics being the most popular publishers (at least in terms of number of issues released) at both the start and the end of the decade.

Meanwhile, dissatisfaction with the wholesale distributor system was evident. As Charles Cridland, a passionate comics sales researcher, remarked in 1949: "Although the industry is enjoying the highest level of sales since it began, it is highly probable that present operations have resulted in the lowest financial return. . . . Many times large bundles of magazines never leave the wholesaler's warehouse but are moved from the receiving platform to the return room." These comics were often mishandled and damaged from being packed into newsstand racks. Some unscrupulous retailers even sold coverless comics to customers, having ripped off the covers to send back to publishers so they could be reimbursed for "unsold" merchandise. Decades of discontent with this system would enable the growth of the direct distribution market in the 1970s.

Most of the era's popular comics were superhero stories, but all-ages and humor comics were also well-loved. Mostly these comics were not intended to be gender specific; boys and girls enjoyed them in equal numbers. Though you might expect war comics to be the most popular, since World War II was in full swing, they really weren't. Readers were looking for escapism, not reality.

At this time, Canada's comics industry had its first (and most significant) boom. With all nonessential goods restricted from import from the United States, comics publishers were popping up all over the country, and with them came exciting new characters. There were still relatively few female creators, at least that we know of, though Shirley Fortune, Pat Dingle, and Doris Slater stand out among those whose contributions have been recorded for history. Nelvana of the Northern Lights, the Wing, and Circus Girl were some of the female characters popular north of the U.S. border, though their names vanished after wartime restrictions ceased and American comic books once again flooded the Canadian market.

Few comics with a female character as the sole lead were widely popular in the 1940s, though women characters often headed the Fiction House anthologies (such as the aforementioned Sheena books). Wonder Woman, Nyoka the Jungle Girl, and Miss America were exceptions, though they were far outnumbered by male characters like Blue Bolt, the Shadow, and Captain Marvel. Nevertheless, women were most definitely present in this new industry—as fans, characters, and creators. Yet female readership was not specifically catered to in this decade, which could be seen as a good thing. Without the imposed categories of "girl comics" and "boy comics," people read whatever they pleased. ⚡

BLACK CAT	Actress and stunt woman turned adventurer and superheroine	"The Black Cat always works alone . . . and succeeds."
		Created by: Alfred Harvey and Al Gabriele
		First appearance: *Pocket Comics* #1 (Harvey Comics, 1941)

After finding propaganda in a recent script, glamorous movie star Linda Turner suspects that her boss is in fact a secret Nazi agent. Also, her pet black cat seems to hate the guy and takes every opportunity to attack him, which is all the proof Linda needs. Inspired by her cat's hatred, Linda decides to create her own super-hero costume . . . and she becomes the Black Cat. Well, her costume is blue and red, not black, and her mask might look like a cat like if you squint. Okay, so her choice of superheroine moniker does seem completely random. But the important thing is that Linda finds out the director of her movie has indeed been using film edits to send messages to embedded Nazi spies!

Along with her costume, Linda (with little explanation) also has a technologically advanced car, as well as her own airplane, for emergency getaways. But other than a skill at beating up bad guys with her fists (jiu-jitsu!), "Hollywood's glamorous detective star" lacked any super gizmos or powers. Not that she needed them. (Her background as an ex-stuntwoman didn't hurt.)

Black Cat is a bit bristly. She tells a persistent pest of a reporter named Rick Horne to shut up and follow her lead, calling him stupid when he calls her beautiful. He does obey pretty well, so Black Cat eventually rewards him with a kiss . . . her style: pinning his arms against his side so he can't move and smooching him until he's dizzy, then taking off into the night.

After a few adventures in *Pocket Comics*, Black Cat moved on to *Speed Comics* and remained there for a good deal of the series over the next five years. She appeared in a variety of comics by her cocreator Alfred Harvey and then starred in her own book at a time when female-led comic series were still pretty rare, even if female characters were popular in anthology comics. But there was the Black Cat on her covers, punching out bad guys and riding motorcycles and doing all sorts of perfectly awesome superheroing.

Linda's dad was the only one who knew her secret identity, and he thoroughly supported her career choice (*awww*). In classic superhero fashion, she starts dating that pesky reporter Horne, who is still obsessed with the Black Cat even though she's pretty mean to him in her superheroine persona.

Eventually, as interest in superheroes started to fade, *Black Cat* inexplicably became a Western comic (with an awkward segue: "and now Linda only makes Westerns!"). After a few more issues, *Black Cat* existed in name only and became a showcase for grisly horror fare. Still, Linda Turner's alter ego had a more than solid run, lasting for nearly two decades. Black Cat should be considered a leading lady of comic book history, and she still has fans among those in the know. "More than most characters, I was drawn to Harvey's Black Cat," says Maggie Thompson, long-time editor of *The Comics Buyer's Guide*. "Mind you, the premise was odd.... But the focus was that real women could and should defend themselves."

ESSENTIAL READING: No full reprint exists, though publisher Lorne-Harvey did reprint some stories in the late 1980s in a digest called *The Original Black Cat* (to distinguish it from the Marvel Spider-Man character of the same name).

GAIL PORTER: GIRL PHOTOGRAPHER	Fearless photographer who dives into danger	*I don't care when you jump, just so you let me know so I can have my camera set up! Go on up higher— it'll make a better shot!*
		Created by: Bob Oksner
		First appearance: *Blue Circle Comics #1* (Rural Home, 1944)

Armed only with quick wit, a sharp tongue, and some pretty fine strength and agility, Gail Porter is the feisty, fiery, and nationwide-famous photographer of the *Daily Photographer*. Not content to snap photos of sports games and political events, she pursues investigative opportunities at every turn, running into dangerous territory time and again, wearing her trademark sharp red suit and oversized hat. Gail will do anything to get the inside scoop on a hot case: crawl down elevator shafts, step in front of loaded guns, and even confront werewolves!

In her first adventure, Gail taunts a man on a ledge threatening to hurl himself off, knowing that her words will make him change his mind and climb down. Finding out that the guy is about to lose his company due to a crooked businessman in league with the mob, Gail sets out to uncover the corruption. She ends up locking the mobsters in an elevator shaft and forcing them into a photo.

In the context of other comics from this era, Gail Porter's adventures definitely stand out. With no romantic interest to distract her, she can concentrate fully on chasing leads. Within the first few pages, the comic passes the Bechdel test (two women in a story who talk about something other than a man) as Gail swaps stories—and a hefty bribe—with a fellow "girl photographer." What's more, Gail's also not treated with kid gloves by the male photographers: In her second issue, when she's investigating a werewolf(!), a rival shutterbug rudely steals the only taxi in town and tells Gail to walk to the story. Of course, that rival turns out to be the werewolf. Okay, he's a fake werewolf, trying to stir up news to spark his journalist career. When Mr. Faux Werewolf begs for forgiveness, Gail takes pity on him and rips up the photographs that reveal his cheap costume. What a sweet gesture from someone who's said to have "developer fluid for blood."

Subsequent adventures involve Gail helping Hans, a young German in an internment camp. When visiting to check if Hans is all right, Gail discovers that a Nazi spy has murdered her gentle friend and stolen his identity. You might expect from previous stories that Gail would find a peaceful solution; instead she kicks the murderer in the hand and turns his own weapon against him. In Gail's next adventure, a gun moll punches her out and impersonates her to escape prison. Tracking down the crook, Gail returns the favor with a punch to the jaw.

Gail Porter's career was short lived. After only five adventures—some drawn by female comics artist Lucy Feller—she disappeared forever. It's a disappointment that this risk-taking, fast-talking investigator—a true jewel from the golden age of comics—had such an abbreviated lifespan.

ESSENTIAL READING: Gail Porter was never reprinted, though she's long overdue. Look for her in back issues of *Blue Circle Comics* #1 though #5.

GALE ALLEN AND THE GIRL SQUADRON	Tough-as-nails space commander, with a squadron of equally tough women	66 Listen to the jealous talk! You still don't think we women can fight as well as you big, strong men. 99
		Created by: Fred Nelson (probably a pen name)
		First appearance: *Planet Comics* #4 (Fiction House, 1940)

Her book premiered as *Gale Allen of the Women's Space Battalion*, but apparently the editors thought that sounded too serious. They changed the title to *Gale Allen and the Girl Patrol*, then finally settled on the slightly better *Gale Allen and the Girl Squadron*.

Whatever the title, Gale is an expert flyer and military commander. But even in the far future (of 1990) she isn't immune to sexist insults. When Gale comes to the aid of Captain Jack North, he taunts her battalion as being just a "knitting circle." Jack soon finds himself kidnapped by aliens and saved by Gale while her squadron rescues a lost battalion and delivers them safely to Saturn. How's that for a knitting circle, Jack?

In her second adventure, the evil Prince Daru wants to force Gale to be his bride. Finding herself outgunned Gale is captured, and this time it's Jack who comes to *her* aid. Even though in the end it's Gale's flying tackle that takes out the

GALE ALLEN and the GIRL SQUADRON
by DOUGLAS McKEE

villain, Jack still declares that women belong in the home. Despite their incompatibility, the two team up to foil Prince Daru's plans to sabotage the Transatlantic Subway, a transport system that stretches clear across the ocean.

After that, Jack and Gale fall in love. Of course.

No, wait! Actually, they remain platonic friends, and Gale considers Jack her best bud despite his taunts and bad behavior. They take turns rescuing each other from political enemies seeking to tear down the Queen of Venus's rule of the universe. We never learn much about the Girl Squadron, but they frequently rush to Gale's aid whenever she's in a jam. Later on, Jack is replaced as a male companion by the charming roguish pirate Captain Saracen, who makes no bones that he wants to . . . well, bone her. Yet Saracen is an outlaw after all, and soon Gale is back traveling with just her girls.

Gale is skilled in all sorts of combat, from traditional swordfights to physical brawls, but her trusty weapon of choice is always her beloved ray gun. Her friends are loyal and her adventures beyond fantastic and bizarre, like getting trapped in a giant spider's web or fighting imaginary dragons. Though she definitely gets tied up at times and finds herself in need of rescuing, more often than not Gale is the one rescuing others. All in all, she is the epitome of a leader whom female readers can look up to, and she's one of the jewels of comics' golden age.

ESSENTIAL READING: You can find reprinted Gale Allen stories in the *Planet Comics* collections published by PS Art Books, organized by comics historian Roy Thomas.

KATY KEENE

**The pinup queen
everyone loves**

*❝I'm the luckiest girl in the world to have
such beautiful dress designs sent to me
from my fans all over the globe!❞*

Created by: Bill Woggon

First appearance: *Wilbur Comics #5*
(Archie Comics, 1945)

In Katy Keene's first appearance in *Wilbur*, one of many interchangeable teen comics of the day, you knew immediately what you were getting. Katy is a perfect, voluptuous, and glamorous woman drowning in too many love interests and dealing with a bratty little sister named Sis (who is chubby with glasses, natch). Sis's primary job is to scare away boys who are unsuitable for Katy (say, if they're too cheap), but Sis also tricks suitors into buying her treats in exchange for time alone with her sister. Sis would pretty much do anything for treats; she was sort of an Etta Candy to Katy's Wonder Woman, without them actually having any exciting adventures.

We're acutely reminded at the start of this series that, though it may star a woman, it was clearly meant for men to read (or at least to stare at). Many stories start with a line like, "Katy's got more curves than a mountain trail!"

By and large, Katy's adventures are fairly mild. They usually revolved around her passion for fashion or such exciting drama as Katy spending a full story trying to keep the wind from blowing up her skirt (a narrative that allows for multiple panels featuring her stockings and underwear). Romantic stories involved Katy's many love interests until eventually she settled into being mostly steady with K. O. Kelly, an Irish working-class boxing champ . . . when she wasn't dating the rich and high-class Randy Van Ronson, that is. I mean, a girl needs luxury sometimes, you know? Added to the cast is poor ice cream vendor Chubby, who occasionally gets a pity date. Also in the mix: the glamorous, vain, and spoiled model Gloria, who's constantly after the same jobs as Katy (a comic starring a woman always needs the frenemy balance).

Interestingly enough, Katy was fully aware that she was in a comic book; she answered letters for requests from pinups from her readers. She may have been intended as just a curvy female character to break up the boy-centric adventures of Wilbur, but she quickly became popular with female fans, who loved seeing the variety of costumes and clothing she wore. Her readers began sending in requests for the dream outfits they'd love for Katy to wear, and the character's artist Bill Woggon happily obliged.

After a few years of bouncing around various Archie Comics titles such as *Pep*, *Laugh*, *Suzie*, and *Wilbur*, Katy finally received her own book. Fangirls redeemed their heroine and she became an outlet for their creative inspirations. Katy Keene was particularly popular not because she had exciting adventures, but because she became a character that readers could project their dreams onto. You couldn't exactly write in to Superman and choose his outfits, but you sure could for Katy! Superstar comics artist Amanda Conner (*Harley Quinn*) even got her start in comics art by submitting outfit ideas to Katy's 1980s reboot.

Katy Keene continued as a popular character for decades, always encouraging readers to think of new inventive fashions, which were the main focus of her adventures. Essentially a paper-doll book disguised as a comic, Katy faded away in the 1960s; brief revivals in the 1980s and 2000s failed to cement long-term interest in the character.

ESSENTIAL READING: No full reprint collections exist, though a more affordable option than finding the original comics might be hunting down the 1980s Katy Keene digests, which feature reprints and newer stories.

MADAME STRANGE	She patrols the outposts of American civilization, looking for spies and saboteurs to unearth (or blow up)	*"They'll never live to try that again!"*
		Created by: Achmed Zudella (probably a pen name for Chuck Winter)
		First appearance: *Great Comics* #1 (Great Publications, 1941)

Though she wears a cape and a mismatched swimsuit (seriously, the outfit clashes something awful), Madame Strange appears to have no superpowers, aside from being pretty strong and rather brave. In her secret identity—not shared until her

Madame STRANGE

BY ACHMED ZUDELLA

ON A MURKY SINGAPORE CABARET MADAME STRANGE IS DISGUISED AS A DANCER.

EDGING TOWARD A TABLE WHERE TWO BRITISH NAVAL OFFICERS ARE DRINKING, SHE OVERHEARS.

BUT HOW DO YOU KNOW, CAP'N, THAT THE SECRET MAP OF OUR DEFENSE BASE WAS PHOTOGRAPHED?

WE FOUND A RED STRIP FROM A ROLL OF FOREIGN FILM ON THE MAP TABLE!

UNLESS WE OBTAIN THAT NEGATIVE .. SINGAPORE IS DOOMED!

third and final appearance—she's revealed to be a "girl reporter"; she then discards her costume and extraordinary strength. But whether civilian or superhero, Madame Strange is ferocious, not hesitating for a second to lock the bad guys in strangleholds. And she's definitely not reading them their rights as she throws gas bombs and grenades in their faces.

In her second adventure, Madame Strange travels to Singapore, where her spy-within-a-spy-ring (it's like an onion of spies) is assassinated while trying to pass on a message to her. As always, Madame Strange's first instincts are to shoot first and ask questions never!

Tactics include her trademark maneuver of running down enemies with her car. An unusual move for a superheroine . . . but this was the 1940s, when superheroines (like the Black Widow, Fantomah, and Lady Satan) hadn't yet adopted a moral code of conduct for their crime-fighting activities. So why not throw a grenade at your adversaries, blowing them all to tiny pieces? I mean, they *are* the enemy after all. Madame Strange's actions even lead her allies in government to laugh nervously, "Ahah, glad she's with us instead of against us . . ."

Madame Strange's lack of morals didn't just extend to inhumane treatment of the bad guys. She was also . . . what's a nice way to put this . . . a straight-up racist. Her first adventure takes place in Hawaii, where she confronts a Japanese saboteur attempting to attack the United States by blowing up parts of Pearl Harbor. Interestingly, this comic was published exactly one month *before* the Pearl Harbor attack. (I suppose if a comic book writer could recognize Pearl Harbor as a strategic attack point, so could the Japanese forces.) But the anti-Asian racism and tension are already well evident. Madame Strange and other characters in her stories use a variety of racial slurs, and issue by issue the villains grow more absurdly stereotyped and caricaturized. The comic also displays a weird sort of pan-Asian stereotyping, with Sikh-looking men in loincloths and turbans scheming with the Japanese.

Maybe these less appealing aspects are why the comic's creator Chuck Winter used a pseudonym, "Achmed Zudella," and passed off to a different artist/writer the character's last appearance.

In a perfect world, if Madame Strange ever returned to the pages of comics, she'd have all that racism excised completely. Then we could focus on her exploits, which would probably entail overthrowing the government and implementing her own form of vigilante justice.

ESSENTIAL READING: Like all golden age comics, Madame Strange's original adventures are hard to find, some pages may be viewed on the internet. You can find a black-and-white reprint in the book *Divas, Dames & Daredevils* (Exterminating Angel Press, 2013).

MAUREEN MARINE	A human girl who rules a land under the sea	*"Die! Fool of fools! My people will ravage your city, destroy all, if you lay one finger on me!"*
		Created by: Harold Delay
		First Appearance: *Blue Circle Comics* #1 (Rural Home Publishing, 1944)

Maureen Marine is the destined child—a human girl selected to live under the sea with mermaids and other exotic aquatic folk. Sneaking aboard her fisherman father's ship against his wishes, young Maureen witnesses him gunned down by Nazis. She sinks into the ocean, only to awaken in the arms of a new father: Neptune.

Essentially, Maureen Marine is living every child's wish. First of all, no parents to govern her behavior. She's chosen to be the special one, treated not as a mere princess but as a queen. And she gets to live with mermaids. Well, technically, mermen. Turns out that since the death of the previous queen, only males are left in Atlantis. But let's not think about Maureen's future.

Oh, did I forget to mention that the city she rules under the sea is made entirely of gold? And that she rides giant sea turtles? Of course she does. In addition, every one of Maureen's many subjects loves her dearly, for she reigns over them elegantly and wisely. I can only imagine this concept came from the brain of a ten-year-old girl put in the corner in a time-out, muttering, "I'll show them. I'll show them all!" Maureen Marine is the perfect Mary Sue, a seemingly flawless character who effortlessly saves the day. But I say that with all the love and affection I have for this character type (which is considerable). An unnaturally perfect, admired, and innocent young girl in a magical world all her own? Surely comics have room for that.

In her adventures, Maureen fights Nazis (of course—it's

the 1940s) along with lighter duties such as refereeing aquatic seahorse derbies. She quickly exhibits a strong sense of command and is fast to defend herself when things get shady.

Maureen Marine was one of those unusual comics from the '40s that doesn't fit into typical genres. It's definitely a comic geared toward young girls, but it's neither a romance nor a humor book. Instead, it's closer to a fantasy epic, though one that sadly lasted only a few issues.

ESSENTIAL READING: You can read Maureen Marine's first appearance in the reprint collection *Divas, Dames & Daredevils* (Exterminating Angel Press, 2013).

MISS FURY	The first female-created superheroine in comics	66 *Somehow I've had nothing but misfortune since my uncle left me the black leopard skin!* 99
		Created by: Tarpé Mills
		First appearance: Bell syndicate, 1941 (newspaper strip); *Miss Fury* #1 (Timely Comics, 1942)

Imagine a time when newspapers covered cartoonists' love lives as if they were celebrities . . . Well, that time never existed. But Tarpé Mills was the exception: she was a fast-living, glamorous woman who lived life the way she wanted, even if that made her the subject of tabloid gossip. A fashion designer who turned to comics, Mills based the look and personality of her groundbreaking character Miss Fury on herself.

The grande dame of all superheroes, Miss Fury is not only one of the first superheroines to see print—she predates Wonder Woman by eight months—she's also the first female superhero created by a woman. Initially known as "Black Fury," the character premiered in 1941 as a syndicated newspaper strip and adopted the Miss Fury moniker soon after. The name "Miss Furry" would have been equally apt; to fight crime, the socialite Marla Drake donned a full-body cat suit, complete with claws and ears. Her Sunday newspaper strip lasted until 1952 and were reprinted in comic book form by Timely Comics (a predecessor of Marvel Comics) starting in 1942.

But there's more to Miss Fury's appeal than being first on the scene. This character was a combination of strength, chutzpah, and sexiness who set a standard of heroic perfection rarely seen even in later heroines. In her eight-year run she had a career that holds up against any of her male contemporaries, battling assorted robbers, murderers, blackmailers, and mob bosses. Not to mention the evil Baroness Erica von Kampf, a Nazi spy who had a swastika burned into her forehead as punishment for a failed mission.

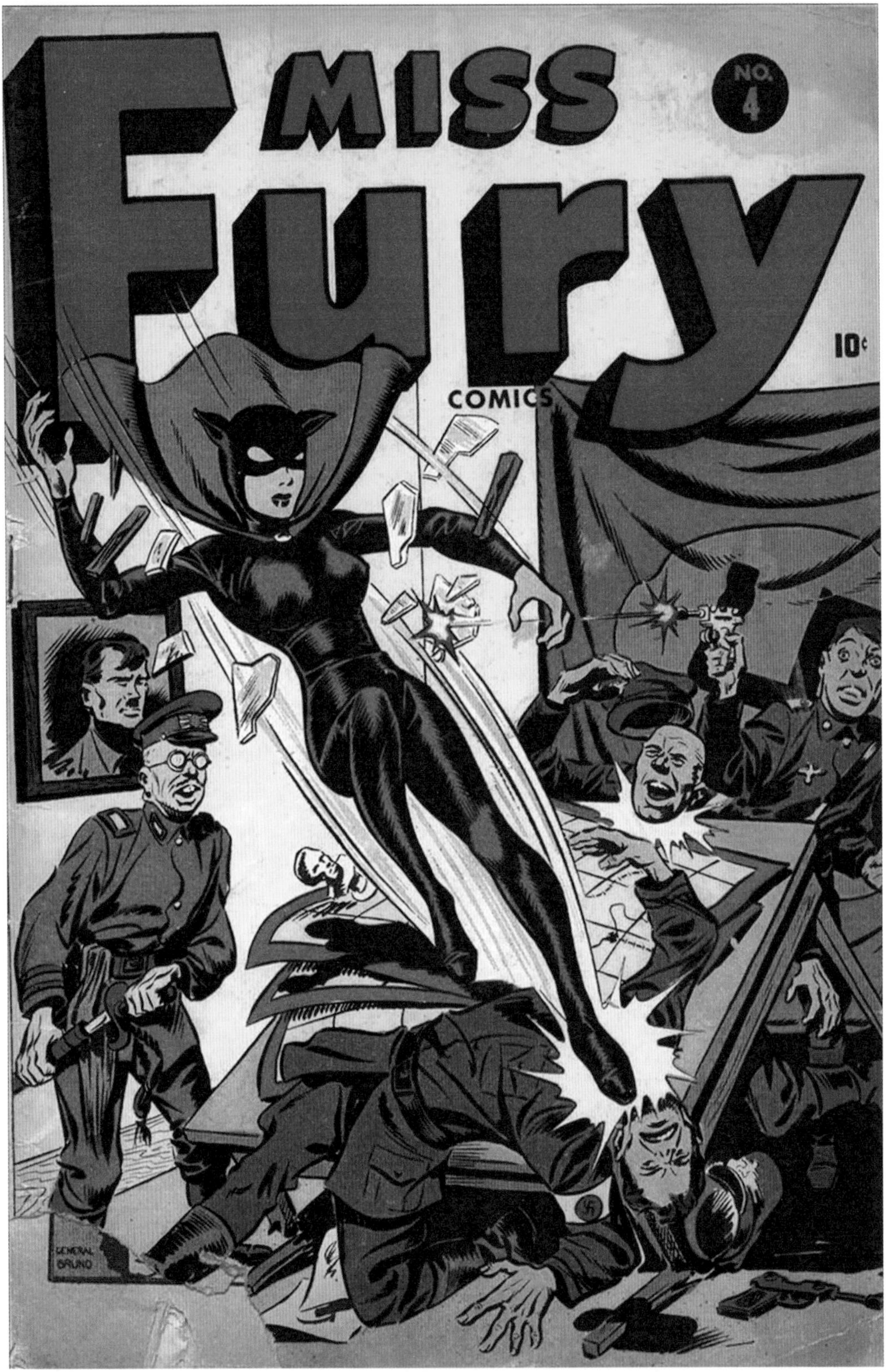
MISS
Fury
COMICS
NO.
4
10¢
GENERAL
BRUNO

Though her black-panther cat suit, given to her by her uncle, was said to grant her enchanted strength and speed, Miss Fury often entered into action wearing just her everyday (albeit fabulous) wardrobe. She had no trouble throwing punches and jumping off rooftops clad in Marla Drake's high heels and mink stole. As artist, writer, and comics historian Trina Robbins puts it: "Marla Drake is the grandmother that Buffy Summers and Sidney Bristow didn't know they had."

To be honest, part of Miss Fury's success was her sex appeal. She was an incredibly gorgeous, well-drawn character who looked incredibly dashing, in or out of her stylish panther suit. There were more than a few scenes of her coyly undressing, but Miss Fury was more than simple eye candy. She was a tough, take-charge hero who gave as good as she got. And like Tarpé Mills, Miss Fury never apologized for her strength of will.

ESSENTIAL READING: *Miss Fury: Sensational Sundays 1941–1944* (IDW, 2011) collects her most dynamic strips. Be wary of modern revivals, which tend to be exploitative. The original Miss Fury, while a powerfully sexy hero, was most definitely not a T&A character.

SEÑORITA RIO	A dashing Latin spy and vigilante out to rid the world of crooks	66 *Mind your manners, mein herr!* 99
		Created by: Nick Viscardi (a.k.a Nick Cardy) and Joe Hawkins (probably a pen a name)
		First appearance: *Fight Comics* #19 (Fiction House, 1942)

Señorita Rio! Global adventuress and perpetual woman of style! From sword-fighting to jiu-jitsu, she was a skilled fighter and an even better spy.

Vowing revenge after her fiancé is killed at Pearl Harbor, Rita Farrar becomes the Queen of Spies, Señorita Rio, in order to root out crime. Using her superior acting abilities to quickly learn new skills, Señorita Rio is a master of languages, fighting abilities, and firearms. Not only that but her quick wit allowed her to solve crimes when the police just couldn't cut it. With an undefined background, Señorita Rio is also a rare Latina presented as a heroine (even to date, that's still fairly uncommon in comic books).

Rio concentrated on hunting crime in Brazil and other South American countries. In her first appearance, we see her dive into freezing shark-infested waters, swim to a deserted wharf, assume the identity of a rich countess, infiltrate a secret Nazi bar, and grab forged documents that could compromise U.S.–Brazil relations. And all this after faking her own death and giving up a high-profile career as an actress.

Señorita Rio was on a quest of vengeance against Nazis and, mourning beloved fiancé, she avoided temptations of romance. In adventure after adventure, she thwarts Nazi plans in South America, parachuting into danger and tossing dangerous men over her shoulders as if they were weightless. The book she starred in was called *Fight Comics* for good reason; all the stories were action packed and full of hands-on violence.

After twelve issues, Rio begins to share space with the jungle heroine Tiger Girl. Rio even appeared in one adventure stealing Tiger Girl's style, wearing cat ears and a leopard suit. But that wasn't enough to save her. After about fifty issues of protecting the world from Nazis and other undesirables, Señorita Rio's story came to an end. (Her rival Tiger Girl continued for twelve more issues.) During her long and impressive career, the Señorita's enemies included men and women, allowing her to rescue her fair share of both pretty damsels and charming rogues.

Señorita Rio was one of the few comics of the 1940s that was drawn by a female artist, in this case Lily Renée. Renée's personal life was just as interesting as the action-packed heroine she brought to life. Born in Austria, as a child she escaped Nazi Germany via the Kindertransport refugee effort and was separated from her parents for two years while they looked for a way to escape wartorn Austria. Eventually, her parents made it to America, and Lily joined them shortly thereafter (though she had to sneak onto a ship because Scotland Yard had accused her of being a spy!). Once in the United States, Lily found work at Fiction House, thanks to the wartime shortage of male artists.

ESSENTIAL READING: Cartoonist and comics historian Trina Robbins has made free downloads of Señorita Rio available on her website, trinarobbins.com. She's also written a biographical comic about Renée (*Lily Renée, Escape Artist*; Graphic Universe, 2011).

STARR FLAGG, UNDERCOVER GIRL	The greatest spy in the world	66Oh, Larry! Stop proposing to me! I have a job to do as foreign correspondent for The Herald *and you know it!*99
		Created by: Gardner Fox and Ogden Whitney
		First appearance: *Manhunt* #1 (Magazine Enterprises, 1947)

Also known as Undercover Girl, Starr Flagg is an action-adventure spy heroine of the James Bond variety, complete with expert fighting skills and a quick wit. She always possesses the best qualities for any scenario. Master of martial arts? You got it. Expert lock picker? Absolutely. Master of disguise? No problem! Most important, she's equipped with a mind that can solve any complicated

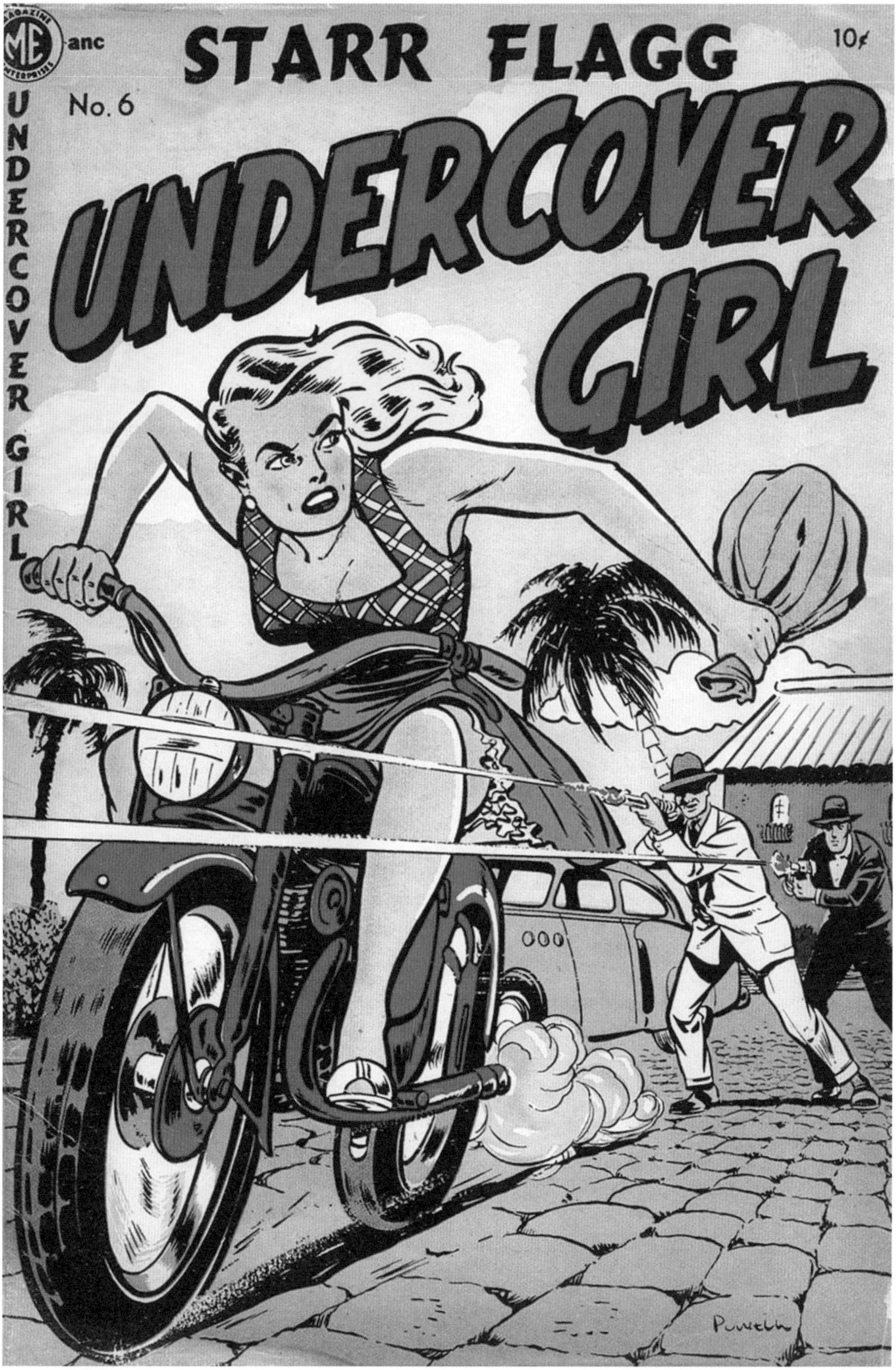
ME
anc
STARR FLAGG
10¢
No. 6
UNDERCOVER GIRL
UNDERCOVER GIRL
Powell

mystery. In every issue, Starr figures her way out of a dangerous situation thanks to some handy last-minute decisions. She also happens to be as ruthless as they come, sniping enemies, hitting them with torture weapons, or even siccing bloodthirsty gorillas on them.

All while being incredibly glamorous in, you know, an effortless kind of way.

In her day-to-day persona, Starr is a foreign correspondent, which gives her the excuse to travel around the world. She has no recurring love interest, though men do pass into and out of her life. Her enemies are clever: spies who send coded messages via their badly applied makeup, and tailors who sew coded patches into unsuspecting victims' swimsuits to reveal secret bomb plans. But in the end their schemes are no match for Starr's superb detective skills.

Though frequently she finds herself trapped or tied up, Starr never waits to be rescued. She escapes using her superior physical skills. Tied to the outside of a plummeting elevator, she uses the friction of the cables to cut herself free.

Thrown into a lake with a rock tied to her feet, she slices the ropes with a sunken boat's propeller. Dropped by a giant animated stone statue, she bounces off a nearby canopy and lands safely on her feet. And like any good action hero, Starr isn't above bad puns. "Try this lamp and see the light!" and "Better table our discussion until next time!" she yells at her foes as she clobbers them with, well, a lamp and a table.

Starr debuted in the pages of *Manhunt*, an anthology series starring G-men, marshals, mounties, and other characters who hunted men (titles were literal in those days). Starr Flagg easily stands out as the most compelling feature. She was quick to get her own series, which unfortunately was just reprints of her original adventures. Nevertheless, Starr Flagg is a highlight of the golden age and one of the most regrettable instances of a character fading from comics history.

ESSENTIAL READING: Read all of her original adventures in the reprint *Undercover Girl: The Complete Adventures of Starr Flagg* (Boardman Books, 2015).

ULTRA VIOLET

A bobby-soxer with the ability to shape-change into her wildest fantasies

"Honest, kids, it was positively weird! I imagined I told old chromedome what a square Mrs. Ratchet is and all of a sudden he was spoutin' the shoutin' to her!"

Created by: Joe Simon, Jack Kirby, and Mort Meskin

First appearance: *My Date* #1 (Hillman Productions, 1947)

Violet Ray is an energetic, quirky teenager who's constantly lost in daydreams. She'd rather *be* Mary Queen of Scots than *learn* about Mary Queen of Scots. Then one day she discovers the ability to shape-change into any human form she desires, and she uses this power to fight crime and better humanity. Just kidding, she uses it to punish her teachers, make time with celebrities, and pretend to be a rich girl to snub bad dates.

Let's not lie; she's living our teenage dreams too.

The Ultra Violet stories are hipper than most square romance comics of the era, with dialogue and fashion that was up-to-date and pulled right from the schoolyards. In fact, Violet defied the standards set by other romance stories, which focused on melodrama, heartbreak, and propriety. She was self-serving, manipulative, and stubborn, and her stories sparkled with a vibrant and fresh sense of humor. This comic seemed as if it was written for teens to truly enjoy, not just sigh over wistfully.

But Violet isn't merely a stubborn teen. In classic romance-comic style, when her best friend Helen is left heartbroken over George, who snubs her for being too plain, Violet takes matters into her own hands. She morphs into a rich and glamorous persona in order to seduce George and teach him a lesson. In a twist on the romance comic trope, the initial snubbing was a ruse orchestrated by George's best friend for him to swoop in and steal Helen away.

In the end, Helen ends up back with George, who makes her promise never to try to be glamorous. Which is . . . an awful lesson? Oh Ultra Violet, you were doing so well until then!

ESSENTIAL READING: Ultra Violet's stories have never been reprinted, so you'll have to ask your grandparents to unearth their copies of *My Date* comics for you to borrow.

THE WING

The wit of Mae West, the career of Stan Lee, and the powers of an angel

> 66 Lift 'em chump. 'Cause baby ain't gonna lay this pistol down. 99

Created by: John G. Hilkert and Murray Karn

First appearance: *Joke Comics* #4 (Bell Features, 1942)

The Wing is the superheroine identity of cartoonist Trixie Rogers, who, like many young Canadian women during the Second World War, contributes to the cause by working in an airplane factory. Her powers come from a magical cape that grants some increased agility and speed as well as, more important, the ability to fly. She fights off saboteurs to her country plus two-bit crooks and the odd murderer. More a detective than a superhero, the Wing solves crimes and brings bad guys to justice using her powers of deduction, often without the aid of her magical abilities. She also uses her adventures as inspiration for her comics about, yep, a character called the Wing.

As far as superheroines go, Trixie was not incredibly unusual, though she was one of the few recurring female characters of the 1940s Canadian comics industry boom, alongside Nelvana of the Northern Lights, Commandette, Circus Girl, and Polka Dot Pirate. These were largely black-and-white comic strips, often with some art traced from American comics. Those that somehow managed to make it past the border, that is; American comic books were banned from entering Canada during the war, as were other "non-essential goods."

The Wing had style and flair that were undeniable. Her superhero outfit—a strapless, backless top and high-waist briefs—was unusual even in an era with scantily clad characters such as the Phantom Lady (see Vampirella, page 92). Her adventures were short, usually no longer than eight pages, and often a bit silly. But they did feature some fairly enjoyable moments. In one memorable adventure, Trixie attends a costume party in costume as the Wing. The hostess sees both Trixie in her party costume as the Wing and the "real" Wing (also Trixie, same costume), but cannot put together that they are one and the same. It's as if Clark Kent never even bothered to put on regular clothes or a pair of glasses to pretend he wasn't Superman.

She might not rank as high as the level of Nelvana of the Northern Lights in terms of Canadian superheroines, but the Wing had something Nelvana sorely lacked in most of her adventures: a sense of humor.

ESSENTIAL READING: Fortunately, Library and Archives Canada (bac-lac.gc.ca) has digitized every issue in their collection, so if you don't mind a bit of searching, you can find all of the Wing's original adventures online.

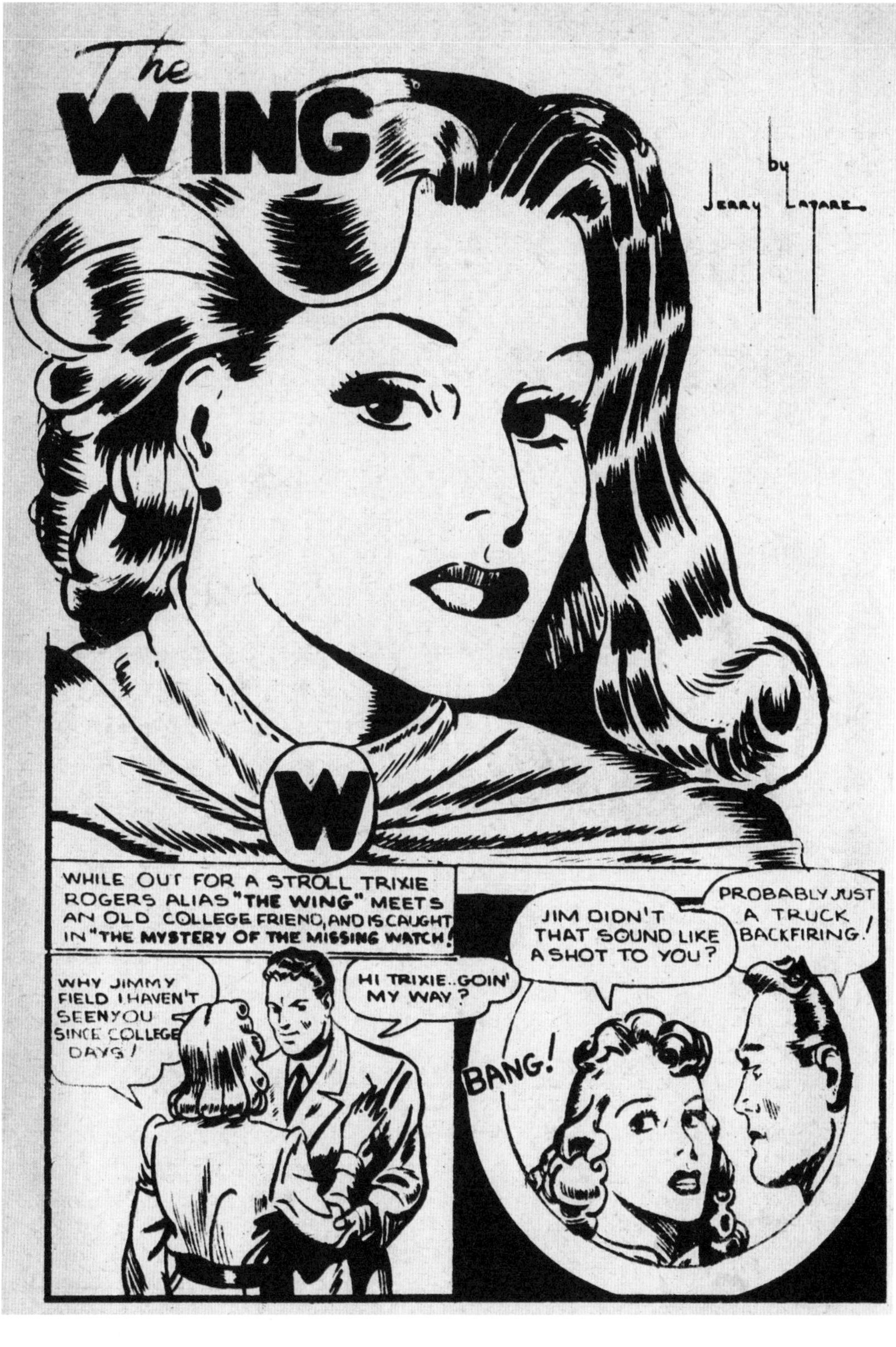
The WING
by Jerry Lazare
WHILE OUT FOR A STROLL TRIXIE ROGERS ALIAS "THE WING" MEETS AN OLD COLLEGE FRIEND, AND IS CAUGHT IN "THE MYSTERY OF THE MISSING WATCH!"
WHY JIMMY FIELD I HAVEN'T SEEN YOU SINCE COLLEGE DAYS!
HI TRIXIE..GOIN' MY WAY?
JIM DIDN'T THAT SOUND LIKE A SHOT TO YOU?
PROBABLY JUST A TRUCK BACKFIRING!
BANG!

WONDER WOMAN	Amazon warrior on a mission of peace for all mankind	66Liberty and Justice for all—all regardless of race, color, or religion!99
		Created by: William Marston and Harry Peter
		First appearance: *All Star Comics* #8 (DC Comics, 1941)

Well, no duh, we all know about Wonder Woman. A year doesn't go by without a new in-depth book, article, or essay on the legendary hero . . . and a hot take on whether she's a feminist icon, a slave to BDSM male gaze, or a paragon of alternative sexuality and romantic relationships. (But isn't it way more interesting that her creator was in a FFM, mutually respectable triad relationship than that he kinda thought chains were hot?)

Sure, you know all about her, and I have nothing to offer you but my own thoughts. I won't pretend to be a Wonder Woman expert, because to be honest I've read maybe five of her comics (albeit good ones from the 1970s, with Wonder Woman fighting Nazis just like in the old days of the 1940s). But in case you've never read a comic in your life (and totally missed the latest blockbuster film, and the popular Lynda Carter television show, and all of the cartoons), I'll give you the rundown:

Wonder Woman's birth origins change at DC's whims. But in the version I always liked, she was sculpted from clay and brought to life on a faraway island full of warrior women as a daughter for their queen, Hippolyte. This daughter, named Diana, grows up a strong woman, learning to repel bullets with her gauntlets, and is given a magical lasso that compels the wearer to tell the truth (and she has an invisible plane!). She's sent as a representative of the Amazons to investigate the modern world beyond their island. Shocked at the brutality and crime that characterize man's world, Diana vows to do her part to fight injustice at every turn.

Wonder Woman is much more than a comic character. And we can all debate on what the "real" version is: the peace-loving, chubby-faced Amazon of her origin; the powerful and regal superhero of the 1950s, fighting a war for humankind; the suave and mod secret agent of the 1960s; the big-haired leader of women of the 1980s; the scantily clad dominatrix of the 1990s; the pants-wearing adventuress of the 2000s; or the fierce warrior-princess we see today.

But no one knows how to define Wonder Woman—what her true essence is. She's what we female comics readers regard as our icon of strength and power, and yet she's as slippery as water to pin down.

And really why shouldn't that be the case? Why should identity be solid, when everybody changes? Why lock down a character to just one version? And why exactly must there be only one, single, iconic, heroic female figure in comics, when there is no one major male comic book figure?

Why does Wonder Woman's identity shift so rapidly; why is it so susceptible to the whims of style, fashion, and marketing choices? Because we've never been lucky enough to have a multitude of popular female superheroes as our icons. Sure, this book is full of candidates, but is their merchandise in the stores? Do they have action figures, T-shirts, movie franchises? Therefore Diana has the added pressure to be everything. And as a result she becomes nothing.

Maybe fans cling too tightly to Wonder Woman when what we need to do is stop putting the pressure to be a perfect feminist icon on just one superhero. Why not share our attention among some of Wonder Woman's sisters in crimefighting instead?

CHAPTER

3

The

19

50s

COMICS CODE CRACKDOWN

THE 1950s

After a decade of surging popularity, the comics industry faced a game-changing cultural shake-up: the introduction of the Comics Code Authority in 1954. Before the CCA, comics could be as saucy and as dirty as they wanted to be. In practice, however, most publishers refrained from situations and images too extreme, in the interest of keeping parents happily buying books for their kids.

Nevertheless, a psychiatrist named Fredric Wertham made it his mission to direct America's attention to exactly what its children were reading. Although his claims that comics were too sexy and too queer didn't convince most parents, his lurid descriptions of juvenile delinquency being influenced by the most violent crime comics certainly did. Such comics, showcasing stories of brutal criminal activity, had already been banned in Canada, the result of a 1948 court case regarding two comics-obsessed kids who'd decided to shoot random strangers. It didn't take much prodding from Wertham to raise similar sentiments in the United States—with his argument strengthened by images of decapitated heads and gruesome murders on the covers of *Crime SuspenStories* (EC Comics), *Crimes by Women* (Fox), *Crime Does Not*

Pay (Lev Gleason Publications), *Lawbreakers Suspense Stories* (Charlton), and *Black Cat Mystery* (Harvey Comics). Following a hearing in the U.S. Senate, publishers decided to police themselves. The resulting Comics Code Authority banned gore, violence, and sexual innuendo and led to the possibly sad, if temporary, death of crime comics (still technically illegal in Canada).

Aside from the precode crime books, the 1950s may have been the start of the popular opinion that comics were really just kids' stuff. And for good reason—kids' comics made up the bulk of the comics released in this decade. *Classics Illustrated*, *Little Lulu*, *Walt Disney's Comics and Stories*, *Tom and Jerry*, and *New Funnies* filled the newsstands.

As in most industries, it was less common to find women working in comics in the 1950s than in the 1940s. With men returning home after the Second World War, many women decided their careers would take a backseat to raising children and trying to the heal the emotional wounds of an entire generation that had fought overseas. It was tough work.

One standout creator of this era was Marie Severin, the idol of comics colorists. Her impeccable skill gave EC comics a particularly vivid appeal, with their blood spatters and gore. Helen Meyer, who may be one of the most significant people in the medium's history, took the helm of Dell Comics, leading the company to its status as the world's largest comics publisher, selling an average of 800,000 copies of their all-ages comics per issue.

Though comics were still fairly popular at the beginning of the decade, they hit a sharp and steady decline after 1952, forcing some formerly popular publishers to cease publication, including Fawcett, St. John, EC (hit hard by CCA regulations), Standard, and Fiction House. Archie Comics maintained its volume of issues throughout the decade. DC, Marvel, and Dell all had steady climbs until decreasing output in the decade's last few years. The decline was largely due to a sudden shake-up in distribution, rather than negative effects from Comics Code rules (except for poor EC Comics).

By and large the female characters in the 1950s were definitely not the forceful, vengeful, and fascinating superheroines of the 1940s. In fact, superheroes in general, outside of DC Comics, seemed to be in a general decline. Little Lulu still ruled the roost, but Lois Lane suddenly went from a tough-edged crime reporter to a wannabe housewife trying to manipulate Superman into marriage. Most of the highest-volume comics in the 1950s starred male characters. Romance comics were starting to make significant headway, with *Young Romance*, *First Love Illustrated*, *Love Romances*, and *Hi-School Romances* gaining fans.

The 1950s was an era of significant upheaval within the industry. But on the surface, the comics were all placid and sweet, especially after the crackdown on horror and crime. ⚡

BLACK PHANTOM	Queen of the outlaws turned deputy sheriff	66 *Now you gents are going to learn the hard way that honesty is the best policy!* 99
		Created by: Frank Bolle and Gardner F. Fox
		First appearance: *Tim Holt* #25 (Magazine Enterprises, 1951)

It's not that women weren't seen in Westerns; after all, *someone* had to be carried away by boys wearing black hats and brought back to civilization by the boys in white hats. But women in such stories were not often seen with a gun in one hand, a knife in the other, and dressed in men's clothes. The exception: Black Phantom. She first appeared in the series *Tim Holt*, a comic that starred real-life Western movie hero Tim Holt as a cowboy who becomes a superhero called Red Mask (aka Redmask).

When we first meet Black Phantom, she's a daring stagecoach robber leading a crew of men—including the fiercely loyal muscleman Beast—to plunder gold from helpless passengers. Upon their success, Black Phantom, whose real name is Helena, strides into town to meet her twin sister, Jacarilla (later changed to Jicarilla), a popular burlesque dancer. Upon being discovered by Jacarilla's paramour Chito, Black Phantom resolves to protect her identity by throwing Chito into a secret whirlpool that will whisk him away to his death. She doesn't figure on Red Mask rescuing Chito, who turns out to be his partner. The hero handily dispatches Black Phantom's crew and comes after the ringleader, who hurls herself off a cliff in defiance rather than be captured alive.

And that's the end of Black Phantom . . . except, wait, then she appeared in twenty more issues and had her own spinoff special to boot!

Black Phantom returns almost two years later, with no explanation save that she was behind bars for a stint. Let me reassure you: she's gone good. Yet thanks to some sneaky villains, Red Mask refuses to believe her tale of redemption. Snitches get stitches, so her own former posse hangs her off a cliff to be eaten alive by vultures. Wow. First drowning to death in a whirlpool, now vulture torture—this was definitely a precode comic (for more on the Comics Code, see page 50). But don't worry; Black Phantom and Red Mask send her former friends plummeting to an early death, with Red Mask suggesting that Black Phantom become his assistant. Hmm. No offense, Red Mask, you're sassy in your own way. But Black Phantom deserves her own book!

Fortunately, someone agreed with that sentiment, because the very next appearance of Black Phantom has Red Mask noticing that she doesn't get enough work to do, even though she's been made a proper deputy. Feeling disrespected by Sherriff Gage (who gives all the choice jobs to Red Mask), Black Phantom sets out to prove her worth against the villain Skullhead and is taken hostage. For once, Red Mask and Black Phantom merely knock the villain out cold, rather than murdering him outright.

In her most interesting adventure, we see the return of Jicarilla, Black Phantom's hard-partying sister. When Black Phantom falls into a fever, Jicarilla steps in to preserve her sister's newfound respectability. Unfortunately, Jicarilla makes a terrible hero. Eventually the real outlaw heroine, fever and all, shoots down the bad guys and rescues both her sister and Red Mask. Sisters got to stick together!

To find an interesting, well-developed female character in a 1950s Western comic book is surprising, to say the least. In later issues, Black Phantom pretty much became a sidekick to the hero Red Mask. But in the adventures that she headlined—in the one issue of her own series—Black Phantom is a powerful, interesting, energetic character deserving of being remembered. The letters that readers sent in proved she had found popularity with both male and female fans of Western comics.

(Postscript: The Black Phantom character was ultimately rebooted into a T&A comic in the 1980s . . . but let's pretend that never happened.)

ESSENTIAL READING: You can check out some of the original Black Phantom adventures in *A-1 Comics* #141: *A Retrospective* (Boardman Books, 2015).

A beautiful and courageous WAC focused more on saving lives than finding romance	66Doctor, I may be a soldier . . . but when it comes to lipstick, I'm still a woman!99
	Created by: Bill Benulis and Jack Abel
	First appearance: *Rangers* #67 (Fiction House, 1952)

War comics were a popular genre even years after the Second World War ended, but rarely did they feature female lead characters. Women were temptresses who acted as double agents, damsels to be rescued, or girlfriends encountered along the way. The nurse genre was one way for women to enter the theater of war as leading ladies, such as Harvey Comics' Pat Parker, War Nurse (who was a kick-ass superheroine).

G.I. Jane was another noteworthy exception. Premiering in the popular action-adventure anthology *Rangers*, G.I. Jane was the story of Jane Walters, starting with her inscription into the army and basic training to her role in the Women's Army Auxiliary Corps (WAAC; later known as WAC). In her first adventure, Jane is working at the atomic research lab in Washington, D.C., when a shipment of radioactive metal goes missing. If she doesn't find it—and soon—innocent civilians will face an agonizing death.

Using her detective skills and her Geiger counter, Jane tracks down the missing material, but the new owners refuse to give it up; they intend to sell it. Trying to silence Jane with a headlock, the thief learns that a WAC is no one to trifle with. Jane easily throws him over. Unfortunately, doing so smears her lipstick, and the story ends with the all-important task of touching it up.

In further adventures, Jane uses her military skills to rescue two smart-mouth pilots from certain death as their plane crashes in the Florida Keys, and then she saves some vacation cottagers from an out-of-control wildfire. In the latter story she takes a moment to bond with a rescued tourist over how long it will be until they can touch up their makeup. Okay, Jane, you're still in the middle of a fire. Maybe you two should have other priorities (and maybe the writer should have asked a member of the WAC to look at his script).

Jane reluctantly sets cosmetic concerns aside when asked to look for her lost jeep and its secret supplies, which of course takes longer than usual because she's just a woman who can't make up her mind which road to follow. Nevertheless, after blithely ignoring catcalls from fellow soldiers while she's busy jumping from a helicopter into the middle of a raging inferno, Jane pluckily manages to hold the flames at bay with a fire extinguisher just long enough to grab the supplies.

Jane was never sent overseas, preferring to focus on domestic survival training. Her comics were educational to a degree, but also entertaining. Young readers got a decent idea of the duties of a WAC, though with strong elements of adventure added (I imagine that, like most jobs, actual WAC duties largely involved waiting around and doing paperwork, which doesn't make for great comics).

Despite appearing in only three issues of *Rangers*, G.I. Jane is notable for being one of the few non-nurse-themed war comics to star a woman, and she shouldn't be confused with other comics characters of the same name (Stanhall Comics produced a humor comic titled *G.I. Jane*, about a daffy blond always getting into mix-ups.) Although Jane Walters didn't delve into the same type of action you might find in the pages of, say, *He-Man Gun-Shooter War Comics Monthly* (sorry action fans, not a real comic), she did prove to be a capable and driven woman dedicated to her career as a soldier.

ESSENTIAL READING: No reprints currently exist of the G.I. Jane stories, but you may have luck finding scans of them online.

GAIL FORD, GIRL FRIDAY	Secretary to a homicide detective, she cracks more cases than he does	66 *Gail the Gumshoe becomes a taxi dancer and waltzes around for clues!* 99
		Created by: Eugene Leslie
		First appearance: *Super-Detective* magazine (Trojan, 1950)

Gail Ford is the dedicated secretary, or so-called Girl Friday, to Inspector Madson of the homicide division in an unnamed American city. She's glamorous, with a Bettie Page sort of style, and an expert at going undercover in dangerous situations. (You want to bet they don't give her hazard pay?)

Gail premiered in the pages of the pulp magazine *Super-Detective* in 1950, before graduating to the *Crime Smashers* comics series that same year. In her first adventure in *Crime Smashers*, we're confronted with a gruesome sight: the corpse of a young girl, posed in a department store window among the mannequins. Gail goes undercover, taking the dead girl's job as a saleswoman. Using clever detective work, she discovers hidden papers naming the murderer. She narrowly escapes death by shooting at him in the dark, then she chases the

suspect through the building using the mail-room chute and finally tackles him. She's a hands-on kind of detective.

It seems that in Gail's city a gruesome murder occurs every few days. In her next adventure the authorities discover another dead woman artfully posed, this time on a cemetery headstone. Gail again goes under-cover, this time as a waitress, and takes on a few dates with a shy, quiet loner. At first she thinks the guy's just weird enough to be the killer. But it turns out he's actually just a sweet weirdo. His twin brother, on the other hand, is a homicidal maniac.

Though she works for the homicide di-vision, that doesn't stop Gail from busting up the odd cocaine ring here and there. Any-thing for the good of the city. Whether that means jumping off fire escapes, cozying up to mob bosses, or posing as a lady of the night, Gail Ford does whatever it takes to crack the case, much in the same vein as other Trojan heroines like Sally the Sleuth (see page 17). Gail even racks up a pretty decent body count by the end of the series; her resourcefulness ex-tends to shooting the odd crook or shoving a lit cigarette in his eye. Despite it all, Gail remains a simple Girl Friday, with no promotion in sight.

Gail wasn't a quippy smart aleck like other female crime-fighters of her era, but she was focused, serious, and passionate about her work. (It may be that her static delivery is more reflective of her writer's abilities than her own personali-ty.) As for her enemies, more often than not they were women almost as cunning as she was, albeit motivated by a cold ruthlessness instead of a zest for justice. They were always easily captured and brought in to be tried by the law (or, on occasion, murdered on their way to trial). Gail Ford may not have had the best dialogue, but she was indicative of the tough lady detectives that were surpris-ingly common in comics before the Comics Code Authority erased their edge.

ESSENTIAL READING: Both Eternity Comics' *Spicy Tales* reprint series from the late 1980s/early 1990s and the *Private Super-Detective* reprint collection by Pulpville Press (2013) feature reprints of Gail Ford's early appearances from her pulp magazine days. Some of Gail Ford's *Crime Smashers* stories have also been reprinted in *Spicy Tales*.

JETTA RAYE		
	Perky teenager in a Jetsons-like future	❝I never thought Arky would turn out to be a space wolf!❞
		Created by: Dan DeCarlo
		First appearance: *Jetta* #5 (Standard Comics, 1952)

In the far future of 2052, flying cars and rocketpacks are all the rage with the kids . . . along with boys wearing their underwear on the outside of their clothes. Jetta Raye, the star of her own series, doesn't have to conform to these awful fashion standards; she pretty much looks like she stepped out of the 1950s (well, with a miniskirt).

Jetta is a hot-headed teenager, jealous of the girls trying to win the attention of her main beau Arky (even more so when he returns those attentions). Her main competition is the slinky and gorgeous Hilaria Hale—because if we've learned anything from 1950s comics, it's that women can't possibly be friends. In her first appearance, Jetta devises a plan to win back her boyfriend through hard work and the accidental humiliation of her rival. This pattern will be repeated again and again, for Hilaria is a most persistent cosmic cutie. At least Hilaria also has the attention of space-wolf Biff, who constantly tries to beat Arky and win Hilaria's heart. Or Jetta's, whichever the plot calls for.

As the "Teen-Age Sweetheart of the 21st Century," Jetta can be easily and accurately summed up as Betty Cooper in space. Each story is a classic teenage adventure with sci-fi twists. If her boyfriend crashes the car, it's a flying car. Instead of a drive-in, the kids go to a blast-in (for a chocolate fission fizz). Dialogue and scenarios frequently reference the "old days" of the 1950s, and the current culture of 2052 is characterized by a lot of nostalgia for the time of chivalry and manual labor. Some aspects of this future are funnier today than when they were written, especially those technologies and fads that are now quaintly obsolete. For example, football programs are shown on microfilm, portable record players are the accessory of choice, and "space drum majorette" is an enviable position at school.

Jetta was one of several popular teen comics of the day, which were largely interchangeable. But Dan DeCarlo's masterful art helped set this one apart, and *Jetta* is a precursor to his later work redefining the *Archie* girls into perfect pinup hotties. With DeCarlo's lush figures and fanciful designs, the *Jetta* teen comic was pretty much the pinnacle of its era. And the dad-joke-worthy humor of *Jetta*'s *Jetsons*-like future provides a pleasant dose of retro-futuristic wistfulness when read today.

ESSENTIAL READING: IDW publishing has reprinted all the Jetta comics in the *Dan DeCarlo's Jetta* collection (2010).

LUCY THE REAL GONE GAL	Teenage princess trying to have it all	66 *That girl makes me so mad, I could peel my nail polish!* 99
		Created by: Lily Renée
		First appearance: *Lucy the Real Gone Gal* #1 (St. John, 1953)

First premiering as "Kitty" in a self-titled series in 1948, and drawn by superstar artist Lily Renée (see Señorita Rio, page 39), this comic was reprinted several years later with the character's name changed to Lucy (and the artist credit removed). In either version, the star is a young, spoiled girl whose focus is on the latest fashions and the cutest boys—indeed, all of her adventures revolve around how to obtain one or the other. Her rival is Wanda Farr and, as is customary in teen comics, the two are constantly rubbing their successes in each other's faces.

Lucy is a strawberry-blonde dreamer, an idealist, and a romantic, but also judgmental and quick to anger, causing sitcom levels of misunderstandings. These usually manifest in fights with her boyfriend Wally, who's infatuated with her despite Lucy's tantrums and jealousy. Rather than inducing eye-rolling, it's actually pretty refreshing to see a teenager acting like a real teenager, full of hormones and misplaced rage.

Lucy's short-lived series also featured stories of "Rita," "Trudi," "Ginny," and "Jelly Bean." All were largely exchangeable with Lucy, save that Rita appeared to be in her twenties instead of her teens, and Rita and Ginny are both brunettes (and not even evil, what a shock!). While not completely immoral, none of these characters is exactly a candidate for sainthood either. They tend to be self-involved, cruel to their lovers, and ridiculously vain (or if none of these qualities, then incredibly dimwitted). For example, Trudi fat-shames and brow-beats her boyfriend; Rita pretends to be helpless to trap a man into an unwanted marriage; Ginny drops from a stage rope just to win a dressmaking contest . . . Not exactly role models then or now.

As for Lucy, she is portrayed as a fickle soul who abandons boyfriends for crushes with the drop of a hat (as opposed to 1960s Bunny Ball, page 81, who happily dates them all at once). But Lucy's world is strange. Having developed a normal schoolgirl crush on her gym teacher (who is a muscle-bound lunk with a crewcut, sharp suits, and a dangerous cigarette habit), Lucy is flattered when he begins to return her affections. Remember, she's in high school. He's her teach-er. No one thought this was weird? Even when he says, "You're older and wiser than you look"?

Apparently the writers quickly tired of writing about teenage girls—after four issues the series changed to "Meet Miss Pepper" and focused on the adven-tures of a new teacher and her love life. And with that Lucy's temperamental teenage adventures vanished forever. Still, Lucy was a fun character while she lasted, despite all her faults.

ESSENTIAL READING: Lucy's adventures have never been reprinted, so looking for the original comics from the 1950s is your best bet.

MAN-HUNTIN' MINNIE OF DELTA PU	A desperate-for-love college girl doing everything she can to catch a man	66Of all the guys who never take me out, I like not going out with him the best!99
		Created by: Jack Bradbury
		First appearance: *Dizzy Dames* #1 (American Comics Group, 1952)

In the comic book anthology series *Dizzy Dames* there were only two varieties of women: dumb pretty ones and dumb ugly ones. While characters like Mo-ronica, Goofy Gertie, Screwball Sal, Daffy Dotty, Looney Lucy, and Broadway Babes were firmly of the cute airhead type, also present were Knothead Nellie (not to be confused with Knothead Nancy, who was a total hottie), the Daffy Damsels, and Man-Huntin' Minnie, whose jokes stemmed from their homely appearances.

In her debut, we meet Man-Huntin' Minnie moping around the sorority house, trying to find the one dress that her crush hasn't seen her in . . . so that

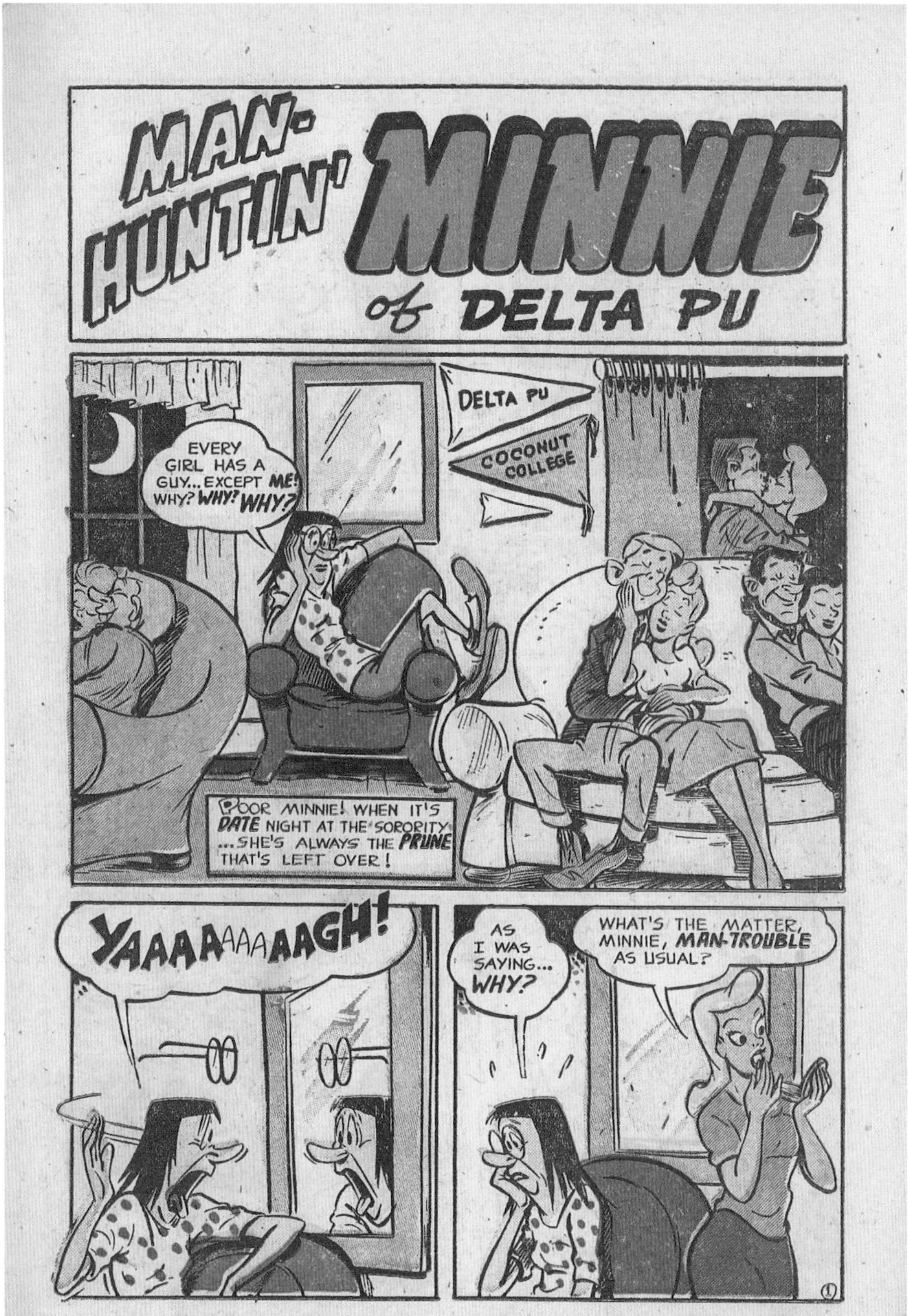
MAN-HUNTIN' MINNIE of DELTA PU
DELTA PU
COCONUT COLLEGE
EVERY GIRL HAS A GUY... EXCEPT ME! WHY? WHY? WHY?
POOR MINNIE! WHEN IT'S DATE NIGHT AT THE SORORITY ...SHE'S ALWAYS THE PRUNE THAT'S LEFT OVER!
YAAAAAAAAAGH!
AS I WAS SAYING... WHY?
WHAT'S THE MATTER, MINNIE, MAN-TROUBLE AS USUAL?
1

she can sit alone at home, pretending that if they were on a date he would like it.

Oh Minnie!

Her roommate Roberta, a cute perky blonde, comes by and chastises her for this foolishness. Why, any woman can get a man, she tells Minnie; you just have to figure out what you can offer them. And since Minnie certainly can't depend on her looks—and the local boys all know her well enough to see that her personality isn't much better—a stranger might just be the best option. So instead of picking a boy to go after just because he's pretty, Roberta urges Minnie to pick someone who needs her help to succeed in life. That's actually . . . not awful advice? Looking beyond physical appearance to find a partner you can connect with, working together to achieve your goals in life, sounds pretty sane, right? I'm suspicious of this . . .

Minnie then decides to skip school in order to look for a man with ambition. Minnie, no! Wrong lesson! So of course she hangs around downtown, where a local builder tries to attach her to the wall, thinking she's a gargoyle. Misunderstanding his fumbles for affection, Minnie loudly proclaims her love only to discover the man in question has a doting family back home. The adulterer!

After a few more similar miscommunications with men whom she tries to ardently pursue—in a fashion reminiscent of Pepé Le Pew romancing that poor cat (i.e., pretty much straight assault)—Minnie eventually ends up in jail, bemoaning the advice that her faithful friend gave her.

In Minnie's only other appearance, the plot pretty much follows the same arc. Roberta advises Minnie to pretend to be intelligent to attract her crush; the plan backfires and her crush goes home with a cute redhead instead. Minnie's would-be beau in this story is a professor twice her age, who really shouldn't be going on dates with any of the girls at the college, but what do I know? It's the 1950s and everything goes, apparently.

You don't see many comics featuring female characters with proportions other than 36-23-38 (comics prefer their characters a bit hippy). So it is nice to see Minnie drawn in the same vein as Big Ethel from Archie Comics. Though her groan-worthy exploits might cause us to cringe at times, we can all relate to chasing someone who just isn't interested. Like Big Ethel, who can't ever land Jughead Jones no matter how hard she tries, Minnie is always the butt of the joke. But she keeps on trying, even though she never seems able to get much positive mojo going for her. Which, all in all, is kind of a bummer.

ESSENTIAL READING: Man-Huntin' Minnie's stories have never been reprinted, so you'll need to hunt out the original *Dizzy Dames* nos. 1 and 2 if you want to spend time with this lackluster gal.

NURSE HELEN GRANT

A sensitive yet practical nurse embroiled in romantic affairs	66Only a woman like nurse Helen Grant could return a man to life and love!99
	Created by: Vince Colletta
	First appearance: *The Romances of Nurse Helen Grant* #1 (Marvel Comics, 1957)

Nurse Helen Grant moves to a new city, looking for challenging employment. She meets Dr. Brian Clark, who definitely challenges her all right: he insults her abilities and suggests she take an easier job elsewhere. Helen Grant then, quite logically, finds Clark to be the most perfect specimen of humanity she's ever met and proceeds to fall head over heels for him. When a rich patient collapses, forcing the pair to make an emergency house call and subsequently remove a tumor, Helen assists with the procedure flawlessly. Thus Clark hires her on the spot—because apparently the standard reference check doesn't cut it for this dashing MD.

The single issue of *Nurse Helen Grant* is the most remarkably overwritten comic story I've ever had the pleasure of reading. From all of the panels waxing poetically about her very many virtues, you would think Helen is a saint. And Dr. Clark! Why, his fingers are strong, gentle, skilled, and warm—all at the same time—as he demonstrates when he lays his hands on Helen's shoulder in a gesture of mild affection, which she interprets as true love, or pulls out a cigarette in order to look distantly cool and professional.

Helen Grant's rival for the good doctor's affections, the Veronica to her Betty, is socialite Diana Hilliard. And you know that Diana's no good because she smokes cigarettes, too (only men can get away with smoking in 1950s melodramas), *and* she loudly proclaims her own skill at running a business (only men can run a successful business in 1950s melodramas). Helen soon grows annoyed at the amount of time that Dr. Clark spends with Diana (who becomes his fiancée). This tension continues until Helen grows to like her rival, after watching Diana stay up all night waiting in the ER while Dr. Clark gives emergency treatment to a little boy.

Shortly after, Diana invites Dr. Clark to visit her at work, where he sees her crack the whip and boss people around. The doc immediately falls out of love with her. Fortunately, they part easily and he returns to Helen to toy with her affections by going hot and cold at a moment's notice. But it was all a purposeful ploy: Diana had in fact decided to *give* Dr. Clark to Helen (that's how fiancées work, right? They aren't actual human beings). She figured her cold businesswoman personality wouldn't provide Dr. Clark with the warmth and comfort he would need after a full day of battling the demons of death.

This hot/cold thread continues for the rest of Helen's adventures (four are squeezed into her first issue alone). In one story she falls in love with a tortured young immigrant from Hungary named Sandor, only for the two to be torn apart for unknown reasons. (They become best friends instead, sans explanation). A jealous Dr. Clark decides to make the ultimate expression of his love and presents his steadfast nurse with . . . a theater ticket. Okay, not exactly a ring, or even a gesture of anything more than mild affection, but that's probably the best Helen's going to get from him, let's be honest.

Nurse Grant is a skilled medical professional, with a soft heart and warm manner, who is pretty much Ideal Wife Material. The hot/cold relationship with her medical colleague is a characteristic problem in romance stories; they're seen as more interesting if they maintain sexual tension without fulfilling it. As a nurse-comic melodrama, *Nurse Helen Grant* is pretty typical of the genre. But its heroine is particularly special. What other nurse has been described as a "crisp clean, shining creature in the service of humanity"?

ESSENTIAL READING: *The Romances of Nurse Helen Grant* #1 (Marvel, 1957) is her first and only appearance.

THE OLD WITCH	The ghoulish host of terror in precode horror comics	66 This is The Old Witch, stirring up her cruddy cauldron, ready to dish out another tasty tale of terror! 99
		Created by: William Gaines and Al Feldstein
		First appearance: *Haunt of Fear* #2 (EC Comics, 1950)

The only woman in the triumvirate of ghoulish horror hosts in the EC Comics stable, the Old Witch was the face of *Haunt of Fear*. In this title she answered letters from dear readers eager for more "revolting recipes from her reeking cauldron." Across all three EC horror titles (*Haunt*, plus *Tales from the Crypt* and *The Vault of Horror*), the Old Witch introduced horror stories that focused primarily on supernatural ghoulies under the bed. Today, she and her colleague the Vault-Keeper are largely forgotten in favor of the Crypt-Keeper, mostly thanks to the latter's massively successful HBO series, cartoon, and feature films. I guess pretty boys really do get it all.

The Old Witch's personal origin was revealed halfway through the series, in "A Little Stranger." In the story we learn that her parents were Elicia, an elegant and ancient vampire, and Zorgo, a rough hermit werewolf. Together they haunted the Bavarian Alps, consuming unlucky travelers who happened across their path. Murdered by vengeful townspeople, the pair married after death in a ceremony presided over by zombies and ghouls, with their ghastly offspring Witch born a year later.

It was the Witch's fearful presence that, in the canon of the EC universe, prompted the company's foray into horror comics. She forced the EC editors into a dank sewer until her contract was signed! In addition, the Witch is no mere sex object pinup. Scorning the advances of both of her fellow horror hosts, she kindly suggests that her two corpselike coworkers go bury themselves alive instead of bothering her.

As for the women in the Witch's stories, most were the classic EC Comics stock of seductresses, two-timers, and murderesses who got what they deserved in the end (usually an incredibly gruesome death or, at minimum, a descent into perpetual madness). Occasionally, if she was lucky, a female lead could be promoted to victim instead (in EC Comics, there is no option for heroine) and seek revenge on her murderer after death.

Horror and crime reigned supreme in comics during the 1940s, with EC Comics the gold standard for purveyors of putrid tales. That is, until its comic books became the face of moral outrage in the United States and Canada. The lurid covers, featuring bloody decapitations and rotting bodies rising from graves, curried little favor in obscenity court cases. Soon after the U.S. comics industry's self-appointed Comics Code Authority went into effect in 1954, horror disappeared from the newly sanitized newsstands. However, in the 1970s, a character called Eve, who looked startlingly like the Old Witch, hosted the tales in DC's *Secrets of Sinister House*. Eventually Neil Gaiman worked Eve into his acclaimed *Sandman* series. So in a way, a little bit of the Old Witch is still in comics today.

ESSENTIAL READING: If you want to catch the Old Witch's origin story, check out *Sucker Bait and Other Stories* (2014).

STARLIGHT	A danger-seeking Huron girl looking to be treated as a warrior	66 *One side, Old Turtle, I will teach them what it means to jest with me!* 99
		Created by: Ann Adams and Ralph Mayo
		First appearance: *Indians* #2 (Fiction House, 1950)

Indians was a comic series intended to provide educational and entertaining stories featuring Indigenous characters to, you know, inform white people of the exoticism in their midst. Of course, the Nations featured were always placed

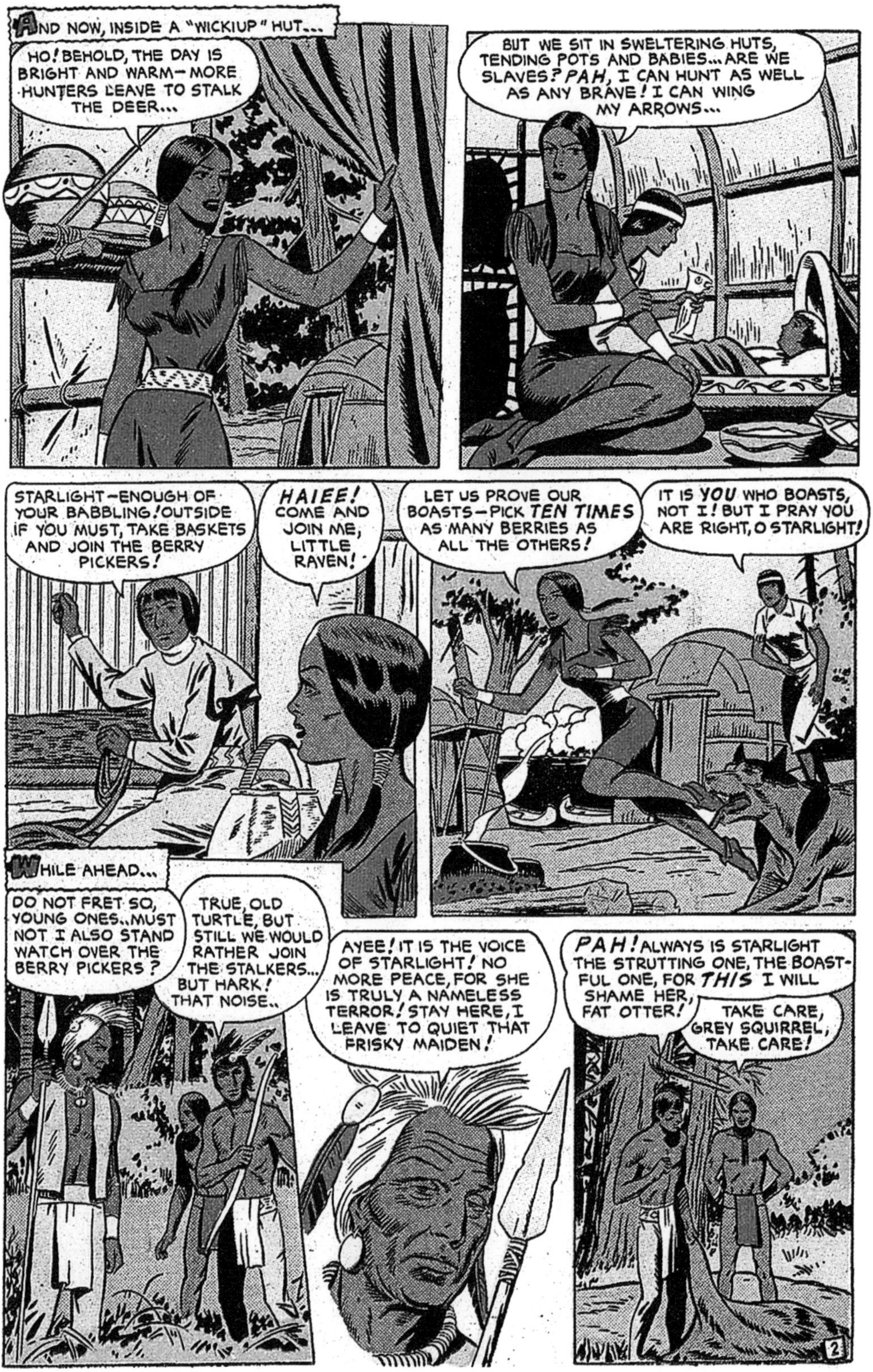
AND NOW, INSIDE A "WICKIUP" HUT...
HO! BEHOLD, THE DAY IS BRIGHT AND WARM—MORE HUNTERS LEAVE TO STALK THE DEER...
BUT WE SIT IN SWELTERING HUTS, TENDING POTS AND BABIES... ARE WE SLAVES? PAH, I CAN HUNT AS WELL AS ANY BRAVE! I CAN WING MY ARROWS...
STARLIGHT—ENOUGH OF YOUR BABBLING! OUTSIDE IF YOU MUST, TAKE BASKETS AND JOIN THE BERRY PICKERS!
HAIEE! COME AND JOIN ME, LITTLE RAVEN!
LET US PROVE OUR BOASTS—PICK TEN TIMES AS MANY BERRIES AS ALL THE OTHERS!
IT IS YOU WHO BOASTS, NOT I! BUT I PRAY YOU ARE RIGHT, O STARLIGHT!
WHILE AHEAD...
DO NOT FRET SO, YOUNG ONES.. MUST NOT I ALSO STAND WATCH OVER THE BERRY PICKERS?
TRUE, OLD TURTLE, BUT STILL WE WOULD RATHER JOIN THE STALKERS... BUT HARK! THAT NOISE..
AYEE! IT IS THE VOICE OF STARLIGHT! NO MORE PEACE, FOR SHE IS TRULY A NAMELESS TERROR! STAY HERE, I LEAVE TO QUIET THAT FRISKY MAIDEN!
PAH! ALWAYS IS STARLIGHT THE STRUTTING ONE, THE BOASTFUL ONE, FOR THIS I WILL SHAME HER, FAT OTTER!
TAKE CARE, GREY SQUIRREL, TAKE CARE!
2

MAIDENS SHOULD BE MODEST... MAIDENS SHOULD BE GENTLE AND SHY—CONTENT TO COOK AND WEAVE FOR THE MEAT KILLERS... BUT THE HEART THAT BEAT IN *STARLIGHT'S* BREAST WAS TUNED TO THE WINDIGO WINDS... TO THE HUNT AND THE CHASE AND THE DANGER DRUMS!

firmly in that nebulous time period popular in American Westerns. And they all lived pretty much the same lifestyle of war, hunting, and gathering, with little differentiation, even though the tribes who were highlighted ranged from across the country.

Comics, as well as films and TV, have always followed a tradition of "pan-Indian" identity, combining aspects of different cultures into one in order to best showcase "the other." I didn't really expect accurate representation from a comic that also starred "Manzar: The White Indian." When the art features wigwams in a Huron village, instead of longhouses, and totem poles on the wrong side of the continent, what can you do but purse your lips and shrug? (And maybe vow to foster an environment in which Indigenous cultures are portrayed and written by Indigenous creators.)

But contrary to a lot of Western comics, Starlight's story does present unique personalities for each character. As the protagonist, Starlight is described as a "firebrand" and "frisky." She takes risks and jumps into danger. While gathering berries deep in the woods with her friend Little Raven, a grizzly attacks, sending Little Raven scrambling up a tree. Starlight dives into action, thrusting her spear deep into the beast as her friend escapes. Elsewhere, local boys who'd been teasing and taunting the two women are kidnapped by a Mohawk tribe and taken downriver. Which is when Starlight sends herself and the grizzly tumbling off a ledge into the water, sending most of the Mohawks scattering while she alone takes care of the enemy attempting to kill her tribemate.

By the next issue, Grey Squirrel has forgotten that Starlight saved his life and blames her for setting a hive of hornets on the village (which in fact he had disturbed). Upset, Starlight follows the timeless teenager tradition of running away from home, again with her loyal friend Little Raven, only to unearth and foil a Mohawk conspiracy to set the nations to war. After capturing the Mohawk leaders, Starlight at last earns her rightful status as a warrior in the community. In later issues her temper gets her into trouble, but things always turn to her advantage as she saves the lives of innocents, teaches children how to hunt, and consistently rescues her male brethren from danger. Starlight is devoted to her community and family, and she uses her above-average strength, skill, and wits in each adventure. She's just a pair of tights away from being a superhero!

Sadly, Starlight lasted for only seven issues, though the *Indians* series continued for another year after her disappearance. A look at the letter columns in *Indians* suggests that, compared to the other stories in the collection, Starlight met with mixed reception. Parents sniffed that her tale was "far too glamorized to be anything near reality." But younger readers, particularly girls, wrote in to say that they enjoyed her adventures. (I wonder what "glamour" these parents were talking about? Was it that Starlight was a woman's action comic written by a woman?) Many of the letters mention the importance of preserving American history, but each discussion is mired in the past, treating indigenous culture in North America as a "was." Not much has changed, save that these days there's largely an erasure of indigenous characters in comics, rather than the romanticization and simplification found in Starlight's stories or the aggressively rude stereotypes in other comics from that era.

However, *Indians* was praised by Indigenous readers as a step in the right direction, citing that the stories featured Indigenous characters as human beings instead of murderous madmen. It's a shame that this approach hasn't progressed, and that we so rarely see native characters in comics pages anymore.

ESSENTIAL READING: *Indians* #2–8 (Fiction House), though good luck finding them!

TOMBOY	Pint-sized superhero with fists of fury	**❝I don't like being pushed around, rat!❞**
		Created by: Mort Meskin
		First appearance: *Captain Flash* #1 (Sterling, 1954)

Janie Jackson is a gentle little lady who respects her parents, does her homework, and behaves properly. But at night she's the scourge of the underworld known as Tomboy! "Disguised" in a simple domino mask and skirt-suit with boots, Tomboy looks little different from Janie, save that her hair is worn down. She has no special powers but is extraordinarily fearless in the face of danger. Swinging across laundry lines to boot robbers in the face, she follows up with a wisecrack and a sock to the jaw. Then she leaves the concussed ne'er-do-wells for the cops to discover, hightailing it outta there before they arrive. Not because she's a masked vigilante and might be prosecuted for interfering with justice, but because the local police lieutenant is her father!

Tomboy's nemesis is the Claw, a mob boss with the hands of a savage beast. Learning that Tomboy has a connection to the lieutenant, he springs a trap.

But of course Tomboy easily escapes. When she ends up on an airplane hurtling through the sky at who knows what speed, Tomboy backflips out the door, grabs the undercarriage, prevents the bomb bay doors from opening, then dives into the ocean and swims away as the plane explodes.

And remember: all without superpowers!

As Janie, she has a bratty brother who worships Tomboy and mocks his sister for being too feminine and weak. If he only knew! Tomboy is a clever girl, and one time she even masquerades as herself to throw her parents and her brother off her trail (and maybe to laugh a bit at their thickness as well).

Janie Jackson's adventures were brief, appearing as a recurring adventure in the unpopular comic *Captain Flash*. She lasted only as long as his run: a mere four issues. But a teenage female protagonist who can beat up crooks and doesn't mind being a femme by day and a tomboy by night? She should have been the star!

ESSENTIAL READING: You can catch Tomboy's first adventure reprinted in *Golden Age Treasury*, vol. 2 (AC Comics, 2003).

WENDY THE GOOD LITTLE WITCH	Wendy's a witch—but one who only does good	**❝I think beauty is one of the greatest things in the world!❞**
		Created by: Steve Muffatti
		First appearance: *Casper* #20 (Harvey Comics, 1954)

A Harvey Comics creation, Wendy the Good Little Witch came from the same publishing family as Casper the Friendly Ghost, Hot Stuff, and Richie Rich. She started as a supporting character in Casper's comic, spun off into animated cartoons, and then landed in her own long-running series. Harvey's comics were designed to be easy to pick up and put down, with no prior knowledge about the characters required. Readers could have a few laughs and simply enjoy pleasant, kid-friendly fare.

Wendy first appeared as a chaste love interest for her ghosty boy costar. As the youngest member of a coven of ancient, evil witches, she had quite a bit in common with Casper. And unlike most people, she wasn't the least bit scared of him. Together they went on adventures in the *Harvey Hits* anthology. Soon the romance angle was turned off, and Wendy and Casper were just the best of friends, solving crimes, traveling through time, and reveling in the opportunity for companionship. When Wendy's adventures don't involve her supernatural friends, she spends her time dealing with her aunt witches, undoing their mischief on the forest creatures while maintaining peace between the ghosts and her family.

Admittedly, the plots were formulaic and the puns groan-worthy, as in most kids' comics. But know what? Every so often you need a comic that lets you giggle at little witches and affable ghosts being friends and having fun. And if it makes you crave a Hostess fruit pie at the same time, maybe it's teaching children the right lessons.

Wendy is a good role model for children, and let's admit it, a lot of adults probably need her too. She cares deeply about her friends in the forest and is faithfully loyal to them. (Though her aunts recommend that she befriend absolutely no one; friends are the worst!) Wendy is a spot of brightness in a family, and a world, that seems kind of messed up, and she does whatever she can to fix people's problems. There's a reason that Wendy's stories were beloved and enduring, running from the 1950s all the way to the 1990s (she even met the New Kids on the Block!). It's because they just make you feel good inside.

ESSENTIAL READING: You can enjoy some of Wendy's best adventures in the Casper-focused reprint *Harvey Comics Classics* #1 (Dark Horse, 2007).

The

50s

SUPERGIRL	Bright and cheerful guardian angel to her adopted planet	*"I won't get any headlines for my feats like my cousin Superman does. But it's still super-fun to work secretly as Supergirl and help others!"*
		Created by: Otto Binder, Al Plastino, and Curt Swan
		First appearance: *Action Comics* #252 (DC Comics, 1959)

Supergirl, the Maid of Steel, has existed in a few different forms and identities. The first test of the waters by DC Comics for a female companion to Superman was in a story in the late 1950s featuring Jimmy Olsen wishing desperately for Superman to have a good girlfriend. Mighty nice of you, Jimmy, but you're the one who has stuck with Superman through thick and thin, so I think you have those duties well covered.

This proto-Supergirl dies tragically at the end of the issue, but she paves the way for a girl with the same powers to enter the scene a few years later. The new Supergirl is the one that sticks: Superman's long-lost cousin Kara Zor-El, aka Linda Lee, whom he promptly abandons at an orphanage minutes after she arrives. Because, well, Superman is sometimes a superjerk.

Supergirl premiered in 1959 to an incredibly enthusiastic response. But that's not to say that comic book trolls didn't exist even in midcentury America. As one disgruntled young reader wrote in to say: "I'm sure most of us boys would prefer the book much better with something else. So how about moving Supergirl over to *Lois Lane* comics and make everybody happy?" Not all boys felt the same, with another reader gushing, "I almost like her better than Superman!" Clearly the divisiveness caused by introducing female characters into comics is not a new phenomenon.

Supergirl's first adventures focused on her maintaining her secret identity while trying her best to improve the lives of the other orphans. Oh, and occasionally saving the world.

In the 1960s Supergirl frequently appeared on the cover of Superman's comics, along with Krypto the Superdog. Girl and pup were treated pretty much the same in Superman's self-titled series. In the pages of *Action Comics*, however, Supergirl enjoyed a more significant presence, often with her own backup strip and star placement on many covers. Like Superman, Supergirl also had her own mini-menagerie, including a flying horse named Comet (a transformed human who later fell in love with her) and her supercat Streaky. Next to *MAD* magazine, Superman was the most popular comic of the 1960s, and therefore Supergirl was the most popular female superhero of the 1960s (at least when Lois Lane didn't have superpowers).

Like Wonder Woman, Supergirl has undergone dramatic changes since her first appearance. She's been killed off, rebooted, and replaced by other Supergirls. She even briefly dated Lex Luthor (*shudder*). Supergirl has appeared in film adaptations and cartoons, and in 2015 she became a cute and bubbly Ally McBeal–esque superhero in her own TV series. She subsequently triggered an internet meme: her incredibly infectious happiness as the Flash delivers an ice cream cone at superspeed was a symbol to fangirls everywhere of everything being right with the world.

Supergirl is a fun, cheery superhero who's a much-needed beam of sunlight amid the seriousness of most comics and downer film adaptations. Sometimes we all just need to read the adventures of a girl in a cape saving orphans with her flying horse. And that's why she's stuck around for so long.

CHAPTER

4

The 19

60s

SUPERHEROES RETURN →

THE 1960s

Like the ghosts of genres past, the superheroes of the 1960s seemed to rise from the dead. DC Comics still dominated the market with Superman and Batman, along with a healthy and popular selection of all-ages humor comics. But Marvel, which a decade earlier had dropped superheroes like an old sock, came out with a fresh and exciting approach to the genre. It was so successful that Marvel's output skyrocketed, from about half as many titles as DC to nearly its equal by decade's end.

Women were definitely working in the industry in the 1960s: colorists like Tatjana Wood, artists like Liz Safian Berube (*Young Romance*) and Ramona Fradon (*Aquaman*), writers like Linda Fite (*The Cat*), and editors such as Phyllis Reed and Susan Lane. Still, most big companies were boys' clubs.

Romance comics were coming into their own, and though they were geared specifically to women, they were written largely by men. The superhero comics of the day were pretty much a gender-neutral genre, appealing equally to male and female readers. Comics marketed toward young women (including teen comics, romance comics, and the strangely popular nurse comics) had fairly strong sales in this decade, roughly matching sales of boys' comics (like Western and war comics). You couldn't say that the 1960s were bad for female fans; comics were still widely available on the newsstand and remained popular among boys and girls alike.

But the most succesful comics were those that appealed equally to both genders, such as superhero, humor, and film/TV adaptations. These titles usually sold twice as well as other, more gendered books. Even their letter pages show a near-equal mix of male and female readers writing in.

Given that, and as superheroes reclaimed the pop-culture status they'd enjoyed in the 1940s . . . where were the superheroines? Sure, Ant-Man had a vain sidekick in the Wasp, and other female side characters debuted here and there in the new Marvel comics (e.g., the Invisible Woman and Marvel Girl). And at DC, legacy characters like Wonder Woman and Supergirl still turned up; Batgirl, the Barbara Gordon version, was prominent in both the TV and comic universes simultaneously. But there were no new women superhero characters fronting their own books, despite being incredibly numerous just two decades earlier.

Jeet Heer, editor of *The Superhero Reader* (University Press of Mississippi, 2013), suggests that romance-comics writers who moved to superhero comics essentially triggered a merging of the two genres. Their melodramatic sensibilities bled into the action-packed superhero stories, and maybe that's why female characters in 1960s comics tended to be love interests or sidekicks. In any case, even though girls were reading superhero comics, it seemed that publishers had no interest in presenting a female superhero who led her own title. Not when there were so many nurses having torrid affairs with vulnerable patients for girls to read about.

Speaking of readers, this decade saw the rise of fan culture and community—including the first comics-specific convention, held in 1964.

As the comics readership aged, there also grew an impatience with the limitations of the Comics Code Authority and the perceived staleness and juvenile tone of genre comics. As a result, the late 1960s saw the beginnings of the counterculture underground "comix" movement. These comics were closely tied to the hippie and youth communities and were often found in "head shops" that sold black-light posters and drug paraphernalia. East Village Other, Apex Novelties, and Parallax were publishers pushing out comics by creators like Joel Beck (one of the first underground cartoonists) and Robert Crumb (probably the best known creator from this movement).

We'll see what women thought of this comix movement in the next chapter. ⚡

ANGEL O'DAY	A martial-arts-trained detective who solves crime with her gorilla partner	66Finger-karate, hai!99
		Created by: Tex Blaisdell, Ed Nelson Bridwell, Al Jaffee, and Bob Oksner
		First appearance: *Showcase* #77 (DC Comics, 1968)

Angel is your everyday drop-dead gorgeous working woman. She runs a faltering detective agency with her partner Sam Simeon, an idealistic artist more committed to drawing comic books than accompanying her on cases. But working together, though frustrating, often leads to them growing closer together as friends, and maybe more . . . Okay, let's get this out of the way: Angel is a human woman. Sam is a talking gorilla. They are not going to end up together. We're still in the days of the Comics Code Authority, after all.

Angel and the Ape was a fun, brightly colored, bombastic, mod series steeped in 1960s style. The title character, a curvy pinup model type, is the brains of her detective agency, with soft-hearted Sam being the reluctant brawn. Not that Angel couldn't take care of herself in a brawl; in the first issue she handily employs her martial arts skills to put away three crooks at a time (while sidekick Sam watches on, analyzing her poses for his next comic strip). Included in the comic was a thinly veiled caricature of rival Marvel Comics president Stan Lee, depicted as an overbearing and egotistical comics editor named Stan Bragg, whom Sam constantly hounds for delayed paychecks.

In addition to being a highly skilled martial artist, superb markswoman, trained detective, and capable go-go dancer, Angel O'Day has yet another side, which was revealed when the book changed its title to *Meet Angel!* We then learn that Angel is also closely connected to the supernatural, with her aunt Evilisha being both a witch and a double agent.

Perhaps not surprisingly, the series was canceled with that issue.

A later reboot in the 1990s expanded Angel's family even more, revealing fellow sixties heroine "Dumb Bunny," of the satire series *Inferior Five*, to be Angel's half-sister. In the 2000s, the series was rebooted yet again, this time as a raunchy sex comedy featuring Angel in the role of the frequently unclothed and clumsy heroine. Thankfully that stint lasted for only a single miniseries. These later incarnations lacked the charm and humor that made the original so compelling. The sixties version looked like a teen comic, read like *MAD* magazine, and somehow was adult oriented without sinking too low.

ESSENTIAL READING: Track down the original 1960s issues. No reprint of this series has yet been issued.

BARBARELLA	An outer-space vixen exploring the expanses of alien sexuality	66 *It won't be the first time an outer-space creature has viewed my nudity!* 99
		Created by: Jean-Claude Forest
		First appearance: *V Magazine* (Spring 1962)

I know what you're thinking: Hold on! Barbarella originated in a French comic book, and this is a book about North American comics. What gives?

Well, here's the deal. Barbarella was published in an English translation within the same decade as its initial French appearance, and then it was turned into a popular film starring Jane Fonda. So, French in origin, but accessible enough to the North American population to warrant discussion.

For the record, the sci-fi comic *Barbarella* was first published as an ongoing strip in the French publication *V Magazine* before being collected and translated into English by Grove Press in 1968. The protagonist is a lone Earth woman wandering the stars, and we're never given an explanation why Barbarella has left the safe confines of her home planet for the wildness of outer-space adventure.

In her first appearance, within minutes of landing on the planet Crystallia, Barbarella's outfit is torn to pieces, leaving her nude and vulnerable. The situation quickly escalates to a make-out session with her handsome young rescuer, and that pretty much sets the tone for the rest of the series. Throughout the comic, Barbarella encounters sexy male aliens and robots and, spurred by curiosity, takes them to bed. From winged angels to handsome traitors, she travels the stars and stumbles into adventure, throwing herself into sex at every opportunity.

In the second volume, published in color in the 1970s, Barbarella returns in all her brash glory. This time, instead of outer-space exploits she travels in-

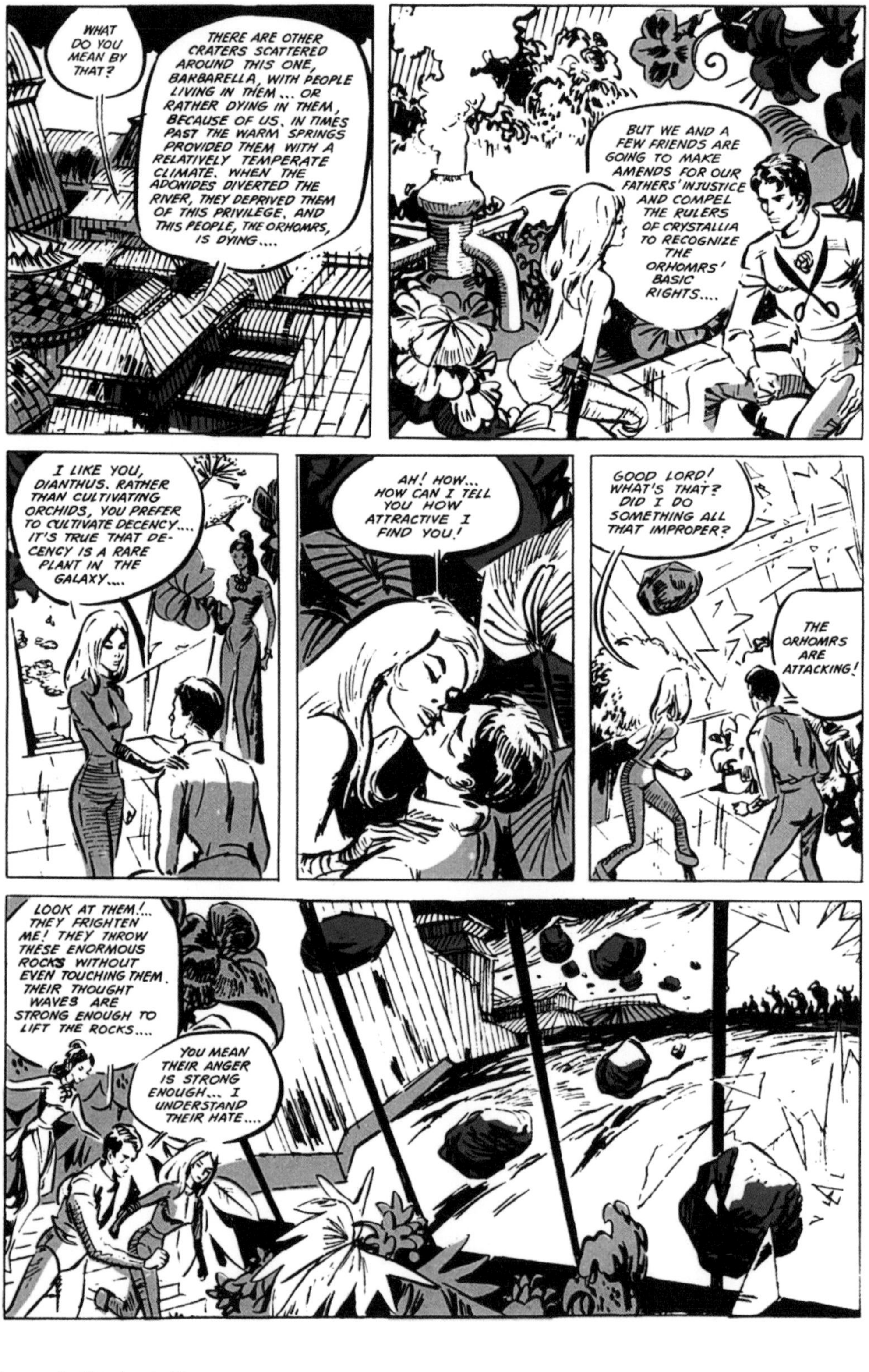
WHAT DO YOU MEAN BY THAT?
THERE ARE OTHER CRATERS SCATTERED AROUND THIS ONE, BARBARELLA, WITH PEOPLE LIVING IN THEM... OR RATHER DYING IN THEM, BECAUSE OF US. IN TIMES PAST THE WARM SPRINGS PROVIDED THEM WITH A RELATIVELY TEMPERATE CLIMATE. WHEN THE ADONIDES DIVERTED THE RIVER, THEY DEPRIVED THEM OF THIS PRIVILEGE. AND THIS PEOPLE, THE ORHOMRS, IS DYING....
BUT WE AND A FEW FRIENDS ARE GOING TO MAKE AMENDS FOR OUR FATHERS' INJUSTICE AND COMPEL THE RULERS OF CRYSTALLIA TO RECOGNIZE THE ORHOMRS' BASIC RIGHTS....
I LIKE YOU, DIANTHUS. RATHER THAN CULTIVATING ORCHIDS, YOU PREFER TO CULTIVATE DECENCY.... IT'S TRUE THAT DECENCY IS A RARE PLANT IN THE GALAXY....
AH! HOW... HOW CAN I TELL YOU HOW ATTRACTIVE I FIND YOU!
GOOD LORD! WHAT'S THAT? DID I DO SOMETHING ALL THAT IMPROPER?
THE ORHOMRS ARE ATTACKING!
LOOK AT THEM!... THEY FRIGHTEN ME! THEY THROW THESE ENORMOUS ROCKS WITHOUT EVEN TOUCHING THEM. THEIR THOUGHT WAVES ARE STRONG ENOUGH TO LIFT THE ROCKS....
YOU MEAN THEIR ANGER IS STRONG ENOUGH... I UNDERSTAND THEIR HATE....

ward, entering the mind-universe of a reclusive scientist. The story proceeds on a much less linear path than in the previous volume, cleverly taking on allegories of gender, childbirth, creation, art, and reality and breaking the fourth wall at several points.

Let's be clear, *Barbarella* is a sex comic, one that is fully conscious of itself. But it's also a comic about sex starring a woman who deeply enjoys it and who is eager to explore, through physical intimacy, the wide array of personalities that exist in the cosmos. The amount of pleasure and enthusiasm that Barbarella brings to her exploits across the universe is refreshing to read. Her sex-kitten nature is an inherent drive of the character, rather than an excuse for her to be used as an object for the eyes of men. The difference between her appearance and bad-girl art from the 1990s is all in the gaze. This is a character whose adventures we can enjoy watching; we aren't just watching her be used.

And the art is gorgeous.

ESSENTIAL READING: *Barbarella* (Humanoids, 2014) features the original story. The translation has been adapted and updated by popular American comic-book creator Kelly Sue DeConnick to better capture the spirit of the French text.

BIKINI LUV	A ditzy mod celebrity who ends up in more jams than a bushel of strawberries	66Gee, Ajax! I don't feel like a secret agent! I don't even have a gold finger or anything!99
		Created by: Jon D'Agostino
		First appearance: Go-Go #1 (Charlton Comics, 1966)

Bikini Luv premiered in what has to be a perfect 1960s artifact: the comic book/magazine hybrid *Go-Go*. The comic is filled with parodies of bands like the Rolling Stones (called the Rotting Stumps, whose members are much pudgier and less charismatic), monster and gothic romance shows such as *Dark Shadows* and *Peyton Place* (called *Return to Peculiar Place*), and irreverent gag cartoons. In addition, it included pinups of real rock bands and crooners that swooning teens could clip out and hang on their walls.

Bikini Luv had her own feature in the comic, in which she is America's typical teenager—in comics terms, that means she gets into every trouble known to humanity and scarfs down food like a hog. Sporting a mop of beautiful silver hair with a thick-cut fringe, Bikini is the star and sweetheart of stage and screen, essentially an homage to (or possibly parody of) Annette Funicello's beach-party movie characters. With the popularity of spy flicks and television shows at an all-time high, it's no surprise that in her third appearance Bikini Luv winds

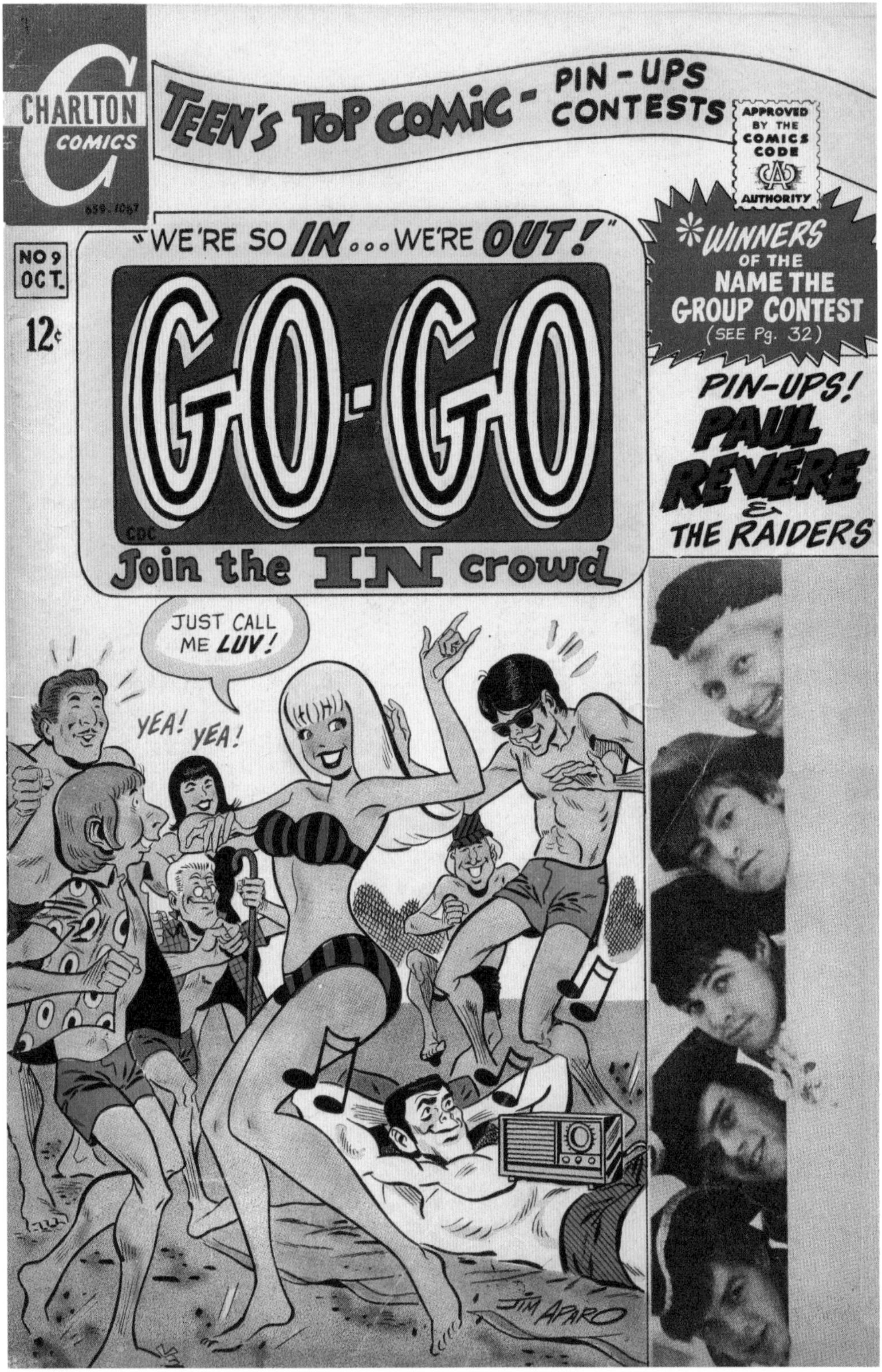
CHARLTON
COMICS
TEEN'S TOP COMIC - PIN-UPS CONTESTS
APPROVED BY THE COMICS CODE AUTHORITY
NO 9 OCT.
12¢
"WE'RE SO IN... WE'RE OUT!"
GO-GO
Join the IN crowd
*WINNERS OF THE NAME THE GROUP CONTEST (SEE Pg. 32)
PIN-UPS! PAUL REVERE & THE RAIDERS
JUST CALL ME LUV!
YEA! YEA!
JIM APARO

up donning an all-black catsuit in order to protect secret microfilm from landing in the hands of communist agents. Her weak-willed (though aesthetically pleasing) beau is Ajax Strong, who at the first sign of danger—or at the thought of having to kiss Bikini Luv—is most likely to faint or cower behind her. But that's fine, because she took a thirty-minute "how to be a secret agent" training session, so she's pretty up on her secret agenting. Well, at least she knows judo, though she can't shoot a gun straight if her life depended on it.

Which it does, since she's going up against murderous mobsters! Not to worry; it's a comedy comic. No one dies, though Bikini and her beau cry so hard in fright that their meticulously styled hair wilts. Luckily, they're saved in the nick of time by a true secret agent, whom Bikini graciously thanks by taking full credit for destroying the head of the spy ring. The cheek!

In further adventures, we see Bikini Luv's finished beach party film (incredibly awful!). She teams up with an Elvis Presley lookalike called Elvin Prisley and falls into the beatnik scene.

Go-Go is a cute, silly comic that seems to be a bit more "with it" than other comics of the same era that tried to take on youth culture. (Ever cringe when you read some of the '60s *Archie* comics attempting to be hip?) It effortlessly mocks the enforced wholesomeness of media geared toward kids, without pushing situations or issues into territory that would get the comic banned by parents. It's *MAD* magazine lite. Bikini Luv is also, unfortunately, an example of a female character who falls into the "dumb cutie" archetype. Which isn't so bad except that it's a type that's significantly more prevalent for pretty girls than pretty guys (though we see the same characterization with Ajax, Bikini's boyfriend). The fashion is good, the story is cute, and Bikini is a bit dim. But this comic is a pretty stellar standout from most teen offerings from this era.

ESSENTIAL READING: Avalon Communications reprinted some of Bikini Luv's strips in the collection *Yeah Baby* (2000).

BUNNY BALL	She's hip! She's mod! She's boss!	66 Groovy—I'm certainly dressed for an outasite party like that! 99
		Created by: Warren Harvey and Hy Eisman
		First appearance: *Bunny* #1 (Harvey Comics, 1966)

Bunny Ball is a California girl who just wants to surf all day and dance all night, so long as her elegant to-the-heavens beehive isn't disturbed, of course. Hailing from a tiny town, Bunny and her little sister Honey travel to the big city (which

city is never mentioned) where they live with their aunt and uncle. Until, that is, Bunny is discovered by a model scout during a bowling game. After winning a beauty pageant—Bunny showed she was equally beautiful on the inside by helping the other contestants get ready—she's crowned Miss Cool Teen Queen.

From that point on, Bunny becomes a supercool model. Star of page and screen, she buys a luxurious penthouse apartment but still makes time for her favorite little sis. It's a pretty shoe-horned origin story, but it does the trick of setting up our title character.

Pitched as a teen book, *Bunny* was also a fashion book, with styles that rivaled anything seen in other fashion comics (such as Katy Keene or Millie the Model). Though, as is common in comics of this era, Bunny is forbidden from showing her belly button, which makes some of the peek-a-boo swimsuits a little disconcerting to look at. We frequently see Bunny sporting bucket hats, mod minidresses, go-go boots, fishnet tights, colorful capelets, architecturally cut coats, and other creative fashion-forward looks.

Though the clothing was pretty, the comic itself was a little bland. Trying to mimic the *Archie* style, with notes of Marvel Comics' *Millie the Model*, Bunny's book lacked much of the charisma of those two series. It contained shades of other Harvey Comics as well, especially seen in the character Arnold van Greenpockets, a type of grown-up Richie Rich. Compensating for his lack of skill with women, Greenpockets uses his excessive wealth to try to impress Bunny. Those attempts involve such items as a weather machine that can instantly change the surrounding area from sun to snow and from day to night. As in other Harvey Comics stories, such as *Wendy the Witch* (see page 68), this one contains an inventive, off-the-wall fantasy element that never ceases to charm.

One story in particular was a definite departure from the bland normalcy characteristic of the series. In issue 4, a psychedelic band enters the scene. The lead singer solemnly arrives to start a Happening. While Bunny and her crew wait patiently, he shoots bolts of color from his hands, and the friends ride the artwork in a dizzying array of brightly hued shapes. As the happening nears its end, Bunny starts to freak out and barricades the doors, but she changes her mind after the Happening Spirits plead for release. Far out! This sudden departure from a cute and wholesome teen book into a drug-fueled kaleidoscope is surprising, but beautifully detailed.

Bunny was nice and kind, which might be a welcoming change from the conniving antics of her contemporaries Betty and Veronica or Chili and Millie, but she didn't really have much else going for her. Well, that's not entirely true. She did have one enemy, the dark-haired (of course) Esmeralda, who's been jealous of Bunny ever since Bunny beat her at the modeling contest (and stole her hairy-chested poet crush). But Bunny can't help it! You see, she's just that effortlessly alluring, and she wins the adoration of boys and men all over without even trying. She's just being her good, wholesome self.

All the boys are in love with Bunny—secret agents, rock stars, millionaires, poets, and beatniks—and for her part Bunny is pretty much in love right back. How nice to see a female character who doesn't have a steady love interest. As Bunny says in her letter column in issue 2: "I am lucky to have many different kinds of boyfriends. The more friends we have, the more we learn about our wonderful world!"

Bunny Ball lacks the competitiveness and cattiness found in other teen comics, and its blandness does make it more than a bit dull. But it happens to be very sweet, too.

ESSENTIAL READING: Bunny's adventures have not yet been reprinted, so search online and in back-issue bins for the originals.

MYSTRA AND DRAGONELLA	An android and a dragon's adopted daughter, in adventures by the legendary Wally Wood	66 *Die, you misshapen mockery of humanity!* 99
		Created by: Wally Wood, Ralph Reese, and Ron Whyte
		First appearance: *Heroes, Inc. Presents Cannon* #1 (Self-published, 1969)

In the late 1960s Wally Wood, best known as the artist behind many of EC Comics' legendary sci-fi stories, made some fascinating female-led comics. These appeared in some of the first examples of quality comics produced by independent comics publishing. (Okay, sure, they also starred a hunky dude named Cannon, but that's not of interest here.)

Wood had no lack of female heroines in his comics. They ranged in quality from the lusty nymph Nudine in his Pipsqueak saga—a diminutive nymphomaniac always needing to be rescued—to the more fascinating characters of Mystra and the fantasy hero Dragonella. Both appear in the first self-published issue of Wood's anthology *Heroes, Inc.*

In the short yet truly epic sci-fi story "The Misfits," we're introduced to an woman named Mystra and her gang of strange companions. Mystra is a mysterious amnesiac looking for clues to her past, while at the same time Earth is nearing destruction by alien forces. It turns out that Mystra is the only one who can stop the aliens, so she busts out of a containment facility, along with a super-strong mutant named Glomb and a little telepathic alien named Shag. Mystra soon discovers that she's not the "normal one" of the group, but is in fact an android. The misfit trio works together to defeat the invaders, saving Earth from malicious aliens. In the end, the president of Earth wants to thank Mystra

for her work. But feeling like an outcast from society, Mystra takes off with her buddies to find a place where they'll all feel accepted.

Mystra's adventures share more than a few similarities with Madeleine L'Engle's 1962 book *A Wrinkle in Time*, from the thought-telepathy battle to the matter transmitter in space to the final showdown with the giant brain named Unit One. Along the way, Mystra's outfit gets ripped (of course), so her breasts are almost fully exposed. Yet her adventure is interesting and had potential to be a grand space epic with a fascinating trio of heroes.

In the same issue, we also meet the character Dragonella in a type of Snow White/Tarzan/Prince Valiant parody. Abandoned in the woods by an evil wizard, baby Dragonella is seen by a cute little dragon baby named St. George, who manipulates his mom into raising her as his sister. Upon growing up and realizing that she'll never find a mate among her lizard kin (despite the romantic adoration of her foster brother George), Dragonella sets off into the wilderness to find a prince.

First mistaking a middle-aged lust monster for her royal mate, Dragonella finally finds a potential sweetie in the character of Prince Hal (a nod to Prince Valiant creator Hal Foster). Unfortunately, a wizard's army and Hal's legion of princess groupies soon separate the two. Dragonella gives up and tries to kiss George to see if maybe that would work instead. But even an embrace fails to ignite a spark, and they set off again on their adventure as Just Friends.

That's a lot of action and plot to squeeze into these short comics! Yet neither feels rushed or burdened, and the quality of the art is outstanding. The variety and skill in these stories are greater than most anthologies of the time, and the difference between the soap opera action of the Misfits and the satirical fantasy of Dragonella showcases the diverse skill of Wally Wood. *Heroes Inc.*, interestingly enough, was never designed for a mass comics audience but for military personnel. Had a few copies not snuck into general circulation (and a large dumpload of them dropped onto the market decades later), the first issue of this comic would have been completely forgotten.

And you're okay that I skipped Nudine, right?

ESSENTIAL READING: The Misfits story has not yet been reprinted, but you can check out Dragonella in *Wallace Wood's Pipsqueak Papers* #1 (Fantagraphics, 1993).

NURSE BETSY CRANE

A dedicated nurse whose personal life will always run second to her patients

66 *Remember! You're a member of the finest profession in the world! You are a nurse, not a sniffling little fool who faints at the sight of a cut finger!* 99

Created by: Joe Sinnott and Vince Colletta

First appearance: *Teen Secret Diary* #11 (Charlton Comics, 1961)

A nurse at Dale General Hospital, Betsy Crane is in many ways a typical young romance heroine. Month after month, she faces challenges of melodrama in her romantic life and in the romantic lives of others, which she can't help but become involved in. Meddling was a common secondary job for women in romance comics.

Of course, the situations she meddles in are always incredibly ridiculous. Take Betsy's friend Lori, who worships physical perfection and can't stand the sight of cripples. What will she do when she finds out her fiancé has . . . *cataracts*?

From time to time Nurse Betsy Crane also fell in love, but it always ended in tragedy, with Betsy bravely and heroically putting her sweetheart's interests above her own. Or she casts him out of her life for his own good. Or she chooses to pursue her career as a nurse instead of becoming a wife. Because, along with Betsy Crane's attributes of exceptional beauty and wisdom, she was also, above all else, a professional: a no-nonsense nurse who doesn't take flak from anyone, especially not egotistical soldiers trying to get her to "loosen up a little" during wartime.

She's Nurse Betsy Crane, gosh darn it. And she has work to do!

For all her romance-comic trappings, Betsy is an admirable character. She's a dedicated medical provider who's focused on her career and doing the right thing at all times. True, she's not a terribly nuanced or flexible character. And the ideals of love, romance, and courtship in her stories are traditional to say the least. In modern comics, Betsy would be laughed off as a too-perfect Mary

Sue. But what's wrong with a strong, successful, career-oriented woman, whom readers can look up to and try to emulate?

Nurse plotlines were once a thriving subgenre in comics, providing a blend of traditional romance and adventure stories. The female protagonist could be heroic and save lives, choose career over love, even occasionally solve crimes and mysteries. Along with *Nurse Betsy Crane*, Charlton also published *Cynthia Doyle, Nurse in Love*; *Sue and Sally Smith: Flying Nurses* (see page 89); *Registered Nurse*; and *Three Nurses*. Competitor Dell offered *Nurse Linda Lark*, and Marvel had *Linda Carter, Student Nurse* and *The Romances of Nurse Helen Grant* (see page 62). DC Comics often featured nurses on the covers of their romance anthology series.

Romance comics had relatively few recurring characters, and Betsy sometimes takes a backseat in her own title to other people's stories. That said, to make it as one of those rare recurring characters, let alone star in your own series, you needed to be a role model to young women. And Betsy Crane was a successful example of that. Not only did she exhibit impeccable professionalism and compassion, but her comic also explicitly promoted nursing as the ideal vocation. The issues included ads for nursing schools and medical-themed toys, as well as strips that explained different types of nursing careers. Say what you want about nurse comics, but I don't think Superman or Spider-Man ever bothered to explain to readers how journalism works.

ESSENTIAL READING: If you can't find the original Betsy Crane issues, try searching for the 1980s Charlton Comics reprint series *Soap Opera Romances*.

PUSSYCAT	The cool and carefree capers of a curvy, cuddly chick	*"I never seem to have any trouble opening doors . . . as soon as I get close to them, the locks always melt!"*
		Created by: Gabe Guttman, Wally Wood, and Jim Mooney
		First appearance: *Male Annual* #3 (Marvel Comics, 1965)

Pussycat's comic ran in the pages of men's magazines published by the parent company of Marvel Comics, such as *Male Annual* and *Stag Annual*. The adventures were parodies of the spy genre, with more than a hint of Playboy's popular *Little Annie Fanny* comic strip. Marvel also put together a comic-format collection of the best Pussycat stories. In retrospect, it's fairly shocking to see Marvel release a full-length comic dedicated to the scandalous adventures of a buxom and barely clad spy, especially during the days of the Comics Code Authority.

THE ADVENTURES OF
Pussycat
35¢
40¢ IN CANADA
OCT,
1968

SEE THE
CURVEY CUTIE
FROM
S.C.O.R.E.
VS.
THE FOUL FIENDS
OF **L.U.S.T.**

I WANT YOU...

...TO **JOIN**
ME IN THE
COOL and CUDDLY
CAPERS OF A
FRIENDLY
SECRET AGENT
---NAMELY
ME!

THE LADY IS A *SWINGER!*

Pussycat is a lowly secretary working for S.C.O.R.E. (clever acronym of the Secret Council of Ruthless Extroverts) when she's selected for an extra-special mission. They need someone stupid enough not to be frightened yet sexy enough to distract the enemy—and the very shapely Pussycat fits the bill. She's then outfitted to face off against the charming Ivan Passion of L.U.S.T. (Legion of Undesirable Super Types). Uh-oh, this might be difficult, because Ivan has the brooding eyes and sensitive lips of a young Rudolph Valentino. Never fear! Pussycat has something even more powerful than mere charisma . . .

I think they mean her vagina. I'm not really sure. But it seems Pussycat is possessed of such irresistible sexual appeal that she can melt metal just by lowering her ample bosom toward it (though you'd think melting would be the last thing it would do). The sight of her in a tiny string bikini is enough to send a thousand men rushing over, crushing a pier to dust. The various artists drawing her adventures must be admired for their dedication to creating the most perfectly bodacious character that comics has even seen—especially the intricate detail paid to her impressive outfits and negligee. (What I wouldn't do to get a pair of those gold metallic patterned tights in her third story!)

Starting off as an ingénue oblivious of her effect on men, after a few issues Pussycat becomes a skilled agent, fully aware of how to turn on her charms to get the information she needs. Snuggling up to enemy combatants or flashing a little leg as she examines a run in her stocking, the "curvy cutie" is able to pretty much solve any international crisis with nothing more than a pout and a bend.

The Adventures of Pussycat is one of those rare sex comics in which the supernaturally hot female lead is able to use her power for good, rather than getting tied up or relegated to being at the mercy of her antagonists (so, far and away better than the exploitative sex comic *Phoebe Zeit-Geist*). Pussycat might be a sex symbol in a men's magazine, but she's a damn good secret agent, too.

ESSENTIAL READING: Pick up the 1968 collected edition *The Adventures of Pussycat*, featuring fifty pages full of Pussycat fun.

'SCOT	The swingiest girl in the modnik crew	66'Cause a go-go gal can be a real go-go pal!99
		Created by: Gary Poole and Lloyd White
		First appearance: *The Modniks* #1 (Gold Key, 1967)

Most of the Modniks were guys, it's true. But in mod-beatnik society, labels such as gender weren't really that important, you dig?

In other words, members of the Modniks were more or less interchangeable. They each had the cool, hip lingo down; they wore the wildest, freshest clothes, and they were in no way squares. Their adventures were fairly Archie-esque, with the clueless youngsters facing up against authority figures and working together to loosen up their uptight classmates.

The girl in the group, referred to (once) only as 'Scot (with no explanation of what that could be short for), is the girlfriend of the Modniks' leader, Wheels Williams. She's got a straight figure (no Dan DeCarlo curves here) and wears a jaunty stylish cap, minidress, fishnet stockings, and of course the essential accessory for any truly mod chick: thigh-high go-go boots. She occasionally varies her look by wearing black tights and a trapeze top (clearly no one bothered to tell her that leggings aren't pants).

Am I paying too much attention to the fashion? Perhaps. Let's get into what we know of 'Scot and her crew.

'Scot may be cool and all, but she's a fairly sweet girl; in one storyline, she takes the squarest boy in town, Billy "Cube" Wilson, under her wing. As one might expect, she and her gang then aim to change him into a swinging hipster. They take him to the dress shop and dandify him, complete with a full floral suit and frilly undershirt, making him look like he just stepped off the streets of London's Carnaby Street. Very Austin Powers. Of course the look is topped off with a shaggy wig whose fringe is so low it hides his lame spectacles. By the end of the adventure, Cube reverts back to his square ways. But the Modniks are okay with that. After all, what would be less hip than refusing to allow someone to be who they truly are? These cats aren't cruel.

Nevertheless, they are fairly loose with their words, even nicknaming one of 'Scot's friends "Reject" because she's the local ugly duckling. Which is a pretty harsh label just because a girl wears a jumper and puts ribbons in her hair. Of course they try to pair her up with Cube, but instead Reject falls head over heels for 'Scot's boyfriend, Wheels. To politely dissuade this "loser" from trying to make time with the leader of the mods, they just go-go at full speed until Reject is exhausted and settles for the slow pace of comparing stamp collections with Cube.

In one memorable story, the school principal Mr. Blair (eternal thorn in the Modniks' side) is in a huff over the miniskirts all the girls are wearing. They're just too distracting to be allowed in school! (Does this debate never cease?) Led by 'Scot, the girls arrange a protest and wisely point out that their grandmas did the Charleston in dresses shorter than minis! So 'Scot and her group turn on all the women in town—regardless of age—and convince them to bring back the miniskirt.

The Modniks is far from the highest point in comics literature. But hey, when a group of groovy kids can get together and find ways to make the establishment work for them (*and* wear some swingingly stylish clothes to boot), it's a hit by me.

ESSENTIAL READING: No reprints of *The Modniks* exist yet, and only two issues were published, so get to back-issue bin-hunting to find these lost treasures!

SUE AND SALLY SMITH, FLYING NURSES	Two sisters who parachute into danger and risk their lives for the common good	❝I am a nurse, mister! When a human being needs our skills, we don't ask whether he is an enemy or an ally before we go to him!❞
		Created by: Joe Gill, Joe Sinnott, and Vince Colletta
		First appearance: *My Secret Life* #47 (Charlton Comics, 1962)

The genre of nurse comics is definitely a hallmark of the 1960s, and the stories showcased a career that was achievable for many women but that held the potential for love and action to entertain female readers. And for Sue and Sally Smith, it's really the action that was essential. The sisters might fall in love with the odd soldier in the field, but mostly they're engaging in one or another high-stakes adventure: Jumping out of airplanes into the middle of war zones! Forced at knifepoint to sew up dying men! Rushing headfirst into

wildfires! Striding confidentially into the most dangerous Vietnam battlefields! In short, they're pretty tough ladies.

Indeed, these women are no shrinking violets. In one story they find themselves pursued by wealthy elite bachelors far off in the Andes Mountains. They allow their natural charms to earn them an invitation to a remote pleasure mansion, only to lecture the men on the treatment of the poor and hungry peasants in the village below. Clearly these women have priorities. Their good looks are merely a means to an end, and that end happens to be making the world a better place. Using terms the capitalist tyrants can appreciate, the Smith sisters explain that if the elites mistreat the poor, they'll band together and revolt in favor of pure communism. Then the wealthy will whine about how there were led to ruin by communism, instead of their own stupidities. The rich guys get it, since the true discussion is about how much money they might lose, not the security of poor people. Still, they remain unconvinced. In exasperation, Sally Smith wagers the health of the people on the outcome of a drag race. Unfortunately, the guy with whom they place the bet falls off a cliff, prompting the women to parachute down to give him an emergency plasma donation.

The sisters also seem to be telepathic, but that's a standard quality of all twins and barely worth mentioning. In one adventure, one twin just happens to know the other is locking lips with her doctor beau, so she joins along with her own suitor. I have to admit that's incredibly creepy.

The Sue and Sally Smith adventures were thrilling, action packed, and usually international in scope. The comics did a good job tackling political issues overseas with some degree of grace and care. If only Sue could stop assuming that all non-white people don't speak English . . .

ESSENTIAL READING: No reprints are available, so check back-issue sources. After the first appearance in *My Secret Life*, Sue and Sally Smith branched off into their own series, which lasted seven issues.

TIFFANY SINN	The world's greatest private eye takes a secret job from the CIA and discovers the thrill of romance	66*Relax, lover boy, the worst thing that can happen is for us to get killed!*99
		Created by: Gary Friedrich, Charles Wojtkowski, and Vince Alascia
		First appearance: *Career Girl Romances* #38 (Charlton Comics, 1966)

Career Girl Romances isn't the worst in terms of female representation in romance comics. In every adventure (usually three to an issue), the protagonist has her own career that drives the story. While the careers are often as secretaries or waitresses, with the odd movie star thrown in, sometimes these women had jobs

TO SAVE AN AGENT

HURRY, REX! I CAN'T HOLD THEM OFF MUCH LONGER!

I'VE MADE IT, BABY! BETTER CLIMB DOWN YOURSELF BEFORE YOU GET TURNED INTO A DEAD RINGER FOR A HUNK OF SWISS CHEESE!

that were substantially more dangerous.

Tiffany Sinn is one such case. She has an origin story worthy of Batman: her parents were killed in East Berlin in the 1950s and she grew up a tough orphan, learning to fend for herself. At age 26, she was already one of the best private eyes in the business, hoping to find time to pursue her quest of vengeance for her parents' death. Romance was pretty low on her priorities list. Top of the list: getting paid. Next on the list: avenge parents' murder. Get swoony-eyed over a boy was, like, twelfth after that.

But this book is called *Career Girl Romances*, not *Career Girl Adventures*, so we better get on to the loving!

It turns out that Rex Swift—who rescued Tiffany from East Berlin when she was 12 years old—has gone missing. Oh no! Despite having a hot date that night, Tiffany agrees to go off and rescue him. Well, it's less "agrees" and more "is forced into," since she's also been hit over the head and kidnapped by the CIA.

In short order she's reunited with her kidnapped savior and, uh, immediately starts macking on him. Evidently Tiffany had fallen in love with Rex back when she was an adolescent. That might be only a fifteen-year or so age difference, but still. Maybe don't make out with a clearly damaged girl, okay Rex?

Rex confesses that he's always been in love with Tiffany, which is pretty awful since this appears to be the first time they've met since she was a preteen. Anyways, he garrotes a guard and she grabs a pistol and they blast their way out of the communist camp. But wait—Rex is shot! Will Tiffany leave him behind? Nope, she's gosh darn Tiffany Sinn. So she hoists him up over the Berlin Wall and drops him safely on the other side. As thanks, Rex promises he'll marry her and tie an apron around her pretty little waist because she's just too dangerous to remain single.

Luckily—and unlike most romance stories—this one does *not* end with the female lead's happy embrace with her future husband. In the very next issue, Tiffany is kidnapped again by the CIA, with Rex held hostage as insurance for her good behavior (otherwise he'll be sentenced for treason). Her new mission? Find Rex's brother, a dangerous Nazi. Along the way Tiffany discovers a wisecracking fellow agent, Terry, who takes her into his arms and kisses her like she's never been kissed . . . without her permission, but you know how these romance comics are. Tiff and Ter keep smooching throughout the rest of the adventure, though our heroine does have a twinge of regret for dear old Rex. As the pair closes in on the Nazi (who has a city-destroying laser!), Terry is shot, dying heroically and tragically in Tiffany's arms.

In Tiffany's next and final appearance we're treated to a one-panel flashback as our heroine wonders why she never wanted to get married after she shot the crazy Nazi. She's promptly put to work yet again by the CIA, this time to infiltrate a secret laboratory with a hunky scientist. Tiffany Sinn, you are not a typical romance heroine!

ESSENTIAL READING: Given the lack of reprints, you'll have to hunt out Tiffany Sinn's three appearances in the original *Career Girl Romances* of the mid-sixties.

VAMPIRELLA	Is Vampirella an alien? A vampire? Who knows, but she's definitely a babe!	❝Hell hath no fury like a woman scorched!❞
		Created by: Forrest J. Ackerman and Tom Sutton
		First appearance: *Vampirella* #1 (Warren Publishing, 1969)

Vampirella isn't really a bad sort. Is it her fault she evolved on a faraway world called Draculon, where blood rains down on the residents instead of water? These aliens, adapted to consume blood for nutrients, would be pacifists if it wasn't for one thing: their world is suffering from a sudden blood drought! And what arrives on their planet all of a sudden? Earth men, traveling around like giant juicy water balloons in a desert.

Vampirella gets her fair share of admiration (and flak) for being a super-sexy character in a uniform that you can only imagine would be incredibly uncomfortable in the pelvic area. But in her first appearance, her getup on the cover (the one she's widely known for) isn't how she's dressed in the story. Inside she wears a low-cut top that flares into a full set of tight pants. The outfit is backless—due her having giant batwings—though no reason is given for why it dips so low that it gives her butt cleavage. In her second adventure, without explanation, Vampirella dons what becomes her classic costume: a daring deep-cut swimsuit clasped at the neck, leaving her side-breasts and navel exposed. Plus, for some reason, a collar, maybe for fancy business occasions. The outfit, surprisingly, was designed by feminist historian and comics creator Trina Robbins. (I guess she can't help it if the artists designed the character with more body than can fit in her clothes . . .)

Like all of her alien species, Vampirella has the power of invisibility and

DRACULON IS --LITERALLY-- A PLANET OF *BLOOD!* BY A STRANGE QUIRK OF NATURE, THE WATER ON DRAKULON IS COMPOSED OF VIRTUALLY THE SAME COMBINATION OF ELEMENTS THAT ON EARTH CONSTITUTE HEMOGLOBIN, THUS ON DRAKULON A RACE HAS DEVELOPED THAT DEPENDS SOLELY ON *BLOOD* FOR SUSTENANCE. EVOLUTION HAS TAKEN STRANGE WAYS ON *DRAKULON*...

shape changing. She's also learned the power of karate (or at least drackarate!). Along with pursuing her own adventures, Vampirella served the same function as the Old Witch did for EC Comics (see page 63), introducing a selection of vampire, werewolf, and other creature features. In her first issue, the intent was for all the stories to star a dynamic (and fairly vivacious) female lead. However, this requirement was cast off by the next issue.

Turns out that Vampirella is not the last of her species. Later stories feature her cousin Evily and her twin sister Draculina (a blonde, of course). Vampirella also had an alter ego, the completely compelling monster-model "Bambi Aurora"; that identity is soon killed off in a fake plane crash. For quite some time after her first few stories, Vampi appeared only as a guest host. When she returned with stories of her own, her gorgeous bat wings have been amputated, and she vows vengeance on the cult of Chaos that kidnapped and de-winged her, pledging to attack and drain the blood of those who are evil.

Vampirella's series lasted for well over a hundred appearances in her own magazine, plus a large volume of spin-off series (which made her origins more mystical than sci-fi). It's hard to get rid of Vampirella, the first lady of horror comics. (Sorry, Old Witch.)

One of the most important legacies of Vampirella, other than being a forerunner of the T&A aesthetic in comics (if Phantom Lady was the godmother of this approach, Vampirella definitely made it popular), is that her creation gave a huge boost to the popularity of the burgeoning cosplay hobby. With publisher Warren Comics holding regular contests to find the best Vampirella to feature in the magazine, masquerade contests at comics conventions were soon flooded with a bevy of what today we would call cosplayers, each with a singular look. The fun wasn't without controversy; one 14-year-old Vampirella and her stage mom elicited jeers and boos. And yes, *cosplay* wasn't the term for costumed fans back then. But just as with the "bad girl" aesthetic in comics, Vampirella was there before the phenomenon's meteoric rise in the 1990s.

Vampirella eventually spun off into a manga series and was also the star of a direct-to-video film that was widely (and rightly) panned. In the '90s she appeared in stories with a bevy of bad girls who were popular at the time, including Witchblade (see page 178), Catwoman, Shi, Dawn, Pantha, Painkiller

Jane, Lady Death, and Purgatori. Surprising enough, just a few years back she also starred in a children's comic as "Li'l Vampi," an adorable young paranormal investigator (with, obviously, a much more modest costume).

Vampirella might be best known for pushing the boundaries of what a costume can cover, but she's had an extensive life on the page. She's persevered through every possible industry change, and her longevity as an independent character must be respected.

ESSENTIAL READING: *Li'l Vampi* by Eric Trautmann and Agnes Garbowska (Dynamite Entertainment, 2014), because it's adorable.

BATGIRL

A crime-fighter and genius tech expert who never gives up

66 *A hero is not measured by what her power may be . . . but by the courage she shows in living, and the warmth she holds in her heart.* 99

Created by: Gardner Fox, Carmine Infantino, and Sid Greene

First appearance (as Barbara Gordon):
Detective Comics #359 (DC Comics, 1967)

Batgirl, like Supergirl, was an entirely different character in her first incarnation. In her initial appearance she is merely Betty Kane, niece to wealthy socialite Kathy Kane (who is secretly Batwoman). Easily figuring out her aunt's identity, Betty joins her as a sidekick and then becomes a love interest to Batman's sidekick, Robin. She's a skilled crime-fighter but, alas, is phased out of the comics in the early 1960s (eventually to return as Flamebird, becoming Batwoman's cousin instead of her niece).

But never fear—she returns yet again! When the *Batman* television series needed some fresh female blood in its third season, a new Batgirl was developed. First introduced by DC Comics in *Detective Comics* in January 1967, the character debuted in the TV show a few months later, giving Batgirl some time to make her way into the hands of young comics readers. In this new manifestation, Batgirl was Commissioner Gordon's daughter Barbara. She's a foxy librarian by day, masked crusader by night, thus giving her the benefit of not one but *two* amazing costumes. In the show, Batgirl wore a super-envy-inducing sparkly purple costume. It looked more comic-booky than even the comics version, which was a more standard black-and-yellow crime-fighting catsuit.

In the 1970s Batgirl became a bit of a feminist icon, first on television, when she demanded equal pay in a televised public service announcement by the U.S. Department of Labor ("I'm paid less than Robin!"). Then, in her comic-book storyline, Barbara Gordon decides that the best way to fight crime is to fix it at its source. So she runs for the U.S. Congress—and despite her youth, she wins a seat!

Of course, this plot turn was a way to write her out of the Batman comics. The character returned to comics eventually but was again written out decades later, when DC gave her an official retirement from crime-fighting and then had the Joker shoot her (in what was meant to be an alternate-universe story). Barbara ends up in a wheelchair, but that doesn't stop her. She proceeds to use her keen, technologically proficient mind to become a force behind the scenes, assuming the codename "Oracle."

Did I mention that she also beat up both Benedict Arnold and Lucifer at one point?

Following a difficult path of physical rehabilitation, Barbara Gordon has since been able to leave her wheelchair and regain her role as Batgirl (others, such as Cassandra Cain and Helena Bertinelli, donned the mantle in between). She even goes off to college, where her adventures have her dealing with the emotional rehab of regaining the life she left behind.

Barbara Gordon was a powerful character right from her original creation. Through everything that's happened to her, she has remained a strong-willed woman who, most important, is adaptive to change. She's a survivor, and we need to see more such female characters on comic-book pages.

CHAPTER

5

the

19

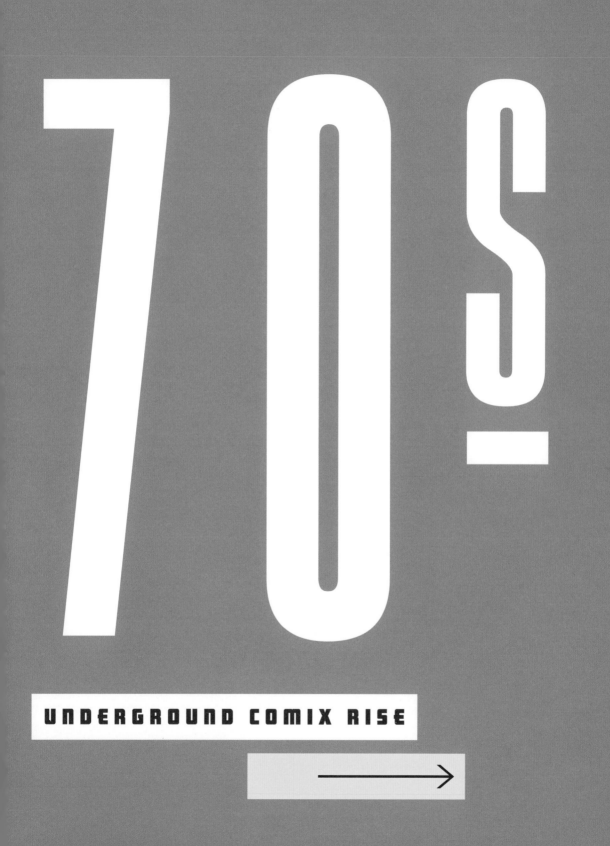

70s

UNDERGROUND COMIX RISE

$\longrightarrow$

THE 1970s

The 1970s was an exciting time for comics starring women. Both Marvel and DC significantly increased output of superheroine-fronted comics, with Spider-Woman, Ms. Marvel, Red Sonja, Supergirl, Isis, Night Nurse, and She-Hulk all headlining their own series. And mainstream publishers finally introduced some (though not nearly enough) female characters who weren't white. *Starfire*, a short-lived sci-fi book published by DC, gave us a rare example of a headlining Asian heroine. Two high-profile black heroines, the weather-controlling mutant Storm (*X-Men*) and bionic detective Misty Knight (*Iron Fist*), debuted at Marvel, along with the Vietnamese heroine Mantis in *The Avengers*.

Romance comics were still well read at the start of the '70s, but their popularity would wane by the end of the decade. Yet all-ages humor titles, like the Archie Comics books, continued to be most popular. Aimed at a general audience, they showcased a variety of female characters, from Betty, Veronica, and Sabrina the Teenage Witch to Li'l Jinx and Josie and the Pussycats.

In 1976 Jenette Kahn became publisher of DC Comics, a post she held until 2002. Around the same time, creators were much more commonly and consistently credited in print than ever before. From these credits we can see that more women were working in comics than we might expect. Writers such as Barbara Friedlander and artists like Elizabeth Safian Berube were doing fill-in artwork (though the majority of art duties, even for romance comics, was still given to male artists). Jo Duffy was a writer in charge of *Power Man and Iron Fist*, an action-packed series influenced equally by blaxploitation and martial arts cinema (with Misty Knight in the supporting cast). Jean Thomas, another Marvel writer, worked on a variety of series including *Night Nurse*, *Werewolf by Night*, and the all-ages *Spidey Super Stories.*

The 1970s also saw the start of the independent comics boom outside the underground market—that is, comics not created by the big publishers, but also not affiliated with head-shops. Wendy Pini, with help from her husband, Richard, created the popular long-running series *Elfquest*; self-published for its first run, the title is still being published forty years later. *Neil the Horse*, a lively musical adventure created by the artist now known as Katherine Collins, was released by Canadian publisher Aardvark-Vanaheim, headed by Deni Loubert and Dave Sim.

Speaking of those underground comix, it was in this decade that feminist comix appeared as a reaction to the male-dominated underground movement. After all, what good is the freedom of underground comix if all the stories are about women being sexed on by dudes? And so *Wimmen's Comix*, *Tits & Clits*, *It Ain't Me, Babe*, *Abortion Eve*, *Dynamite Damsels*, and *The Further Fattening Adventures of Pudge, Girl Blimp*—among others—addressed this need for comics authentic to women's experiences. These were stories about women's bodies, minds, and lives, and they often revolved around social issues and showcased feminist communities. Finally, comics were reflecting social changes *while* the changes were happening!

Where comics fans bought their comics was also changing, thanks to direct market distribution. Retailers of specialty hobby shops could purchase comics directly from publishers; these orders were nonreturnable, sparing the publisher the pain of taking back unsold comics. In return for shouldering the sales risk, retailers were given greater discounts and could fine-tune orders to match customers' interests. The reign of the comic-book shop had begun.

In some ways, the 1970s could be seen as the golden age of women in comics. Women populated the pages, diversity was increasing, and independent comics were showing new stories unburdened by the Comics Code Authority. Not only that, but a woman was in charge of the most popular comic book empire: DC Comics. Yet DC was also canceling many of its solo superheroine titles. And by decade's end the romance comic—the one genre specifically marketed toward women—had vanished. ⚡

DELL 15¢
04282
OCTOBER

friday foster ®

ACTION-PACKED
EXCITEMENT IN
THE FASHIONABLE
WORLD OF
THE JET SET!

© 1972 by The Chicago Tribune. World Rights Reserved

FRIDAY FOSTER	Jet-set fashion photographer turned world-class model	66 My beautiful people live in Harlem and Detroit and Selma and they, not her, are the original beautiful people. 99
		Created by: Jim Lawrence and Jorge Longarón
		First appearance: As a comic strip, *Chicago Tribune* (NYT Syndicate, 1970); as a comic book: *Friday Foster* (unnumbered issue, Dell Comics, 1972)

Premiering in 1970 and running until 1974, "Friday Foster" was a newspaper comic strip detailing the adventures of a fashion photographer's assistant (and sometime photographer herself). A strong and confident woman, Friday boasted an on-point sense of style that was showcased in all of her adventures. She didn't wait to be cornered before voicing her opinions; instead, she analyzed the situation and then boldly and clearly said what was on her mind. For example, in her first, and only, appearance in a full comic book, Friday photographs a rich princess and realizes that not only are the fashions of Paris and Harlem worlds apart, but also that the princess has no idea how privileged she is. Of course, when Friday tells this observation to her boss, he begs her not to say anything or let her opinions interfere with work.

A nice aspect of that Dell Comics one-shot is that female friendship is placed front and center. Friday's feelings toward the privileged princess turn to amity as the two women get to know each other. Eventually, along with an editor from a *Vogue*-like magazine, they protect one another from a manipulative photographer. In addition to female friendship, Friday's family is important in her life, with her little brother Cleve (who lives with her) assuming a key supporting role in the comic strip. Cleve tends to get threatened by the villains *du jour* who hope to force Friday to do what they want. But Friday always triumphs, and her brother stays safe.

In the newspaper strip, Friday Foster started as an assistant to a high-profile photographer. After paying her dues, she becomes a world-traveling model, entering that high-income and celebrity life she once so despised.

Premiering decades after *Torchy Brown* (see page 20), Friday Foster was the first lead black character in a comic strip that appeared in a mainstream daily newspaper. The creators were writer Jim Lawrence, who already had several newspaper strips to his name, and artist Jorge Longarón, a Spanish illustrator with several international comic strips published as well. Together they worked out the unique style of Friday Foster, a character who was not only free of stereotypes but also incredibly hip and fashionable (being a fashion photographer, one would hope so!). Like many of the female characters in comics of the 1970s, Friday was a career girl. Her professional life took priority above other interests, including romance.

The strip's subject manner was on par with other career-girl-themed comics of the time, such as *Brenda Starr*. But it still provoked controversy in some circles. *Friday Foster* was carried by newspapers only in the northern United States because those in the South refused to publish it. Longarón recalls that some Southern papers accepted the strip not knowing that it starred a black woman, and upon seeing the art they refused to run it.

After several years of good reception but weak sales, the *Friday Foster* newspaper strip ended. Yet its legacy endured in the form of a 1975 blaxploitation film based on its character and starring Pam Grier (along with Eartha Kitt and Yaphet Kotto). Later, Jim Lawrence wrote a series of detective novels featuring a character similar to Friday, with cover art once again by Longarón.

ESSENTIAL READING: It might be hard to find the Dell issue of *Friday Foster*, or microfiche of the newspaper strips, so why not check out the 1975 film?

FRIEDA PHELPS

A member of the sisterhood of women

Created by: Roberta Gregory

First appearance: *Dynamite Damsels* #1
(Nanny Goat Productions, 1976)

❝The only thing worse than being a burned-out feminist is being a poor one.❞

If you're looking for a feminist role model and are uncomfortable with Bitchy Bitch and Bitchy Butch (though you should be, that's the point! See page 160 for more on these characters), Roberta Gregory has created a milder-mannered heroine. Frieda Phelps is a 23-year-old virgin new to feminism. As the story progresses, Frieda realizes that her sexuality may be less rigid than she believed, and while taking comfort from being able to discuss anything with women, her gentle nature thrives. Eventually she comes out as a lesbian to those who support her.

The comic also includes the one-time appearance of Superdyke, a lavender-wearing righter of wrongs who snaps to attention at the sound of a woman being harassed. We could use a heroine like that today at some comic conventions.

Though written in the 1970s, the Frieda comics are by and large still relatable. Issues faced by Frieda and her friends, like poor economics, sexual harassment, and misogyny from other women, are still relevant, it's sad to say. Surprisingly, the comics even discuss intersecting social identities within feminism, a rare topic in underground comix of the day. No—a rare topic in comics, period.

For example, when Edie, a black woman, attends her first feminist meeting, she remarks that she thought feminism was for WASPs, an attitude that's met with anger. Gregory is careful to show how Edie's experiences led to this assumption. In her own home, Edie is rebuked for neglecting black rights in favor of women's rights. Feeling out of place among both largely white feminists and male-oriented black rights activists, she forms a black women's liberation group.

One of the most groundbreaking aspects of the Frieda strips, which are formulated as one- to two-page stories, is the representation of internalized misogyny among women. In one example, Frieda believes that all women should be sisters, and be of one mind. This worldview is challenged when she sees a female sportscaster use her first time on air to proclaim that she's not one of those "women's libbers," throwing her sisters under the bus.

In another adventure, Frieda goes to a local high school and learns that young girls think feminism means hating men, neglecting your partner, and refusing to have children. Another time she tries to plan an event where women can come together without being scared off by the word *feminism*. But Frieda is physically attacked by a woman who accuses her of trying to corrupt her daughter; she's also stomped by angry protesters even as she tries to tell them that the rights she fights for benefit them, too. It's a sobering reminder that not all women are feminists.

Later, Frieda meets a powerful older woman named Doris (who looks suspiciously like Superdyke), who proclaims that she is in fact one of those rare feminists who hates men, sports a short crop of hair, and rides a motorcycle. Frieda is about to joke that people will think Doris is a lesbian, only to catch her in a passionate embrace with her girlfriend. This is the first time Frieda has met a lesbian, and she's shocked to realize that they seem just like regular people! In other adventures we are privy to the lives of supporting characters including Shelley, who is a size 18 and struggles to fit into affordable clothes at women's shops; she finally finds a nice middle ground wearing Western gear from men's shops. It's later revealed that both Shelley and Frieda have huge crushes on each other but never act on them, each thinking the other is hopelessly straight.

The *Dynamite Damsels* comics provide a valuable insight and primer into 1970s feminism that's still relevant today, especially with the diverse individuality displayed by the women in the stories. The characters, including Frieda, stand up for what they believe in and are determined to express their identities and live their lives boldly, just the way they want to.

ESSENTIAL READING: You can read the full series online at the Queer Zine Archive (qzap.org), posted with the permission of the creator.

LAURA CHANDLER	A frightened orphan looking for the secret to her friend's murder in a creepy mansion of weirdos	"I'm sure, somewhere in this house lies the answer to your death!"
		Created by: Anonymous, Dorothy Woolfolk, Ethan Mordden, and Tony DiZuniga
		First appearance: *Dark Mansion of Forbidden Love* #1 (DC Comics, 1971)

In "The Secret of the Missing Bride," a grieving Laura Chandler is attending the funeral of her best friend Bettina, who disappeared into marriage some time before. Through a set of unusual circumstances, Laura finds herself whisked away to the foreboding mansion that Bettina lived in with her husband and his family. The house has secrets à la *Wuthering Heights*. Behind every door, it seems, there's another mad family member locked away. Even though technically she was abducted, Laura stays at the manor by choice to find out what happened to her friend . . . and to mack on her friend's late husband. Yes, less than a day after Bettina is buried, the two are sucking face. It's a romance comic, so what do you expect? Laura's new beau is creepy to the max, constantly referring to how "soft and vulnerable" she is. As though she's a baby bird. Because baby birds are what every woman wants to be compared to by a lover.

ALONE, IN THE MASSIVE BED, LAURA BROODED...

THAT PHONE CALL WAS THE LAST TIME I HEARD YOUR VOICE! YOU DIED THAT NIGHT-- THAT WAS *NO ACCIDENT*, I'M SURE, SOMEWHERE IN THIS HOUSE LIES THE ANSWER TO YOUR DEATH-- AND I'LL *FIND IT*, MY DEAR FRIEND. I PROMISE YOU!

Anyway, Laura investigates the house, discovering at last a hidden diary written by Bettina and for which she was killed. It showcases a deep and dirty history of murder instigated by the matriarch of the family, which continues to that very day!

Laura isn't exactly the most interesting protagonist—she's prone to faint in times of stress and is easily swayed by a handsome man (even though he was her best friend's husband just days before). Yet she manages to push past these shortcomings and Nancy Drew her way into finding the secret of a house of lies and slayings. At least before it's burned down by a madman relative escaped from the asylum to seek his revenge. What can I say, it was an extremely action-packed issue!

You can almost hear the howls on the moors and the shocking swells of operatic music as secret after secret is revealed throughout the course of the story (the comic is billed as a "full novel," and at fifty pages of plot, that's fairly accurate). Though entertainment media have a long history of gothic romances set in creepy castles, it's most likely that this series, with its melodramatic plot twists, was inspired by the popular spooky television soap of the time, *Dark Shadows*.

The gothic romance genre in the 1970s was short-lived but prolific, with every publisher getting in on the trend. Charlton had its *Haunted Love* series, Marvel had the *Gothic Love* prose magazine, and DC had two series: *Dark Mansion of Forbidden Love* (which became *The Forbidden Tales of Dark Mansion*) and *The Sinister House of Secret Love* (which became *Secrets of Sinister House*). DC's name changes were an attempt to go straight horror, getting rid of all that yucky romance stuff. The *Sinister House* series was remarkably progressive compared to other comics of this time, highlighting stories about a gay rabbi and his Catholic priest boyfriend (unless they really were just dear, constant companions) who defeat demons together, and a white heroine falling in love with a Sikh man in India. The series wasn't without its complainers; one reader wrote in that the issues edited by Dorothy Woolfolk were too "female-oriented." Later issues showed there were readers who liked Dorothy's editing just fine, with one saying how much her mother and grandmother enjoyed the comic. I guess reading tales about making out with your dead best friend's husband is fun for the whole family. The writer of Laura Chandler's adventure is unknown, though it's stated in the letter pages to be "an Englishwoman who for reasons of her own, wanted to be anonymous." A mystery in the comic's very creation, how meta!

Each succeeding issue of *Dark Mansion of Forbidden Love* focused on one or two swooning young heroines mixed up in a Hitchcockian maze of love, mystery, and spooky houses. The issues were so lengthy and densely plotted that they almost became full-length graphic novels, a far cry from the horror anthologies of short stories that were in vogue at the time. You definitely got your money's worth with these comics. Laura was typical of the heroines, being alternately shaky and brave, relying mostly on her cleverness to solve the whodunit of the day.

ESSENTIAL READING: Laura Chandler appeared in only one issue, though any issue of *Dark Mansion* (or *Sinister House*) is bound to have a similar sort of story. After four issues, the title was changed to *Forbidden Tales of Dark Mansion* and it became an anthology book. *Sinister House of Secret Love*, aka *Secrets of Sinister House*, most recently became available in a black-and-white trade paperback, *Showcase Presents*, from DC (2010).

LEETAH	A gentle elfin healer whose stories sparked controversy with their uninhibited sexuality	66*I hold the power of life and death in my hands—with confidence! But I am afraid of things that I cannot anticipate or control!*99
		Created by: Wendy Pini and Richard Pini
		First appearance: *Fantasy Quarterly* #1 (self-published, 1978)

Leetah is the main female protagonist in the ensemble cast of *Elfquest*, the high-fantasy independent comic-book series that was one of the sparks of the black-and-white comics boom in the late 1970s. She's an ancient, though young-appearing, healer of the dark-skinned Sun Tribe in the World of Two Moons. She's also the reluctant love interest wooed by the male lead Cutter in the first book of the series.

But this is no one-dimensional damsel by any regard. At times stubborn, selfish, and arrogant, Leetah matures during the course of the series thanks to exposure to the younger, more primal Wolfrider tribe that invades her peaceful village and whose community she eventually joins.

Over time she does fall in love with Cutter (after at first simply falling in lust) and eventually becomes a devoted wife and mother. But Leetah is quick to answer the call of danger whenever a family member is in trouble. One of the

most powerful characters in the *Elfquest* universe, Leetah faces down formidable enemies, such as bloodthirsty trolls and the deadly but beautiful Winnowill, a twisted healer whose curiosity led her to dark discoveries.

Leetah's appearance is also striking: she's a curvy figure in a series in which both male and female characters showcase their form at every opportunity. Her exaggerated features were supposed to instill a sense of awe in the reader. The book was one of the first American comics to be heavily influenced by the Japanese manga style, evident in the large eyes and delicate features of the cast. The art is wholly unlike the heavy lines of the pulp and superhero styles popular at the time.

Beyond that, Leetah is a complex character. When she first appears, you're not supposed to like her. She's stubborn, dates a jackass, and is, frankly, a bit of a know-it-all. But her personality changes through exposure to new ideas and situations. As the long-running series unfolds, Leetah becomes a character who, although you might not identify with her because she is just a bit too perfect, comforts you with her discovered peace and wisdom. Her story teaches that change is good, that accepting the inevitable is necessary, and that you can be a good person but still make mistakes because of arrogance.

Elfquest was self-published by Wendy and Richard Pini, a husband-and-wife creative team who first met in the letter pages of Marvel's *Silver Surfer* comic. Their creation was a forerunner of the independent comics wave—especially of black-and-white comics—that started in the late '70s. The *Elfquest* books quickly gained a reputation for controversy and were banned in some shops because of content that included discreet group-sex scenes, consensual polyamory, and queer coupling. But the Pinis persevered, and the series is still running, forty years since its debut. The story has continued across hundreds of comics issues, as part of dozens of trade collections, and in multiple prose anthologies. The devoted fan base has grown from children to adults, with many proudly reading the comics they grew up with to their children and even their grandchildren. Wendy Pini was leading the charge of one of the most successful independent comic books being published, a rarity in any circle but most certainly for a female creator.

ESSENTIAL READING: Get a sample of the series by perusing it online; all the pre-2014 stories are available. Then dive into *The Complete Elfquest*, vol. 1 (Dark Horse, 2014). Although many publishers have reprinted *Elfquest* over the decades, this most recent reprint is most likely to be available and features the introduction of the grand quest that started the series.

PAGE PETERSON	She shows up in times of need to lecture you about what you're doing wrong in dating	**"** *Romance goes out of the window when rollers stay in, Maria! Good grooming is a private affair!* **"**
		Created by: Steve Englehart and DC Comics
		First appearance: *Secret Hearts* #151 (DC Comics, 1971)

Romance comics get a bad rap, though partly for good reasons: the stories, by and large, are meant as prescriptive lessons to women. Giving them hope for the future, assuring them that the love of their life is right around the corner, and chastising them on the proper way to act in order to attract a man. But the intense popularity of the genre, and its anthology format, meant that every so often truly good stories appeared. Stories about unwed mothers finding love, stories with characters of color, stories that promoted honesty and directness over evasion.

Starting in the 1970s, DC Comics, which had taken over the *Young Romance* and *Young Love* lines from Prize Comics, began to introduce a little more diversity onto the pages of its offerings. The first move in this direction was the introduction of the one-page fill-in comic "Page Peterson."

A common feature of the era's romance comics was an advice column, in which readers asked for help with their love lives and were answered by a fictional columnist whose illustration appeared at the top of a text page. "Nancy Hale," "Charmaigne," "Laura Penn," and other impeccably dressed professional women dispensed dating wisdom, and all were white as the driven snow. That trend changed with the appearance of black romance counselor Page Peterson, a welcome addition to the genre. Unlike her advice-doling peers, Page appeared in fully illustrated comics pages instead of text pages. In her one-page "Do's and Don'ts of Dating" strips, readers witnessed a date gone awry and then read Page's calm explanation to a hapless teenager about where she went wrong. (Don't invite your kid sister on a date, don't abandon your date for a better dancer, and other morsels of insight.)

Given that she appeared on only a single page for a few issues, Page Peterson didn't change the status quo much. Soon, however, racially diverse background characters and friends began to appear in romance stories. Although the lead characters in DC's romance lines remained overwhelmingly young white girls, Page was a clear signal that change was in the air. But change would take its time. The only story about an interracial relationship ended with one half of the couple dying tragically (perhaps to avoid the controversy of depicting an interracial wedding scene).

In a 2015 interview with romance comics scholar Jacque Nodell, Steve Englehart, who wrote Page's advice strips, stated that another comics writer told him that white men were the only characters they could really write. Englehart disagreed. "My instinctive reaction was to say 'No, a writer should be able to write anyone'—and I tried to do that—not only with romance, but with black characters, and so on. So I think I have a decent empathy and appreciation for people who don't look like me." A writer willing to go against the status quo and increase diversity in an overwhelmingly white genre was rare. Page Peterson remains a welcome break in terms of diversity and format in 1970s romance comics.

ESSENTIAL READING: These strips haven't been reprinted, but you can check out Jacque Nodell's romance comics blog *Sequential Crush* (sequentialcrush.com) for more information and scans from Page's adventures.

PAULINE PERIL	A clueless reporter whose good luck intervenes from her certain death time and time again	**"Ooh, this is all so lavishly lavish!"**
		Created by: Jack Manning and Del Connell
		First appearance: *Close Shaves of Pauline Peril* #1 (Gold Key, 1970)

A mix of Lois Lane and Moronica (an unfortunately unredeemable 1950s dumb-blonde comic), Pauline Peril is a voluptuous (that's a nice way of saying that her chest is the size of her head and her waist is the size of her wrist) reporter for the *Daily Noose* in Bigburg. Once a spoiled young playgirl, Pauline is transformed when her father, who grew tired of watching her cavort her life away, bought a newspaper chain just so that his daughter could get a job as a "girl reporter." The sinister editor of the paper realizes that if Pauline were to perish

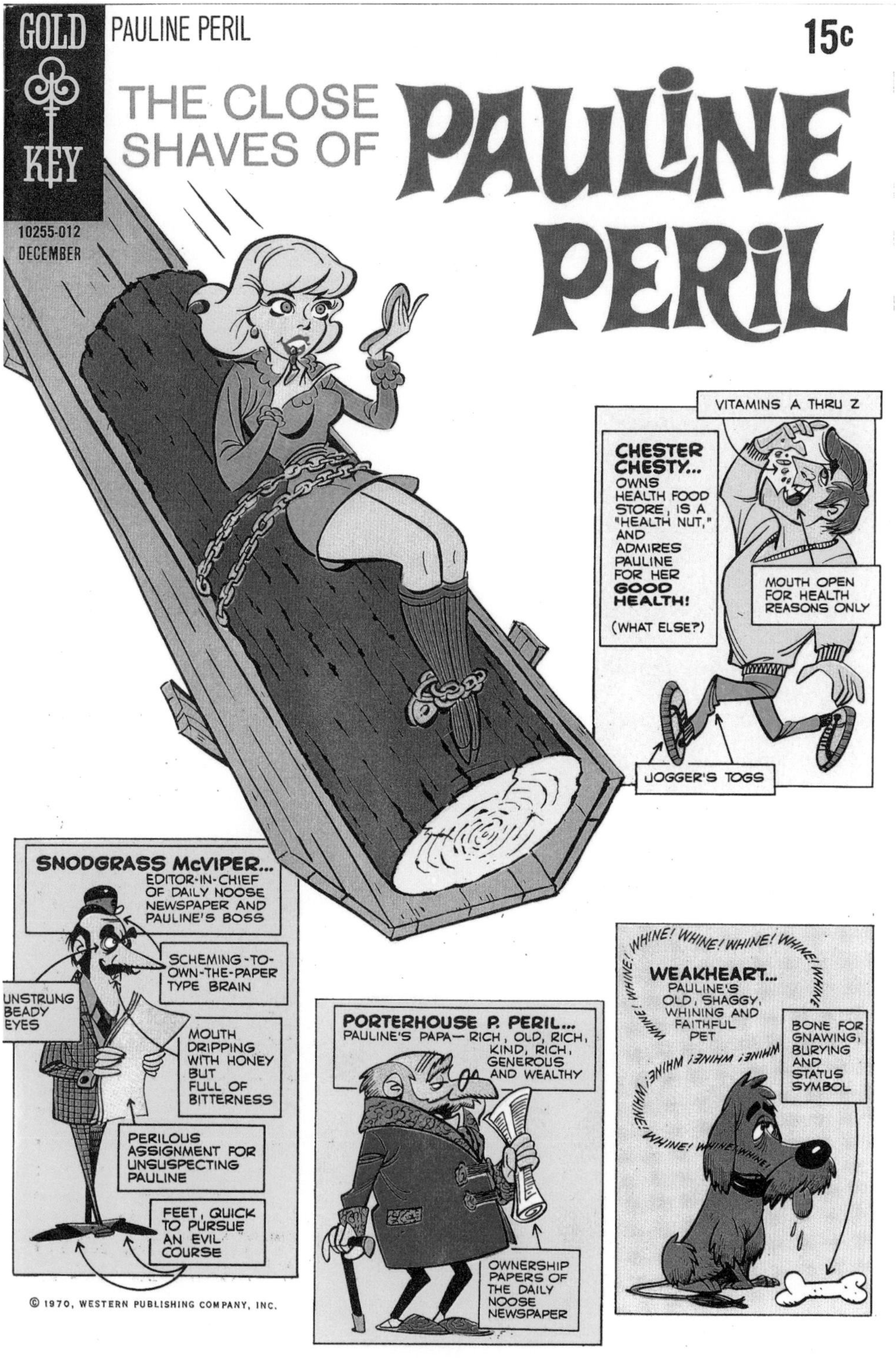
GOLD KEY
PAULINE PERIL
15c
THE CLOSE SHAVES OF PAULINE PERIL
10255-012
DECEMBER
VITAMINS A THRU Z
CHESTER CHESTY... OWNS HEALTH FOOD STORE, IS A "HEALTH NUT," AND ADMIRES PAULINE FOR HER GOOD HEALTH! (WHAT ELSE?)
MOUTH OPEN FOR HEALTH REASONS ONLY
JOGGER'S TOGS
SNODGRASS McVIPER... EDITOR-IN-CHIEF OF DAILY NOOSE NEWSPAPER AND PAULINE'S BOSS
SCHEMING-TO-OWN-THE-PAPER TYPE BRAIN
UNSTRUNG BEADY EYES
MOUTH DRIPPING WITH HONEY BUT FULL OF BITTERNESS
PERILOUS ASSIGNMENT FOR UNSUSPECTING PAULINE
FEET, QUICK TO PURSUE AN EVIL COURSE
PORTERHOUSE P. PERIL... PAULINE'S PAPA— RICH, OLD, RICH, KIND, RICH, GENEROUS AND WEALTHY
OWNERSHIP PAPERS OF THE DAILY NOOSE NEWSPAPER
WHINE! WHINE! WHINE! WHINE!
WEAKHEART... PAULINE'S OLD, SHAGGY, WHINING AND FAITHFUL PET
BONE FOR GNAWING, BURYING AND STATUS SYMBOL

on a dangerous mission, he would be able to buy up the now-useless newspaper at a bargain price and own the whole darn thing. Genius! So poor Pauline is set upon a perilous assignment to interview Tartar, king of the apes (and violent caveman misogynist, of course). Through sheer luck, however, Tartar becomes enamored of Pauline, probably because she's too dim to show him up.

Not exactly a role model, is she? At least the men in Pauline's life are no brighter than she is. There's her faithful and supernaturally strong-willed dog Weakheart, who pursues his master across the ocean and uses his magical whine to save her from danger. And Chester Chesty, a health-food nut who uses the power of raw eggs and yogurt pills to plow through any obstacles on his way to his lady love. Not one to be left out of the fun, Pauline's newly acquired caveman adoree Tartar pitches in, too. With their aid, time and again Pauline avoids the treacherous traps laid out for her and delivers her assignments on time (albeit poorly typed).

The artwork of *Pauline Peril* is unusually charming, looking a bit like *MAD* magazine and a bit like classic 1970s print advertisements. A few groan-worthy plotlines pepper the series, which is also hindered by mentions of women's all-consuming obsession with shiny things (literally at the risk of their own lives), their tendency to gossip, and the benefits and troubles of wearing stiletto heels and short skirts.

But at least Pauline inhabits a world where everyone is a fool. There's something refreshingly fun about that level of unconstrained zaniness. Plus the clothes were pretty amazing. Having just emerged from the 1960s, the characters still had a flair for patterns, minidresses, and keyhole blouses; revisiting these comics is like a walk down retro-fashion lane. If you're looking for anything deep, you won't find it here. But it's okay for adults to read nonsense once in a while, so don't feel guilty if you indulge.

ESSENTIAL READING: *Pauline Peril* ran for just four issues and has not been collected since.

PUDGE, GIRL BLIMP

A Martian's child just looking to get laid

> *If getting laid is bust . . . what is there to life? Sex is nothing? All those movies . . . books . . .is it all lies?*

Created by: Lee Marrs

First appearance: *The Further Fattening Adventures of Pudge, Girl Blimp* #1 (Last Gasp, 1973)

A fat girl from Normal, Illinois, shunned by her parents, Pudge is an outcast and desperately unhappy. Since this is 1973, the best way to escape her humdrum existence is to become a hippie and run off to San Francisco. If only Pudge knew the truth—that all chubby folk are in fact Martian offspring, created to spy on the human race!

Pudge's comic explores the free love culture of the 1970s, complete with drop-outs, hippies, drugs, and casual sex . . . all seen through the exploits of an unlikely protagonist who's a bit dense but incredibly lovable. Soon after her San Fran arrival, Pudge, a 17-year-old involuntary virgin, quickly tries to seduce a man in a trench coat hanging out in the park. Unfortunately, her would-be paramour turns out to be a female undercover police agent. Released by the cops when they figure out she isn't a heroin drug lord, Pudge continues on her quest for sex, which lands her in the slammer again and again. In one case, she's arrested after trying to take advantage of a passed-out neighbor at a commune. Another time, she discovers a guerilla feminist collective, and they're all arrested for teaching one another the ins and outs of biology with speculums and mirrors (this may be an underground comic, but at least it's educational).

Pudge's carnal quest sure isn't easy. Her female friends, exasperated by the girl's naiveté and wanting to protect her from getting mugged, finally decide to help. Except that the guy they set her up with turns out to be . . . the only real gentleman in San Francisco. He refuses to ditch his girlfriend for casual sex (despite really, truly enjoying Pudge's company), so back to the drawing board goes Pudge, discovering a new women's group where she builds her own identity, becomes comfortable in her body, and realizes that we're all weird. Ultimately Pudge decides that sex isn't as important as being respected (cheer!!). Yet time after time, her new resolve is put to the test. After every situation she lands in, Pudge learns to stand up for herself a little more and figure out what she truly wants in life—not just what she *should* want.

Lee Marrs, the creator of Pudge, was a popular underground cartoonist in the 1970s and cofounder of *Wimmen's Comix,* an underground all-female comics anthology. Marrs went on to become active in the digital comics medium,

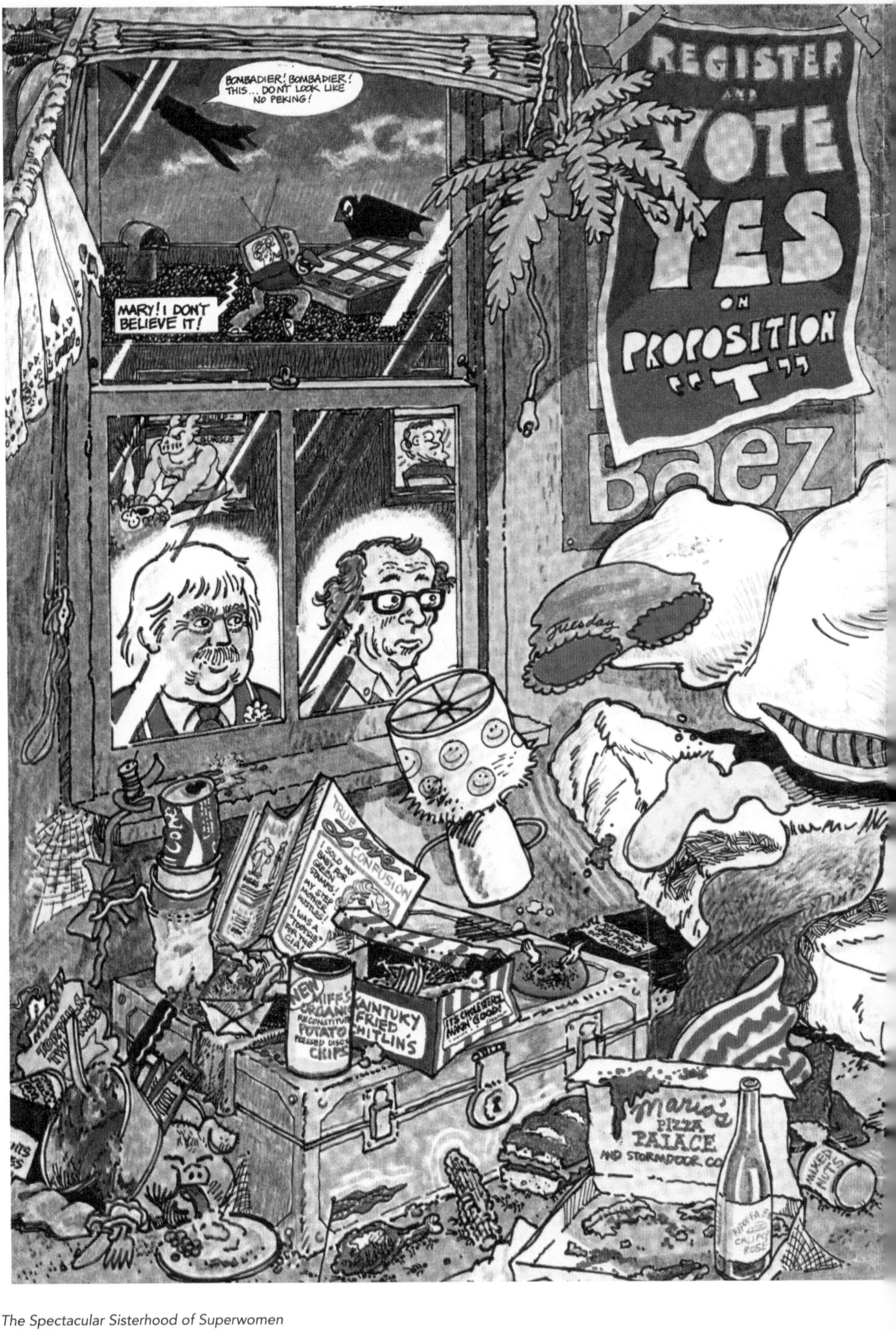
BOMBADIER! BOMBADIER! THIS... DON'T LOOK LIKE NO PEKING!
MARY! I DON'T BELIEVE IT!
REGISTER AND VOTE YES ON PROPOSITION "T"
Baez
Tuesday
TRUE Love CONFUSION
I SOLD MY BABY FOR GREEN STAMPS!
MY STEP MOTHER HUSTLES!
I WAS A "TOOTSIE" FOR THE CIA!
NEW
KAINTUKY FRIED CHITLIN'S
IT'S CHOLESTEROL AKKIN' GOOD!
POTATO
CHIPS
Mario's PIZZA PALACE AND STORMDOOR CO.
MIXED NUTS

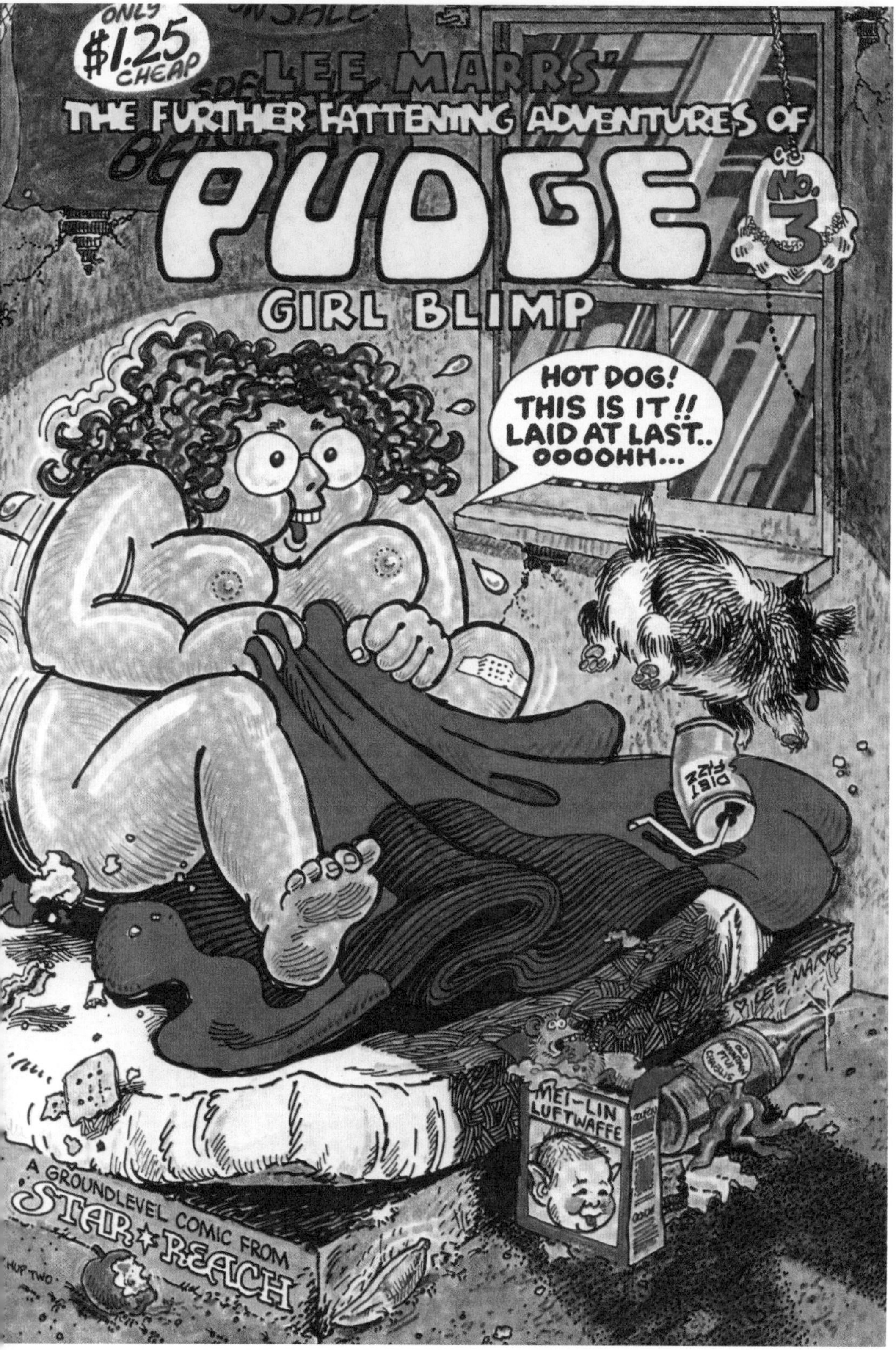
ONLY $1.25 CHEAP
LEE MARRS'
THE FURTHER FATTENING ADVENTURES OF
PUDGE
No. 3
GIRL BLIMP
HOT DOG! THIS IS IT!! LAID AT LAST.. OOOOHH...
LEE MARRS
MEI-LIN LUFTWAFFE
A GROUNDLEVEL COMIC FROM STAR*REACH
HUP TWO

creating interactive comics and working in animation. She's a creator who's not afraid to be the first one in the water, whether at the forefront of digital publishing or leading the charge for the feminist underground comics movement. Her *Pudge* series explores issues of unfair labor practices, police brutality, homophobia, racism, sexism, self-respect, anger control, polyamory, fake feminist men, and pretty much every other issue that women still face today. It's a sensitive and funny comic that delves deeply into the human condition.

The ever-adorable protagonist blunders her way through life, with not only the protection of her friends but also the secret supervision of her Martian parents. (I wasn't kidding about the Martian thing.) The latter are excited at the development of their daughter's personality and materialize on Earth to speed up her self-actualization. (They're disguised as Woody Allen and Captain Kangaroo, just FYI.) Spoiler alert: by the end of the series, Pudge becomes a full-fledged human being, in charge of her future, whatever that might be. As the author says: "You can let her grow up yourself."

ESSENTIAL READING: You can read all of Pudge's adventures by tracking down the 1974 series by publisher Star Reach.

STARFIRE	A slave who rebels against her alien masters	"Come and meet the woman who'll drive your entire empire to its knees!"
		Created by: David Michelinie, Mike Vosburg, and Robert Smith
		First appearance: *Starfire* #1 (DC Comics, 1976)

On Starfire's world, hideous reptilian monsters called Mygorgs keep the human race in chains. Because of her unusual heritage, being half Asian and half white, Starfire grew up as a novelty among the Mygorgs and was raised from birth to be a sheltered and educated servant rather than trained for physical labor. On her eighteenth birthday, Starfire learns that this privilege comes with a price: she will be forced into marriage with one of the most gruesome alien masters.

After running away, she is rescued by a mysterious swordsman named Dagan. This stranger teaches her to value her own worth, to expand her mind, and to view herself as a person not as property. Soon they fall in love and live happily together in the woods. At least until Dagan is captured and brutally tortured to death by the slave drivers.

From that point forward, Starfire vows to destroy her masters and lead the human species to freedom. She travels across her world, amassing an army of freed humans as she destroys all the Mygorgs foolish enough to stand in her way.

One of her new team members is a mute giant named Thump, previously forced to kill other humans for the pleasure of their inhuman masters. Initially she fears that he won't be able to recognize freedom or develop autonomy. But Thump rids the band of a savage warrior intent on raping Starfire, earning her trust. As they progress, more humans join their cause, including the scout Moonwatcher, who falls in love with Starfire. Which turns out to be his nice way of saying he wants to assault her, too. But Starfire doesn't always need to be saved, and she deftly deals with this traitor on her own.

In one of her short run of adventures, Starfire comes across an enslaved city, except no Mygorgs are living there. Instead, all the men are enslaved by the female human leader Karoleen. Like Starfire, Karoleen had been a servant destined for concubinage, but she used her physical skills to escape. Unlike Starfire, she witnessed a concubine being raped, which drove her to seek vengeance not just against her alien captors but against all males, regardless of species. Physically scarred during her escape, Karoleen vows eternal hatred against men as well as those women who side with them.

Okay, I get it: good feminist vs. bad straw-feminist plot. Pretty girl vs. ugly girl. Feel pity for the survivor warped forever by what she's seen, but don't let her be the hero. Eugh. Well, clearly the series has its flaws.

Starfire is often more at risk from her own band of men than she is from the monsters she vows to destroy, which adds an unwelcome tension to the series. The only man she can trust is Thump, who accompanies her to find the legendary Lightning Lords, holders of the weapons capable of defeating the Mygorgs. We then learn that Thump is more than he seems . . . as is the world that he and Starfire live in. It turns out everything is under the power of a sorceress who merged forces with a massive computer-like artificial intelligence; Thump is in fact a powerful computer programmer who's been magicked into forgetting his abilities. The series ends as the refugees whom Starfire collects set their sights on a way to rid the world of the evil emperors once and for all.

Starfire was an energetic, fast-paced sci-fi story that blends action, adventure, drama, and romance. Starfire was the paragon of a furious and proud warrior woman, complete with an elaborate costume that constantly changed from a half leotard to full armor to a hot pants and bikini combo. (The changes were possibly due to copyright concerns: artist Mike Vosburg apparently copied her first outfit faithfully from the Italian comic *Valentina*.) Despite some flaws, the story was well driven, with plots and adventure that kept you reading. All in all, it's a strong, surprising, and sadly short-lived comic.

ESSENTIAL READING: The full eight-issue series of *Starfire* has never been collected, which truly is a shame.

SUPERBITCH	A superpowered fox who takes her special abilities into space	66*If brains were balls, you'd be bow-legged!*99
		Created by: Ira Harmon
		First appearance: *Superbitch* #1 (California Comics, 1977)

Freda Foxx, aka Superbitch, is the star of the one-issue comic anthology named after her. It was marketed as "adult entertainment" and I won't lie: there's some explicit nudity, including lascivious close-ups of our title character.

The very first page showcases our heroine lounging naked in bed with a pet jaguar at her feet, while the news broadcast announces that the first black astronauts will go off into space. They're being sent because of millions of protest letters written in by the public. Wow! How lovely is this alternate view of 1970s society! Oh wait . . . the letters are protesting that liquor bottles and golf clubs have been left up there by white astronauts, and the public wants a black crew sent up to be lunar garbagemen. Adding insult to injury are newscasters and advertisements discussing the specific diet of the black astronauts, all presented in language that's about as racist as you might expect.

That's actually surprisingly good social commentary for a sex comic.

Back to the story: when the spaceship malfunctions and gets lost in deep-freaky space, the head of NASA calls for the help of Superbitch. Using the power of her radioactive vagina and a form-fitting space suit (complete with prosthetic, anatomically correct breast designs), Superbitch launches into action. She soon discovers the lost astronauts buried deep within an interstellar body (literally) and follows them inside, where she

uses tit-fu (that is, her breasts grow to enormous size and smash all aggressors) to ward off the dangerous aliens that lie in wait.

As a character, Superbitch is a mixed bag. On the one hand she's enthusiastic and powerful, and she gets the job done in a focused and practical fashion. On the other hand she punches out annoying white guys with her boobs . . . wait. Maybe that's a check in the positive column, too.

Though the book is an exploitative comic, and is marketed as adult entertainment, the sex in the story is bizarre to say the least. Imagine a spaceship out of control heading straight for a cosmic galaxy in the shape of a woman. Dagwood cheating on Blondie with a grown-up Little Orphan Annie. Aliens who look like Richard Nixon trying to convert an entire civilization of lesbian women with their nympho-ray, which is pitted against the femme society's lethal scrotum-scramblers.

Also, Superbitch's radioactive equipment prevents any type of sexual activity without lethal consequences for her partner, as one unfortunate spaceman finds out.

Freda Foxx isn't the first comics character to be strongly influenced by blaxploitation cinema (Marvel's Luke Cage and Misty Knight, and DC's Black Lightning, precede her). But she is one of the few black female characters created by a black cartoonist. Ira Harmon is a skilled artist, and his work has a better sense of visual style and humor than most underground comics of the period. This is still a sex comic created by a man, and his influence shows strongly. But it's a better example than most of the bizarre innovation characteristic of underground comics.

ESSENTIAL READING: You can read the entirety of Superbitch's story on the creator's website, harmonart.com.

SURVIVAL-WOMAN	The embodiment of Canadian culture	**I feel innocent, pure, virtuous, and well-meaning! I feel easily duped! I feel . . . Canadian!**
		Created by: Margaret Atwood (as Bart Gerrard)
		First appearance: *This* magazine (January 1975)

Survivalwoman is a tongue-in-cheek parody by legendary Canadian literary icon Margaret Atwood, best known for her works of philosophical fiction that delve into the core of humanity. Unbeknownst to many, Atwood makes silly cartoons, too.

The character of Survivalwoman premiered in the pages of the controversial, liberal education publication *This Magazine Is about Schools* (or simply

Gosh ... my hair has curled! I feel innocent, pure, virtuous, and well-meaning! I feel easily duped! I feel ... Canadian! And I've quit smoking!

This). In these strips, she attempts to best her overbearing American neighbor Superham, puts up with the exclusively feminist superheroine Womanwoman, and envies the pride of Quebec, Amphibianwoman. Survivalwoman also tries to earn art grants as a poet, attempts to survive a harsh Canadian political economy, and is chased by randy bears (it's a metaphor—and a nod to the controversial award-winning Canadian novel *Bear*).

Survivalwoman's origin story is simple. One night, a bitter and lonely woman sits in a bar, looking for a passable man to show her an okay time. Fortunately, a sleazy guy picks her up and she follows him back to his place, where he reveals himself to be a magical (and fairly kinky) Mountie! Upon touching one of his semisexual artifacts, the ordinary woman is transformed into the clean-cut, healthy-minded superheroine known as Survivalwoman. Her hair curls and she gains a costume: an *S*-emblazed shirt and cape. Then she realizes she can never change back . . .

Atwood's creation, from its very origin, is a metaphor for Canadian identity. Canada cannot have a superhero; it's not part of the cultural zeitgeist. We Canadians can only survive, not win, so if we do have a superhero—which we cannot—it must be one based on the concept of survival.

Get it? Oh, it's fine. We're talking about Canadian national identity, so no one does.

During Survivalwoman's adventures, we learn about other superheroes in her world. The country's neighbor to the south is portrayed as a thick, overmuscled, yet friendly giant named Superham. Survivalwoman tries to trounce him with her knowledge of Canadian cultural icons—only to be rebuffed by the fact that he simply does not care. Meanwhile, Womanwoman is on the cutting edge of socialism and ultrafeminism. To her, "manhole" is a sexist term. But she makes some pretty good points, like suggesting that the government's Whore Measures Act—which analyzes the bustlines of women on the street—might just be a male power trip. (That's a reference to Canada's War Measures Act, for you Americans.) Womanwoman encourages Survivalwoman to run for the office of prime minister simply because she's a woman, ignoring the fact that Survivalwoman has no experience with, interest in, or aptitude for this position.

In many ways, Womanwoman is similar to Roberta Gregory's creation Butchy Butch (page 160), with the same overexaggerated cartoonish presentation of feminist values, yet the story is still written in a feminist way. It's a tricky line to walk, but ultimately Atwood does it well (as does Gregory).

Americans might not get some of the jokes, such as Survivalwoman's hearty cry of "Yay, yay, John A.!" or the Canada Council refusing to renew her grant for a docudrama on the Toronto Blue Jays. But what's important is, Canadians get it. Okay, maybe most Canadians don't get it either. But really, what's more Canadian than a complete ignorance of our own culture?

ESSENTIAL READING: Ask a Canadian friend to go to the library and send you copies of *This* magazine's cartoon section. That's what I did.

ZELDA THE WITCH	A sexually provocative witch who stumbles back in time	66*Time just slips away when you never age!*99
		Created by: Will Meugniot
		First appearance: *Faerie Star* #1 (Moon Press Productions, 1977)

Zelda the Witch premiered in the first and only issue of *Faerie Star*, a fantasy-comic anthology put together by John David Cothran showcasing creator-owned stories that were not limited by the Comics Code Authority constraints. In the 1970s, that meant a good amount of nudity featuring young, pretty women, rather than biting social commentary or increased character diversity. Zelda is no exception, and her prominent chest and areolae are displayed quite thoroughly in her adventure.

We meet Zelda enjoying yet another beautiful day in Salem, Massachusetts, when she discovers a letter from two old friends, Mr. Younge and Mr. Olde, suppliers of supernatural materials, whom she hasn't seen in two decades. Being ageless, twenty years is no time at all to Zelda, so she's shocked to discover that Mr. Olde has passed away, leaving the business in the hands of his cowardly son.

Trying to determine the date of an ancient Egyptian artifact, Zelda accidentally transports herself and the wimpy son back in time, to the days of Cleopatra. When the time travelers meet the Egyptian pharaoh, she's a beautiful woman clad in a sheer gossamer gown, waited upon by yet more beautiful nude women (the male slaves are allowed a loincloth). In short order, Cleopatra orders them executed for trespassing.

From here the comic takes a surprising turn, with visitors bringing Cleopatra gifts such as exotic bananas (which she eats slowly, with great pleasure and enthusiasm) and intergalactic space-alien guard pets. What? Well, yes. See, in this story Cleopatra appears to have long been in contact with outer-space inhabitants, who plot to bring her empire to a close and claim Earth for themselves.

All in all, Zelda appears to be an adult version of Sabrina the Teenage Witch, with her misadventures in spells prompting the start of her journey and with humorous and bizarre twists peppering the storyline. Despite these similarities, the generous amount of nudity indicates that this comic is definitely aimed at adults. Then again, just a few years before Zelda the Witch appeared, Sabrina was starring in the extremely gory and graphic *Chilling Adventures in Sorcery as Told by Sabrina*, a series that showcased the depths of comic-book horror in an EC Comics style.

The nudity in Zelda's story is certainly exploitative, but it's a funny comic, lacking anything truly offensive. As far as adult underground nudie-comics go, Zelda isn't that bad and is even quite entertaining. I wouldn't have minded reading more of her time-traveling adventures if she hadn't vanished after just one issue.

ESSENTIAL READING: *Faerie Star* #1, if you can find it.

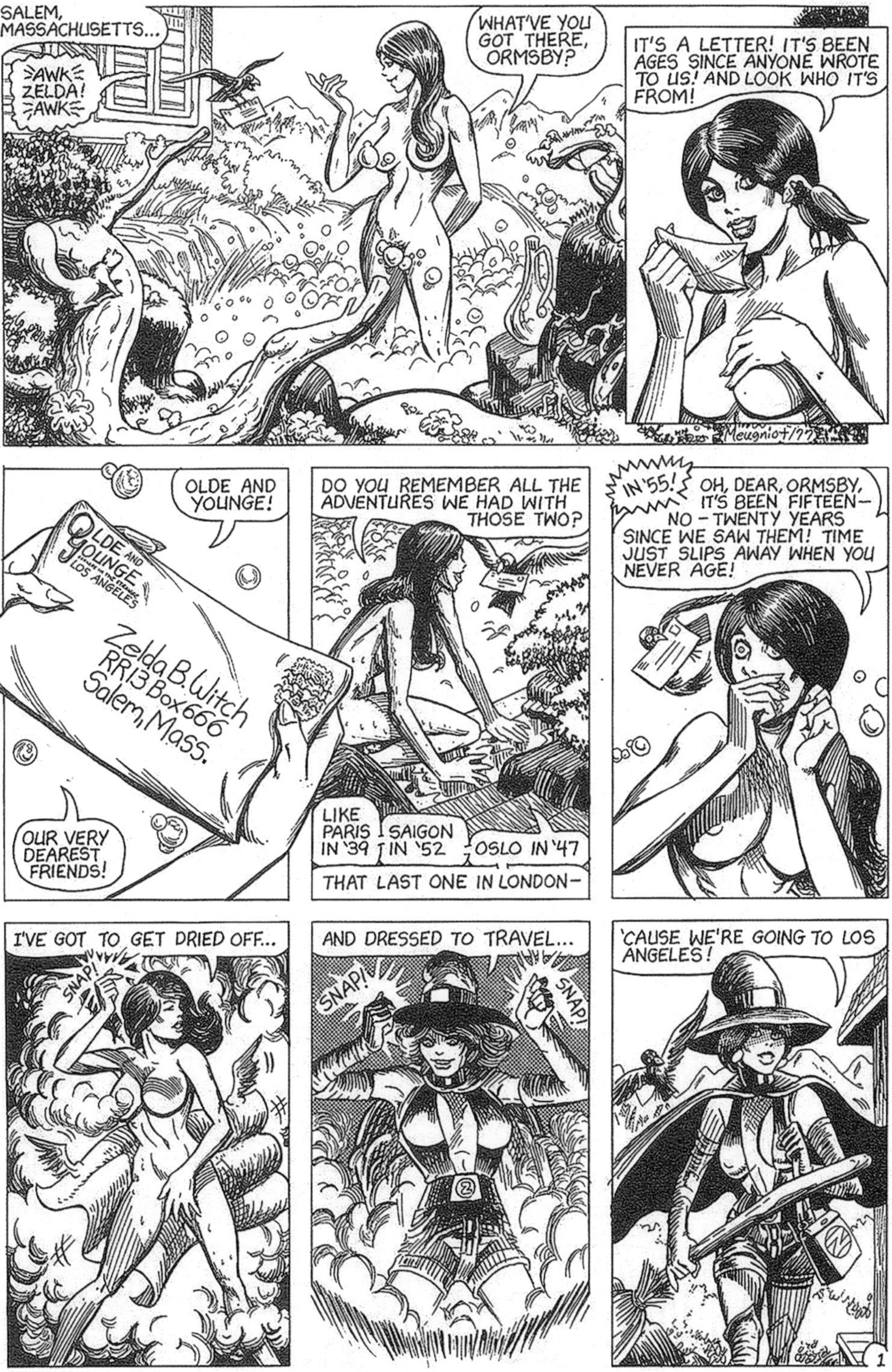
SALEM, MASSACHUSETTS...
AWK ZELDA! AWK
WHAT'VE YOU GOT THERE, ORMSBY?
IT'S A LETTER! IT'S BEEN AGES SINCE ANYONE WROTE TO US! AND LOOK WHO IT'S FROM!
Meugniot/77
OLDE AND YOUNGE!
OLDE AND YOUNGE
LOS ANGELES
Zelda B. Witch
RR13 Box 666
Salem, Mass.
OUR VERY DEAREST FRIENDS!
DO YOU REMEMBER ALL THE ADVENTURES WE HAD WITH THOSE TWO?
LIKE PARIS IN '39
SAIGON IN '52
OSLO IN '47
THAT LAST ONE IN LONDON–
IN '55!
OH, DEAR, ORMSBY, IT'S BEEN FIFTEEN– NO – TWENTY YEARS SINCE WE SAW THEM! TIME JUST SLIPS AWAY WHEN YOU NEVER AGE!
I'VE GOT TO GET DRIED OFF...
SNAP!
AND DRESSED TO TRAVEL...
SNAP!
SNAP!
'CAUSE WE'RE GOING TO LOS ANGELES!
1

ICON
OF THE
DECACE

The

70ˢ

MS. MARVEL (CAROL DANVERS)	Government military leader turned cosmic superheroine	Carol Danvers created by Roy Thomas, Gene Colan, and Paul Reinman; Ms. Marvel created by Gerry Conway, Carla Conway, John Buscema, Joe Sinnott, and Marie Severin
	66 *Some women prefer being protected. Some don't.* 99	First appearance as Carol Danvers: *Marvel Super-Heroes* #13 (Marvel Comics, 1968); First appearance as Ms. Marvel: *Ms. Marvel* #1 (Marvel Comics, 1977)

Carol Danvers turned up in comics almost ten years before she earned her superpowers and a costume. She's introduced as a supporting character in the Captain Marvel stories, given the role of head of security for the Cape, a government military base. She's cool, commanding, and instantly suspicious of alien hero Captain Marvel, who's using the form of a dead eccentric scientist to try to infiltrate the compound. Good instincts, Carol!

She begins to investigate him thoroughly, not letting his rudeness and sexism get in the way of her detective work. Her instincts aren't always so on-point, though, like when she starts flirting and making out with the good captain without realizing he's the same guy she's been investigating. Despite her inconsistent detective abilities, most of Carol's early adventures involve being one corner of a love triangle or needing to be rescued from the Monster of the Week.

Not all readers immediately warmed to Carol Danvers, with some fans writing in to yell at her for being just another "batty blonde." Maybe that's why she was written out of the comic and didn't reappear for several years, save for a brief appearance in *The Avengers*. When she did return, she had a completely new form: Ms. Marvel. Turns out that exposure to alien technology altered her genetic structure. Marvel Comics hyped her as "a superheroine for the seventies . . . and equally well set for the eighties and nineties too!" (In fact, they were right—Carol is still a lead character in comics.) Upon starting her career of champions, Carol switches from security to journalism and lands a job writing about women's issues for the *Daily Bugle*. As soon as there's trouble, she throws on her revealing costume and flies through the air as Ms. Marvel, using her "seventh sense" to predict danger. Trouble is, as Ms. Marvel she has no memories of being Carol Danvers. In fact, she has no memory of anything!

That little problem was eventually resolved, though unfortunately it was only the beginning of Carol's long history of having her mind messed with. In the more than forty years since her first appearance, she's made out with MODOK, been impregnated and brainwashed by an interdimensional creature, had her mind stolen by the *X-Men* character Rogue, become a being of pure cosmic energy, fallen into alcoholism, been canned from the Avengers, died, and been reborn. That's a lot of stuff to deal with.

Still, she has a lot going on in the plus column. Not only a successful solo star, Carol Danvers has been a member of the Avengers, the X-Men (even though she's not a mutant), the Starjammers (even though she's not an alien), the Thunderbolts (even though she's not a villain), and Alpha Flight (even though she's not Canadian). Along the way, she became a prominent and perennial member of the Marvel universe.

Later issues expand her skill set and background. She's revealed to have a long history as a U.S. Air Force pilot before joining the Cape. She eventually returns to her military roots, trading her black unitard for a more military-inspired getup that showcases her original costume's bright colors, and takes the name Captain Marvel.

Carol Danvers has come a long way from her damsel-in-distress roots, assuming her place as the most significant heroine in Marvel comics (with her own feature film to boot). Fangirls flocked to her newest incarnation, which showcased a proud, powerful superwoman focused on her duties and rocking a pretty damn cool uniform at the same time. Ms. Marvel was a feminist icon in the 1970s, and she's firmly in charge of her iconic status today.

CHAPTER

6

The 19

80s

BLACK-AND-WHITE BOOM (AND BUST)

THE 1980s

Ah, the 1980s! The decade of the boom and bust of the black-and-white independent comics market and the continued growth of the direct market system that fed a growing number of comics shops. To calculate the sheer volume of comics publishers that started business in the '80s only to disappear after an issue or two would be difficult. (But not impossible; at least 425 new publishers formed, and roughly 80 percent folded in the first five years.) So, what triggered this sudden boom in small start-up publishing?

Well, the launch of a little comic book sensation called *The Teenage Mutant Ninja Turtles*.

A black-and-white comic self-published by creators Kevin Eastman and Peter Laird, the book benefited from good luck and the smart idea to advertise in *The Comics Buyer's Guide*. The result: a successful and highly sought-after published run, soon followed by a popular merchandise line. Hungry for the same level of overnight success, publishers inundated the industry with a flood of black-and-white indie comics. Some, such as *Love and Rockets*, are still popular today. Many, including *Hamster Vice*, *Clint the Hamster Triumphant*, and *Adolescent Radioactive Black Belt Hamsters*, are long since forgotten.

During this era, publishers began making comics specifically for the direct market that had developed in the 1970s. These books would not be sold on newsstands; the first was Marvel's *Dazzler* (page 135), starring a disco-sound-powered superheroine mutant. Marvel's head of direct sales, Carol Kalish, spearheaded the specialization of sales into direct market channels. Not only did she push for strong relationships between publishers, distributors, and retailers, but she also made it her mission to advise retailers pro bono on how to make their comics stores better.

Sadly, it's likely that the push into the direct market and comics shops and the decline of comics on newsstand racks—while necessary for the industry to survive and thrive—was a heavy blow to the female reading public. Although the industry still had many female comics fans, the number was no longer close to parity with male readers, as it had been in the 1940s. The theory is that many female readers were happy to read comics when they could buy them in well-lit stores and markets. But for some reason, hobby shops—usually located in dim, dingy basements and run almost exclusively by men—held little appeal.

Where were the women in this indie comics boom? Well, Colleen Doran was there, creating her space-opera fantasy epic *A Distant Soil*. Alison Bechdel, creator of the media analysis method known as the Bechdel Test, was releasing *Dykes to Watch Out For*, a semiautobiographical strip. Louise Simonson was creating moving melodramatic arcs for Marvel in the pages of *X-Factor*, *New Mutants*, and *Power Pack* (this last drawn by artist June Brigman and colored by Glynis Wein, a rare, almost all-female creative team). Roberta Gregory was releasing her popular *Naughty Bits* series through Fantagraphics Books. With tenacity, women creators were hanging in there and creating content. But the majority of the black-and-white boom comics were T&A oriented, perhaps because women were not well represented among the creators. For example, in its 80-creator roster, Pacific Comics had only three women: Lela Dowling, Carrie McCarthy, and April Campbell.

Comic book conventions continued to increase in popularity, and female fans cosplayed (though this term was not yet used) as their favorite characters. Female creators were not often invited as guests to these conventions, and when they were, they were looked down on and treated poorly by many of the male executives and creatives. As Colleen Doran put it bluntly (in email correspondence): "It sucked like you wouldn't believe."

By and large, comics from the big publishers were dominated by superheroes—particularly male superheroes. Marvel was again selling more issues than DC, and both companies enjoyed significant growth throughout the decade. Comics, too, were growing in number each year. But the days of genre comics from the big two publishers seemed to be over. If you were in the mood for anything but superheroes (or Conan the Barbarian), you had to look elsewhere. ⚡

AMANDA WALLER	Tough non-superpowered woman in charge of a group of villains turned reluctant heroes	"I will make it my personal business to see your butt is used for shoe leather!"
		Created by: John Ostrander, John Byrne, Len Wein, and Tom Ziuko
		First appearance: *Legends* #1 (DC Comics, 1986)

We first meet Amanda Waller as the head of the mysterious "Task Force X," in which she takes no crap from the square-jawed Colonel Rick Flag, who shows up to assist her. With the Justice League reviled by the public as vigilantes acting without concern for the good of common people, Task Force X is soon revealed to be an elite squad of superpowered villains charged with crimes, who've been sent by the U.S. government on missions likely to be suicidal. If they survive, the criminal charges against them will be dropped.

Now, you might wonder how a normal human like Amanda Waller could get all these superbad supervillains to obey her every whim. The answer: "The Wall" is one incredibly tough and confident woman. Okay, she has also clapped an explosive bracelet to each criminal, which she can detonate at will. Their mission? To eliminate Brimstone, a villain lackey of the powerful outer-space tyrant Darkseid.

With a bunch of supervillains setting out to do good under threat of execution, you might expect the group—soon known as the Suicide Squad—to headline a dark and bitter comic book about the dynamics of power and control. And though it can be that at times, the first series is actually a fairly wacky good time!

Best of all, Amanda Waller is a powerful female leading character unlike any other in comics. For one thing, she's a solid, tough, middle-aged woman of color in charge of a powerful government agency. She also has no superpowers, though she still manages to scare supervillains and stand up to anyone who thinks they knew better than she does. She even berates U.S. president Ronald Reagan for canceling social programs that had helped her family. After crime on the streets leads to the deaths of two of her children and her husband, Amanda Waller puts her last three kids through college before pushing herself to do the same. Having earned a political science degree, and armed with knowledge of her community, she launches a successful political career and achieves a White House post, eventually discovering past versions of the Suicide Squad. She decides to update the program and fill it with powerful but completely expendable people—supervillains.

Over the course of the Squad's early adventures, Amanda Waller makes mistakes, learns, grows, and makes more mistakes. She's powerful and she is very, very human—a compelling character to watch. Don't just take my word for it. Amanda Waller's cult popularity has led to her appearing in hundreds of DC comic books as well as animated movies, TV episodes, video games, and feature films.

Decades after her first appearance, the powers that be rebooted Amanda into a perfect supermodel's body. Because the comics biz just can't let us have anything nice for very long.

ESSENTIAL READING: I'm partial to Amanda Waller's early adventures, which you can read in the recently collected *Suicide Squad: The Silver Age* (DC Comics, 2016).

A bombshell bunny set
out to stop crime on
Earth and in space

*❝This has gotta be the dumbest
story I've ever seen!❞*

Created by: Joshua Quagmire

First appearance: *FAN-tastic* #2 (fanzine, 1982)

Cutey Bunny is the superheroine name of Corporal Kelly O'Hare who, if you're not getting the puns yet, is an anthropomorphic rabbit. Her name is both a play on her animal nature and a nod to the series *Cutie Honey*, one of the first Japanese manga to feature a female protagonist. In fact, Cutey Bunny's creator Joshua Quagmire draws inspiration from a wide array of comics artists, both Western and not, including Will Eisner (*The Spirit*), Tex Avery (Bugs Bunny), Osamu Tezuka (*Astro Boy*), Walt Kelly (*Pogo*), and Harvey Kurtzman (*MAD* magazine). With such diverse influences, this series manages to touch on superhero, sci-fi, and jungle genres, making Cutey Bunny a truly innovative character.

That said, the stories also include strong elements of T&A comics, featuring the main character in a variety of cleavage-sporting costumes (with prominent nipples in most panels). The protagonist unapologetically breaks the fourth wall on the first page of her self-titled comic to let you know that the action will focus on her tight tights. Which, incidentally, are made of torsion-stressed, steel-reinforced hosiery, so they never get runs even in the toughest situations. Well, I guess we have to give *Cutey Bunny* points for transparency!

That fourth-wall breaking continues throughout the series and adds style and charm. Guest stars from other forms of popular media frequently drop in, such as Humphrey Bogart (renamed Bogart Basset . . . yep, he's a dog), Ronald Reagan, Bob Hope, and Inspector Lestrade from Sherlock Holmes. Between stories, Cutey Bunny chats with the writer's assistant, a tiny tabby who does the lettering and Zip-a-Tone (and becomes the masculine power hero in one of the comic's backup features).

On to our heroine's backstory. Cutey Bunny is a former archaeologist who was granted a magical amulet by the Egyptian sun god, Ra-Harahkte. The amulet grants her flight, speed, and strength, as well as the ability to change clothes and hairstyles at will. She lives in a world with both anthropomorphic animals and humans (meaning, yes, it would be theoretically in the realm of canon possibility for a human to . . . ask Cutey out on a romantic date). Cutey's archnemesis is Ashtoreth, named for the goddess of sex and violence. Aptly, this Ashtoreth is an S&M-obsessed fox—I mean she's *literally* a fox, in addition to being pretty cute. Ashtoreth fluctuates wildly between wanting to kill our heroine or seduce her.

Cutey Bunny has a few beaus, such as chubby duck Stevey Ramrod, whom she loves and desires desperately, at least between her other lovers. But Cutey doesn't know that Stevey is the Tuxedo Mask to her Sailor Moon . . . aka Captain Huey! A thinly veiled parody of Captain America, Captain Huey might have two brain cells to rub together if he gained one more. He's more of an obstruction than anything else. Luckily, he fades away after the first issue, leaving our heroine to pursue other romantic interests (such as the dreamy, and mysteriously human, fighter pilot Lt. Lewis Clark).

Cutey also stars in a backup sci-fi series called *Space Gophers*. There's something to be said for a comic that's not afraid to switch genres on a whim.

A really interesting aspect of *Cutey Bunny* is that most funny animal comics humanize animals but give them primarily Caucasian features (light eyes, long flowing hair, etc.), but Cutey Bunny clearly represents a character of African ancestry, with dark skin and hairdos that change from long braids, to curls, to relaxed bobs, to a natural style. Plus, in one story it's stated that she's a princess of the Nubian dynasty, clarifying that aspect of the character.

In Cutey Bunny we have a protagonist who is tough and smart, starring in a T&A comic that somehow manages to be winky-cute rather than overbearingly sexual. Sex and comedy are like peanut butter and chocolate—they just go good together.

ESSENTIAL READING: You'll have to track down the original *Cutey Bunny* comics, since they've never been reprinted. Check the creator's website, cuteybunny.com, for leads.

DAKOTA NORTH	A stylish private eye who rocks a leather jacket and a handgun	**"What is it with all this kissing? Am I supposed to like it? Does anyone?"**
		Created by: Martha Thomases, Tony Salmons, and Christie Scheele
		First appearance: *Dakota North* #1 (Marvel Comics, 1986)

Sporting a clean-cut bob, leather jacket, and cigarette jeans, Dakota North had style and smarts, plus a keen eye for detection and no patience for fools.

Though often compared to Ms. Tree (see page 143)—whose publisher, Renegade Press, ran a parody ad mimicking Marvel's ads for Dakota North—Dakota is less of a hothead and definitely boasts a lower kill count. And while Ms. Tree was dealing with hot-topic political issues, Dakota North just ran around the world looking good and kicking butts.

Dakota runs the North Agency, along with her underpaid and smart-aleck assistant Mad Dog, and welcomes the occasional drop-in visit from studly

Detective Amos. In Dakota's first appearance, she contracts to protect a famous fashion designer, Luke Jacobson, who is as beautiful as he is brainless. Dakota makes quite an entrance on the fashion-shoot set, riding up the elevator on

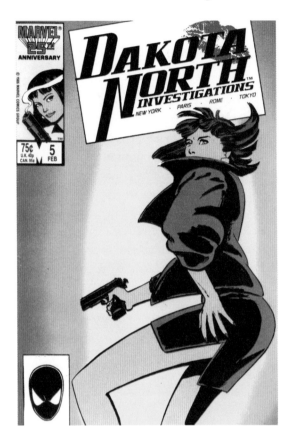

her motorcycle. Given a makeup case to make herself look "presentable" upon arrival, she suspects a trap and throws it out the window. She has great instincts, for it promptly explodes.

It turns out that the villain in charge of the mayhem, Miss Vanderlip, is in league with Jacobson's assistant Anna (in a vaguely homoerotic way that had to be coded); Anna is also in love with her boss. At the same time, Miss Vanderlip is trying to seduce Dakota's much-reviled father—a wheelchair-bound former spy, who turns out to be a past paramour of Vanderlip. Sadly, the series ends abruptly in the middle of a cliffhanger, with Vanderlip approaching Dakota's father with a kiss and a gun. The storyline ends with this bitter note: "This is where we usually put the blurb for the next issue, if there was a next issue, but there isn't."

Though *Dakota North* existed in the Marvel Comics universe, you didn't see superheroes walk through the halls of the North Agency. Only after her miniseries ended was the character integrated into Marvel's superhero world, first facing off against Spider-Man, then getting a major supporting role in Luke Cage's *Cage* series in the 1990s. Marvel sent Dakota into hibernation after that, allowing her to make sporadic appearances until she joined Daredevil in the mid-2000s as a private investigator (and eventual lover to his alter ego, Matt Murdock). In this role she gains the additional honor of being one of Daredevil's rare girlfriends who doesn't die tragically.

In her own miniseries, Dakota seems to function separately from Marvel canon, almost as if she was a creator-owned comic. The situation is explained by creator Martha Thomases on her blog. The character was based, at least in appearance and style, on Thomases's friend Norris Church Mailer, a well-known artist, writer, and model in New York City. Thomases explains that though she had to cede ownership of Dakota North to Marvel Comics for practical reasons—i.e., getting paid—the character was developed with limited input from the company. In her eyes, Dakota North's struggle was that of the father-daughter dynamic, with Dakota trying to win her dad's approval while simultaneously pushing him away. Had the opportunity to create such a character come a decade or two later, Thomases admits that she never would have signed away the rights. It's a familiar story in comics. Many creators who invent new characters under a publisher's banner later regret it, for the characters fall out of their control after their contract ends.

Dakota North had promise, style, humor, and action. It's a shame the book was canceled in its prime and the character relegated to the back burners of Marvel's roster.

ESSENTIAL READING: Since they've never been released in a collection, the five single issues of the 1986–87 *Dakota North* miniseries are the only place to read her solo adventures.

DAZZLER	Disco-powered supermutant in a bedazzled jumpsuit and roller skates just trying to lead a normal life	66I'm no witch, turkey! Just your average everyday mutant—a regular child of the atom!99
		Created by: Chris Claremont, John Byrne, Terry Austin, and Glynis Wein
		First appearance: *Uncanny X-Men* #130 (Marvel Comics, 1980)

Okay, fine. Giggle about the disco-themed superheroine named Dazzler. But don't laugh too loud or she's liable to burn out your eyes with her laser powers. A mutant in the X-Men franchise of Marvel Comics, Alison Blaire possesses the power of "sound transduction," which means she can change sonorous vibrations into various forms of light, including blinding flares, lasers, and hologram-type illusions. She's a handy woman to have in a crisis—as long as her boom box is working.

Born to a controlling father and abandoned at an early age by her mother, Alison grew up with one dream: to be a singer. A reluctant hero for most of her early adventures, Dazzler was often pitted against foes way out of her league, including Doctor Doom, the Hulk, the Enchantress, and even the cosmic planet-eater Galactus (whose herald and love interest she became, albeit in an alternate universe). Known for her bad luck in love as much as her startling powers, Dazzler has dated a bevy of Marvel hunks, such as Angel, Beast, Quasar, and Longshot, whom she eventually marries and later abandons. (In her defense, she thought he was dead. But how many times have we heard that excuse before?)

Pushed into heroism by circumstances beyond her control—notably the ruination of her musical career after being outed as a mutant—Dazzler eventually joins the X-Men. She learns to be a superhero and, eventually, a rebel leader, relinquishing her musical dreams. Though she ditched her disco trappings,

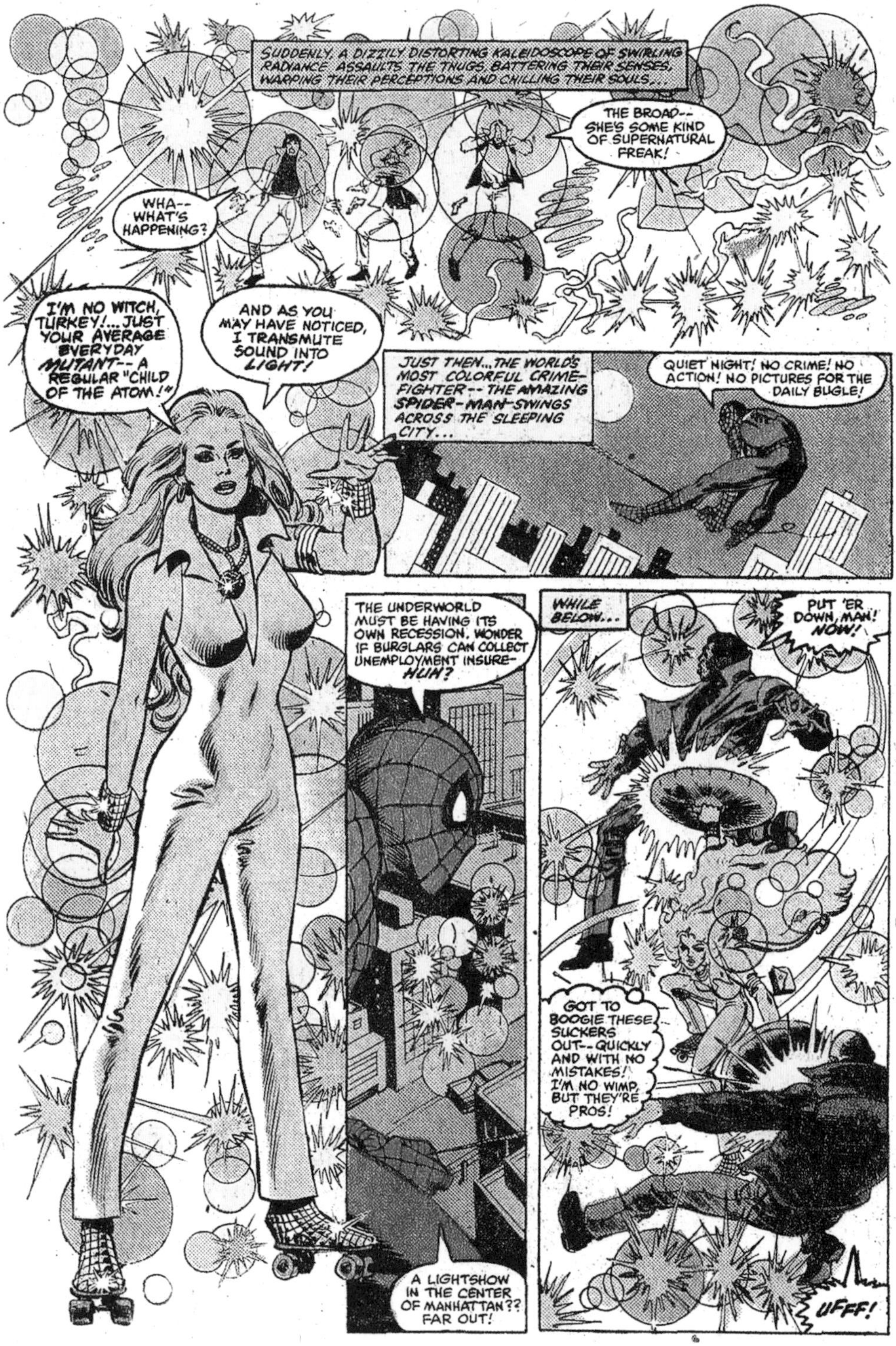
SUDDENLY, A DIZZILY DISTORTING KALEIDOSCOPE OF SWIRLING RADIANCE ASSAULTS THE THUGS, BATTERING THEIR SENSES, WARPING THEIR PERCEPTIONS AND CHILLING THEIR SOULS...
THE BROAD-- SHE'S SOME KIND OF SUPERNATURAL FREAK!
WHA-- WHAT'S HAPPENING?
I'M NO WITCH, TURKEY!... JUST YOUR AVERAGE EVERYDAY MUTANT-- A REGULAR "CHILD OF THE ATOM!"
AND AS YOU MAY HAVE NOTICED, I TRANSMUTE SOUND INTO LIGHT!
JUST THEN... THE WORLD'S MOST COLORFUL CRIME-FIGHTER -- THE AMAZING SPIDER-MAN SWINGS ACROSS THE SLEEPING CITY...
QUIET NIGHT! NO CRIME! NO ACTION! NO PICTURES FOR THE DAILY BUGLE!
THE UNDERWORLD MUST BE HAVING ITS OWN RECESSION. WONDER IF BURGLARS CAN COLLECT UNEMPLOYMENT INSURE-- HUH?
A LIGHTSHOW IN THE CENTER OF MANHATTAN?? FAR OUT!
WHILE BELOW...
PUT 'ER DOWN, MAN! NOW!
GOT TO BOOGIE THESE SUCKERS OUT-- QUICKLY AND WITH NO MISTAKES! I'M NO WIMP, BUT THEY'RE PROS!
UFFF!

Dazzler has faded in popularity over the decades and she makes only semiregular appearances. Most recently she's been hitchhiking her way around an alternate reality and been promoted to an agent of S.H.I.E.L.D., the premier spy group of Marvel Comics.

Oh, forgot to mention—Dazzler is also the adoptive mother of a tribe of miniature X-Men clones, the X-Babies, who live in the Mojoverse dimension. Busy gal!

Dazzler was the first superhero comic I remember reading, thanks to my parents discovering a complete set in the garbage bin of a comics shop (the issues suffered only moderate flood damage). Despite the crinkled pages, I was obsessed with this character. She was cool! She was struggling in her career! She had dates all the time! Even her battles were unlike those of any other superheroes I can think of (she frequently lost). Her story's humanity and melodrama drew me in just as much as the characters' costumes and superpowers.

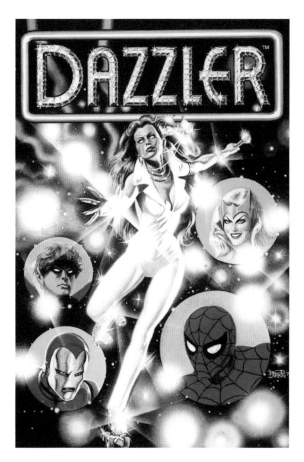

Admittedly, Dazzler's disco getup was already behind the times when she debuted in 1980. But in a way she was riding the wave of the future: *Dazzler* #1 was the very first Marvel comic to try direct-market-only ordering. Distributed exclusively to comics specialty shops, the initial issue sold over 400,000 copies. But why the Studio 54 look? Because Dazzler was *created* during the disco era. She was originally imagined as African American rather than the white gal she ended up being, and her book was supposed to be cross-promoted with a movie and record tie-in featuring a real-life version of the character. Obviously that all changed. But Dazzler's persistence in the Marvel universe, even though she was intended as a fad, speaks to the need and desire for female characters that we all can relate to.

ESSENTIAL READING: Sadly, none of Dazzler's escapades have been reprinted in color. So unless you comb through back-issue bins, you'll have to settle for Marvel's black-and-white reprint collections. *Essential Dazzler*, vol. 1 (Marvel, 2007) includes her dazzling debut and early exploits. If you hate disco and jumpsuits (what, do you hate puppies, too?) you can jump forward to Greg Pak's run of *X-Treme X-Men*. Volume 1 of that collection (2013) showcases Dazzler jumping through dimensions, leading her own rag-tag team of adventurers.

FASHION IN ACTION	The most skilled, and best dressed, celebrity-protection agency in the world	66 *We live in a world where no rules apply. Sometimes, only our friends can remind us that it's still a place worth living for.* 99
		Created by: John K. Snyder III
		First appearance: *Scout* #1 (Eclipse Comics, 1985)

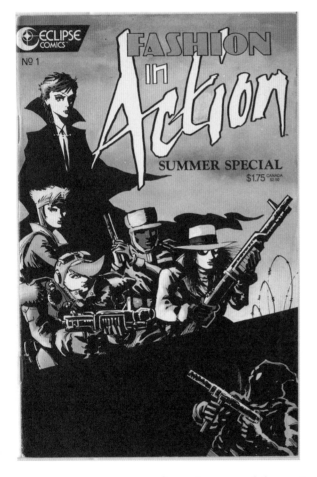

I can't choose just one character from *Fashion in Action*—they're all so wonderful. The series ran as a backup feature in *Scout* in the mid- to late 1980s, before graduating to two of its own full-issue specials and then fading into obscurity.

Fashion in Action was hugely influenced by its era's pop culture. From characters inspired by pop stars (main character Frances Knight is partly a mix of Annie Lennox and David Bowie) to plots that echoed current events—such as Sean Penn and Madonna's wedding—this series was topical for the 1980s. But it was set in the 2080s! This is a future that had lived through world wars, featured flying cars and jetpacks, saw humans settle on Mars . . . yet fashion designers still reigned supreme.

Each of the characters in *Fashion in Action*— that's the name of their security agency—had her own style and specialties. Frances was the tough and capable leader. As a young journalist and freedom fighter, she lost her eye in an incident that is never talked about but that, when finally revealed, showcases her resilience to survive and her resolve to punish those who take advantage of innocents. Her outfits of choice include dark, dramatic capes and sharp suits. Frances's oldest friend and head of security is Kelly, a tough woman with a practical, militaristic style. Talia is the cool, calm pilot who's dependable in the face of danger, rocking an eccentric '70s-influenced look. Sarah is the sarcastic know-it-all who is usually right and who dresses like a modern-day cowboy. And Ursula is the glamorous funder of the agency as well as a powerful psychic.

The plot of the first eight issues revolves around the team trying to stop the mysterious Dr. Cruel and his henchmen, Roxanne and Boss One, from kidnapping celebrity late-night host Johnny Mars (partially inspired by Wayne Newton). They seem to have succeeded, until they learn that the Mars they rescued is in fact a robot who's transmitting a virus designed to turn all the guests at a high-profile celebrity wedding into gorillas. At the same time, Frances is drawn into a fight to the death with her biggest fan, the violently unpredictable (and eccentrically fashioned) Roxanne.

The plot ends unexpectedly, with twists and sudden tragedy. Luckily two additional special issues followed the main series and helped expand the universe. One pitted Fashion in Action against their equally glamorous and deadly mercenary rival Antje, who was plotting to assassinate a counterfeiting fashion designer (who happens to have been part of a military dictatorship that took over Europe). The second adventure continued the plot from the main series, with Frances finally making peace with Roxanne as well as her own violent past.

The women of *Fashion in Action* are unique. Not only did the characters wear clothes straight out of designer catalogs, which draped and flowed instead of being vacuum-sealed to their bodies, but they also had vastly different looks and personalities. They were tall, short, thin, chubby, black, Asian, white, flat, buxom . . . This was a comic very much ahead of its time, one that modern comics should look to as an example of how to create female characters who are strong and well defined.

ESSENTIAL READING: All the issues were collected and restored by Canadian powerhouse publisher Bedside Press in 2016 (disclaimer: this is my publishing company).

GINGER FOX	CEO of a failing film company, beset by assassins at all turns	66 *Just deliver a simple, everyday blockbuster and I'll be happy.* 99
		Created by: Mike Baron, Mitch O'Connell, and Les Dorscheid
		First appearance: *The World of Ginger Fox* (Comico, 1986)

Ginger Fox was not actually ginger (she was blonde). But in everything she did, she was definitely as cunning as a fox. Star of her own graphic novel and miniseries, Ginger Fox was an icon for the 1980s, full of glitz, glamour, and intrigue!

Ginger is the hardworking CEO of Peppertree Studios, a dying Hollywood motion picture company that hasn't had a hit in years. At the start of her story, Ginger joins the all-male-led studio to revitalize it and quickly faces gossip

about "how she got the job." Despite the aspersions cast against her character and her abilities, and with the aid of a trusty assistant named Cozy, she rapidly turns the company around, taking a hard stance against directors who go over budget.

Ginger soon falls for leading man Jason Wu, star of Peppertree's new action movie series. This relationship is immediately tested with threats of violence against both the studio and its star. The source: a secretive underground crime ring that thinks their secrets of "negative kung fu" will be exposed in Wu's films. At the same time, a disgruntled director sabotages Ginger to get back at the "cold bitch" who tried to ruin his career. Through all of this, Ginger handles situations with calm and thoroughness, the perfect picture of a successful 1980s businesswoman.

Along with managing difficult talent, sustaining her dynamite chemistry with a film star, maintaining her personal style, and running a corporation, Ginger Fox is also a single mom raising a son, Huck. Women really can have it all!

After the initial graphic novel, Ginger Fox's saga continued in a four-issue miniseries under the same name; it was drawn with super-stylized artwork that showcased the pop art sensibilities of the day. The colors were bright, the lines were angular, and the personalities were exuberant. This follow-up series was pure 1980s, even campier and more bizarre than the original graphic novel. It was also extremely topical: AIDS is brought up within the first few pages, whereas most comics of the day were sweeping the subject under the rug. In addition, drug use in Hollywood was a common theme in both the graphic novel and the miniseries (though in the former it was treated as A Very Serious Problem that could be dealt with through careful healing and mental comfort; in the latter, drug use usually just indicated that A Bad Dude was present).

Life for Ginger might be more complicated than for your usual film executive. But what fun would her story be if there wasn't a little murder and mayhem?

ESSENTIAL READING: You can read the first graphic novel for free online at co2comics.com.

MAGGIE CHASCARILLO	Punk-rock spaceship mechanic looking for love in all the wrong places	*"Heck no! I'm not crazy! Do I look crazy? I mean, I just kind of like this guy, y'know . . ."*
		Created by: Jaime Hernandez
		First appearance: *Love & Rockets* #1 (Self-published, 1982; later republished by Fantagraphics Books, 1982)

Maggie is really an everyday girl struggling to get by in Hoppers, a fictional barrio near Los Angeles. She hangs out with her core group of female friends, such as wannabe superhero Penny Century, gothic gal Izzy Reubens, rich-girl-slumming-it Daffy Matsumoto, and her on-again off-again best friend and occasional lover, Hopey Glass. Added to this mix are the men and women who wander into her romantic life: the cute-but-thick mechanic superstar Rand Race, the tragic James Dean–like crush Speedy Ortiz, the complicated artist Ray Dominguez, and the fiery-tempered Vivian "Frogmouth" Solis.

Maggie also happens to, on rare occasions, travel into outer space on rocket missions and meet up with superheroes. But mostly she stays on Earth and repairs cars or maintains apartments. I mean, in a world where rocket travel is possible, not every person is going to be able to jut out to space any time they want!

From the beginning, these girls in Jaime Hernandez's *Locas* narratives—which appeared in the long-running *Love and Rockets* series—were a rarity in comics, especially those created by men. They weren't glamorous. They were living their lives, scrambling for jobs and money to make ends meet (and to buy those cute, super-indie-as-hell wrestling boots). Maggie is a character who gains weight, yet never stops being the hottest girl on the block; in each issue she still has rakish men chasing after her. We watch her progress from a tough little punk-girl mechanic with a heart of gold to a divorcee landlord in her forties. We even get peeks at her origin as an adorable tyke.

Maggie's romantic misadventures form the crux of the *Love and Rockets* series. Just when we think we know who her true soulmate is, we watch her life veer in a wildly different direction. But that's good, because that's exactly how life happens.

Usually in comics we aren't fortunate enough to see characters age. But for decades, Maggie and her friends have gotten older, grown together and apart,

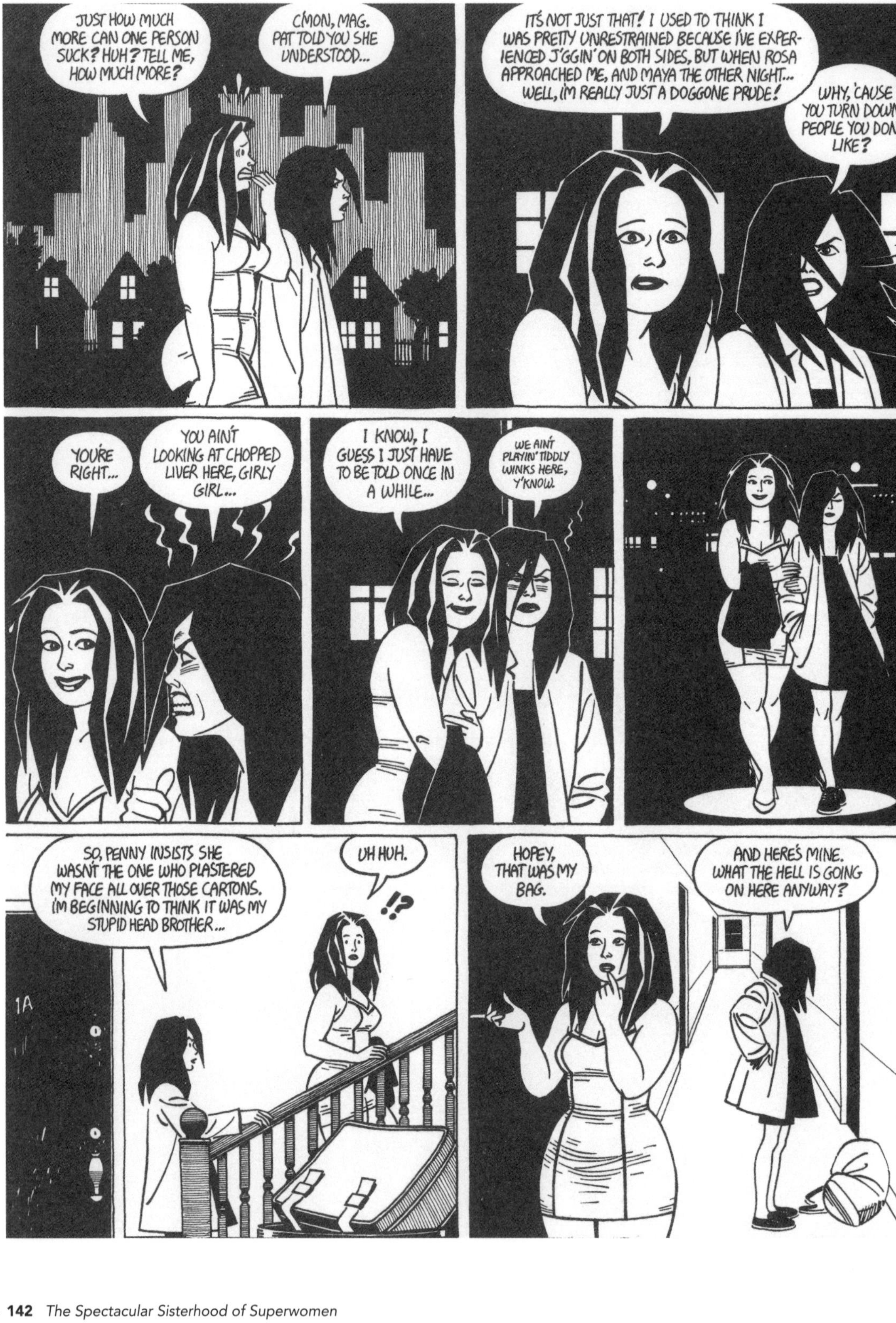
JUST HOW MUCH MORE CAN ONE PERSON SUCK? HUH? TELL ME, HOW MUCH MORE?
C'MON, MAG. PAT TOLD YOU SHE UNDERSTOOD...
IT'S NOT JUST THAT! I USED TO THINK I WAS PRETTY UNRESTRAINED BECAUSE I'VE EXPERIENCED J'GGIN' ON BOTH SIDES, BUT WHEN ROSA APPROACHED ME, AND MAYA THE OTHER NIGHT... WELL, I'M REALLY JUST A DOGGONE PRUDE!
WHY, 'CAUSE YOU TURN DOWN PEOPLE YOU DON'T LIKE?
YOU'RE RIGHT...
YOU AIN'T LOOKING AT CHOPPED LIVER HERE, GIRLY GIRL...
I KNOW, I GUESS I JUST HAVE TO BE TOLD ONCE IN A WHILE...
WE AIN'T PLAYIN' TIDDLY WINKS HERE, Y'KNOW.
SO, PENNY INSISTS SHE WASN'T THE ONE WHO PLASTERED MY FACE ALL OVER THOSE CARTONS. I'M BEGINNING TO THINK IT WAS MY STUPID HEAD BROTHER...
UH HUH.
!?
1A
HOPEY, THAT WAS MY BAG.
AND HERE'S MINE. WHAT THE HELL IS GOING ON HERE ANYWAY?
7

married, divorced, and changed careers and hairstyles. Their comics follow them as if they were friends we grew up with, and every year I look forward to another chapter in their lives.

ESSENTIAL READING: *Locas: The Maggie and Hopey Stories* (Fantagraphics, 2004). Don't be put off by the first few issues; the dialogue-heavy story about life as an outer-space mechanic doesn't feature our ladies at their best. Things pick up steam around the storyline "100 Rooms," featuring Maggie falling in love with a dastardly rogue—or is he a prince in disguise?

MS. TREE

A tough-as-nails P.I. on a mission of vengeance to find the killer of her husband	66That's Ms. Friday to you.99
	Created by: Max Allan Collins and Terry Beatty
	First appearance: *Eclipse Magazine* (Eclipse Comics, 1981)

Former cop (well, meter maid) Michael Friday is the perfect image of a hard-boiled private eye straight out of the grittiest pulp novel. Hard as steel, fast-loving, and sharp-witted, Michael finds her match at last with the sexually provocative P.I. Michael Tree, only to see him murdered on their wedding day. Vowing vengeance against the mob family who ordered the hit, Michael ruthlessly tracks down the dirty cop who betrayed her husband and quickly gets embroiled in the tangled web of mob politics.

Spinning out of the anthology series *Eclipse Magazine*, Ms. Tree soon gained her own series, in which she headed a private investigation company while continuing to dig into her vendetta. An homage to classic pulp novels, *Ms. Tree* displays a wit and charm that breathed new life into an old genre while retaining its characteristic grittiness and style. The comic frequently referenced current news events, including the Vanessa Williams/Miss America nude photo scandal. Controversial and sensitive topics such as abortion, child prostitution, pornography, homosexuality, mental health, and gun rights were raised, and the stories didn't always take the side you'd expect. Angry essays from both liberals and conservatives filled the letter pages in issue after issue.

As her series progressed, Ms. Tree investigated murders, missing persons, and blackmail, all somehow attached to the mysterious Muerta mob who badly wanted her dead. And if a particularly heinous criminal or pimp ended up shot down by the unrepentant detective along the way? So much the better. In fact, Ms. Tree's body count by the end of the series rivals that of Marvel's Frank Castle, thanks to her forays into gunning down warehouses full of mobsters in seconds. As for her romantic life? Spoiler: every single man

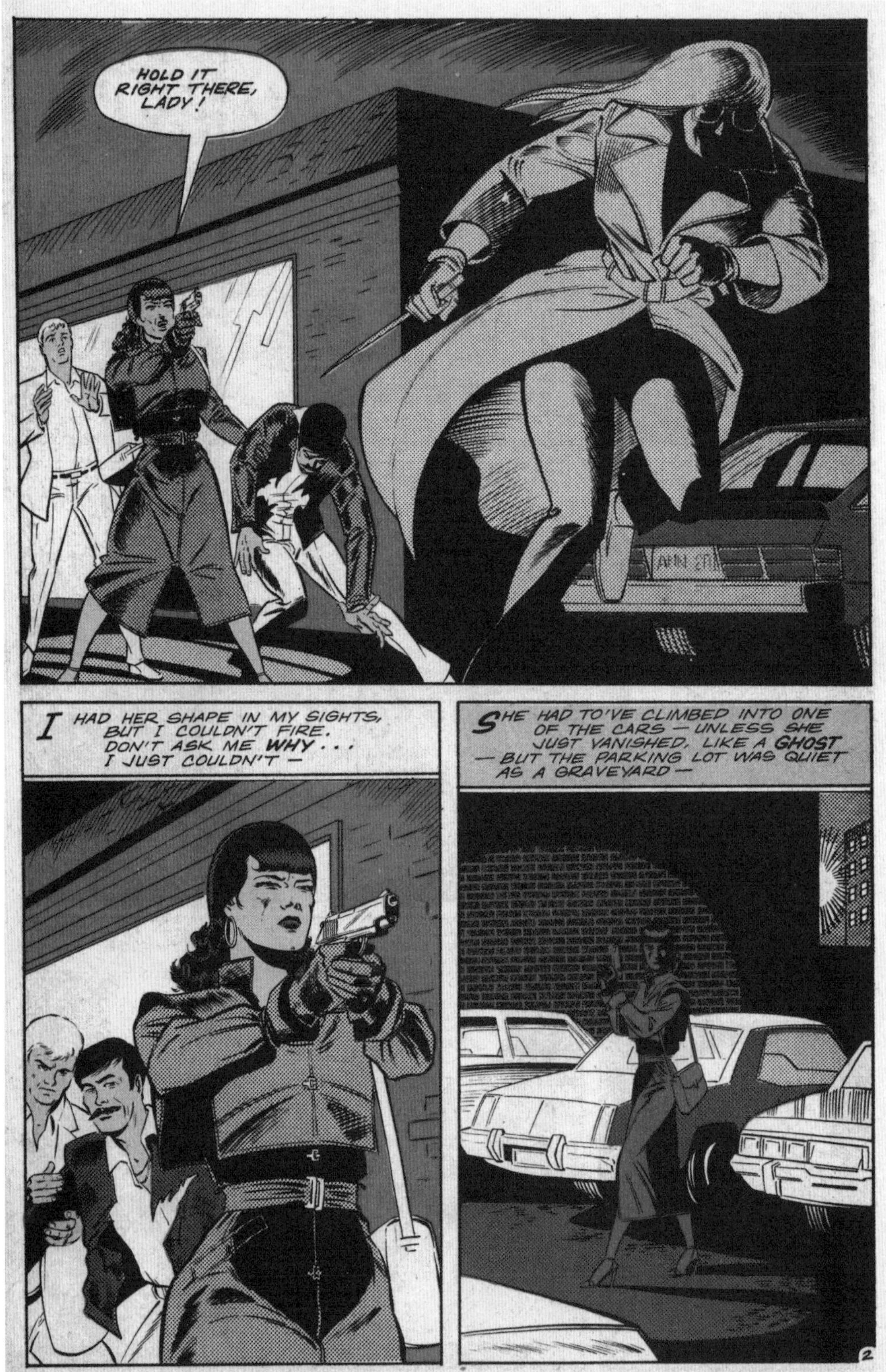
HOLD IT RIGHT THERE, LADY!
I HAD HER SHAPE IN MY SIGHTS, BUT I COULDN'T FIRE. DON'T ASK ME WHY . . . I JUST COULDN'T —
SHE HAD TO'VE CLIMBED INTO ONE OF THE CARS — UNLESS SHE JUST VANISHED, LIKE A GHOST — BUT THE PARKING LOT WAS QUIET AS A GRAVEYARD —
2

Ms. Tree sleeps with (and hey, she wasn't exactly celibate) ends up betraying her and dies, including the adulterous father of her baby at the end of the series.

Ms. Tree was a tough, no-nonsense woman. And the writers definitely realized they were over-the-top, proudly proclaiming the book to be an exaggerated melodrama more than a realistic crime drama.

ESSENTIAL READING: The *Files of Ms. Tree*, vol. 1 (Aardvark-Vanaheim, 1984). In this first collection of Ms. Tree's early appearances, she faces the death of her husband and begins her vendetta against the murderous Muerta family.

SINDI SHADE	Sindi is trying to commit the greatest crime of all: checking out a library book	66 *What's the point of having all this stuff if most of the people can't get near it?* 99
		Created by: Peter Milligan and Brett Ewins
		First appearance: *The Johnny Nemo Magazine* #1 (Eclipse Comics, 1985)

In the far future exists the Library, not just a repository of information but an entire self-contained society. Inhabiting this world is Sindi Shade, an edgy young woman looking to access the knowledge of the Inner Library. But not everyone is allowed access to the sacred halls. Declaring her a traitor just for attempting to enter, the Librarians seek to kill Sindi, hoping also to root out their opposing faction, the Heretics, who the Librarians suspect have a connection to her.

You see, the Library holds a secret: books appear mysteriously on their own, faster than the Librarians are able to dispose of them. And the Librarians' entire role is to keep the Big Machine active and running, because the machine is said to control all reality. They do so by feeding it magical urine from the Grand Librarian inquisitor, along with random human sacrifices. Okay, admittedly the story is a bit strange . . .

Sindi is no rebel leader; she's just a young woman looking to grab some books and run away before anyone catches her. Unfortunately, she is caught by the Junkyarders (a group that worships the burning of the Library's books) before being rescued by a brash young man named Huckleberry, who takes her to the Hall of the Heretics. It's there that the series suddenly ends, a purposeful decision by Peter Milligan, who knew he was granted only a few issues for the story.

Brightly colored and frenetically paced, with a mix of pop art and photo-collage backgrounds, Sindi Shade's story was as gloriously illustrated as it was densely written. An epic and vastly ambitiously plotted series, it's an example of the heights that independent creators can reach if given room (in this case, I wish the story was given more). A backup feature in the *Johnny Nemo Magazine*,

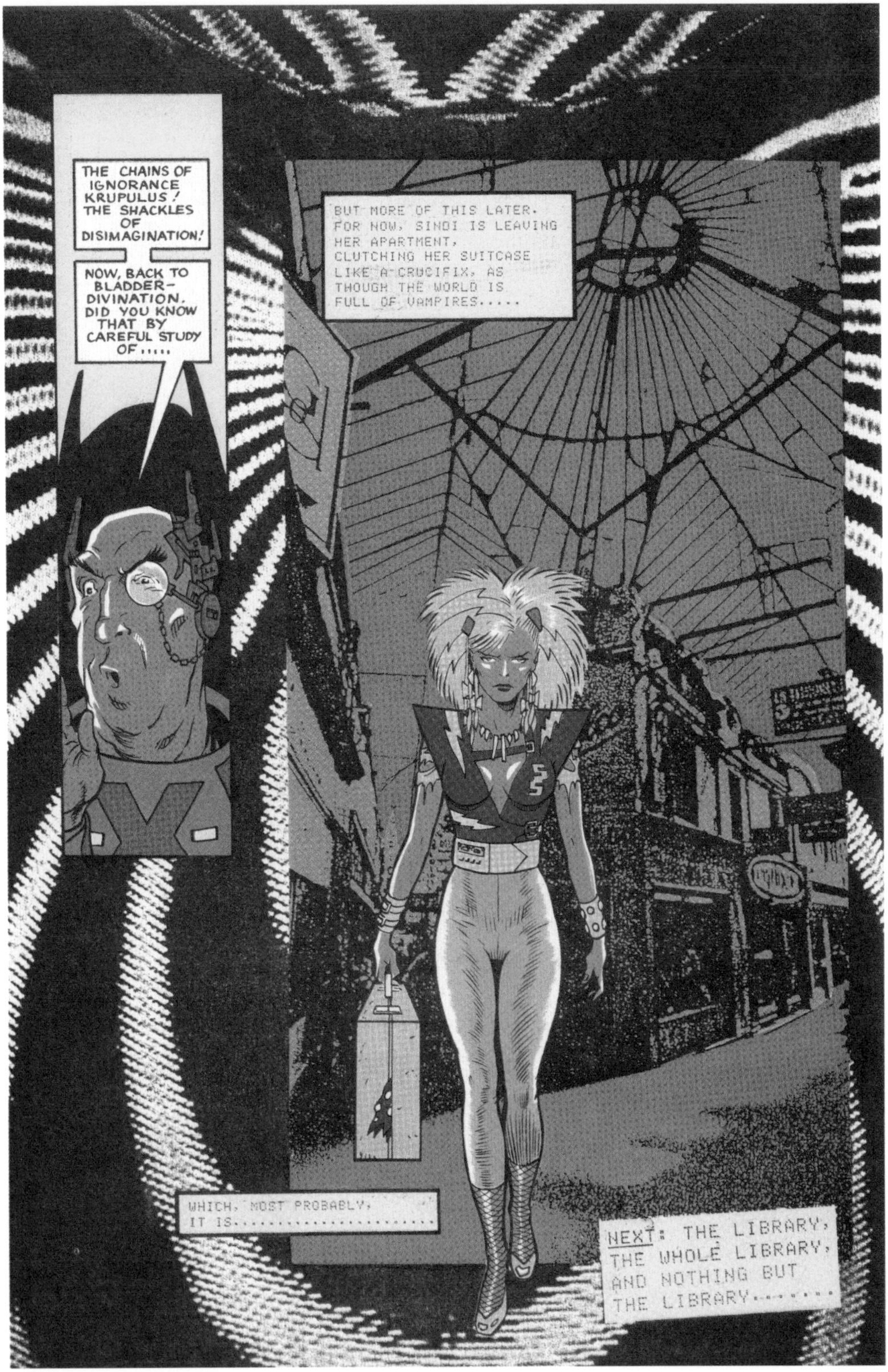
THE CHAINS OF IGNORANCE KRUPULUS! THE SHACKLES OF DISIMAGINATION!
NOW, BACK TO BLADDER-DIVINATION. DID YOU KNOW THAT BY CAREFUL STUDY OF.....
BUT MORE OF THIS LATER. FOR NOW, SINDI IS LEAVING HER APARTMENT, CLUTCHING HER SUITCASE LIKE A CRUCIFIX, AS THOUGH THE WORLD IS FULL OF VAMPIRES.....
WHICH, MOST PROBABLY, IT IS.......................
NEXT: THE LIBRARY, THE WHOLE LIBRARY, AND NOTHING BUT THE LIBRARY........

which lasted for only three issues, poor Sindi ended her series on a cliffhanger: doomed to spend the rest of her days in comics purgatory under the spell of the Babblers, a distressed people who infect others with their incessant talk about nothing.

Hey, I think Sindi Shade predicted the rise of social media!

As her creator, Peter Milligan, reveals: "The first thing I liked about Sindi Shade was that the word *sin* was in her name. Somehow this was the key to her character for me: here was a young woman who sinned and who probably enjoyed sin." Yet what exactly constitutes sin in this strange world run by "the Library" is another matter, Milligan notes. "In essence Sindi is a kind of female Joseph K with a better sense of fun and more futuristic dress." The short-lived nature of the series adds to the Kafkaesque quality of Sindi's adventures. Milligan again: "I knew we'd never have the chance to fully explore her possibilities, but I liked this. Sindi would never quite have to come into focus, and this fugitive quality was intentional and pleasurable."

At the end of the Sindi Shade series, readers desperately want to know what happens next. But that anger and frustration are all part of the plot.

ESSENTIAL READING: Look for the original *Johnny Nemo* magazines, since reprints of the originals have yet to exist.

SUNFLOWER	Wanderlust hippie turned interstellar Madonna	66 *There's just got to be more to life than acid and Nixon and venereal disease.* 99
		Created by: J. M. DeMatteis and Jon J Muth
		First appearance: *Moonshadow* #1 (Marvel Comics/Epic, 1985)

Moonshadow was a 1980s sci-fi miniseries by Marvel Comics' independent imprint Epic that centered on the adventures of the young man for whom it is named. Following Moonshadow's life from birth to death, the series was lushly illustrated and fully painted, offering an involving, deeply layered storyline that stands out in comics history as one of the most innovative of the medium. Unusual for a fantasy series centered on a plucky young protagonist, the early issues prominently featured Moonshadow's mother, Sunflower, who traveled with him.

Born to a sanitation worker and his wife, Sheila Fay Bernbaum had the eyes of her late aunt Ettie, who died in an asylum. Sheila grew up a serious child, preferring Dostoyevsky to Nancy Drew, and experienced unpredictable mood swings that weren't eased despite the care of family members, doctors, and rabbis. Taking off in her early twenties and adopting the name Sunflower, she roamed across 1960s America, finally settling in a commune in New York State. Wishing upon a shooting star for answers to the meaning of life, Sheila is visited and abducted by an alien from the species G'i-Doses: a giant ball of light motivated by nothing but pure whim. At first thinking she has been visited by God, Sheila soon realizes that she's in the aliens' immense zoo, where they collect random citizens from species throughout the universe, granting them immortality and then abandoning them.

Frightened at first of her otherworldly neighbors, Sunflower soon realizes she is no more isolated here than she was on Earth, and so she accepts her lot, including an unprecedented marriage to and subsequent impregnation

by her alien captor. With her child anchoring her to reality, Sunflower teaches him to read, sing, dance, and love. And when her alien husband spirits his son away on a ship to start his adventure, Sunflower joins him. Kind and gentle, Sunflower shows compassion when their first escapade leads them to a plague-ridden planet, where an alien mother suffers from labor pains. While Sunflower plays midwife to her, the ravenous organism that emerges tries to consume her as food. Sunflower dies slowly from her injuries as her son watches.

In some ways, Sunflower wasn't exactly an unusual female character in comics. Her role and sense of being was centered on her importance as a mother. She was traditionally beautiful and dedicated to her child, with little personality outside that function. Like many female supporting characters, she died a horrible death early on, leaving her son orphaned and on his own (a classic beginning to the hero's quest). The difference is that Sunflower remained part of the story for longer than most such characters, joining her son's adventure at least for its beginning. And after she's gone, her gentleness and unusually compassionate nature give her child the ability to survive his upcoming trials. Thanks to her, Moonshadow is flexible and adaptable to any change that comes along.

Sunflower was indeed a powerful character, gone too soon from this series.

ESSENTIAL READING: *The Compleat Moonshadow* (DC Comics, 1998) includes an additional story set long after the series that works as a conclusion. If you're looking for a mother whose space adventures with her child keep going, check out Image Comics' *Saga* series, by Brian K. Vaughan and Fiona Staples, for a modern take on the sci-fi epic.

VANITY	Jungle girl turned sci-fi adventurer	66*You and the Soviets better keep out of my way!*99
		Created by: Will Meugniot
		First appearance: *Vanity* #1 (Pacific Comics, 1984)

Vanity was a short-lived (only two issues) series from Pacific Comics that seemed determined to mash as many genres as possible into one. And though this comic was by no means a parody, it definitely presented its story with a wink and a nudge. The introduction describes the book as "blending science-fiction, romance, humor, espionage, and slam-bang action into a smooth and creamy graphic that will leave you refreshed." I wonder if the writer had a past career as a frozen yogurt salesman?

The story jumps around a lot, using flashbacks set in a variety of times and worlds to tell the tale. The main character, named Vanity, starts her life on Earth during the Stone Age. She lives as an outcast: her slight frame is mocked by her sturdier, more muscular sisters, and she's constantly under attack by bullies. The only person to treat her well is her lover, the "handsome hunk" Ma'nan, whom she adores desperately despite him being, well, a caveman. One day, a spaceship crash-lands nearby. With the help of the dying pilot, Vanity quickly learns how to fly it. But she's warned by the pilot never to allow her people to leave the planet with her—if their violence leads to the development of a nuclear weapon, and it comes near the moon, it will trigger a beacon to send an armada to attack and destroy the Earth! What's that? You say his plan makes no sense? Maybe . . .

Flash forward to the present. Vanity, accompanied by her now-consort and still caveman-like Ma'nan, her best friend the supersmart Prof, and her crew of loyal former cavemen, is exploring planets and solving crimes. Beholden to no government, following their own moral code, she and her team are called on to aid Earth in situations that no ordinary human can solve. Eventually, Vanity is asked to investigate a mysterious signal on Earth's moon. She races to beat the Soviets and the United States so that she can stop the aforementioned beacon and prevent an alien army from destroying the planet.

What next? Well, when her ship's large weapons are wiped out, Vanity whips out her own travel blasters from holsters on her hips as her bandana sways in the breeze. Then she goes in, guns a-blazing but . . . doesn't kill a single soul. See, it turns out that the lunar civilizations are some pretty nice dinosaur people looking for a place to live, and Vanity negotiates a truce before the terrestrial troops arrive. In the meantime, she reprograms the beacon to send the potential (never seen) alien invader forces back to their own planets.

Isn't it nice when things wrap up without violence?

Vanity is an interesting character. Though dressed in skin-baring outfits, she's imagined with a sense of humor and a zest for life and adventure that are infectious and charming. She's also mighty quick with her space pistols, and proves to be a surprisingly good computer programmer for someone who grew up during prehistoric times.

ESSENTIAL READING: *Vanity* nos. 1 and 2 from Pacific Comics.

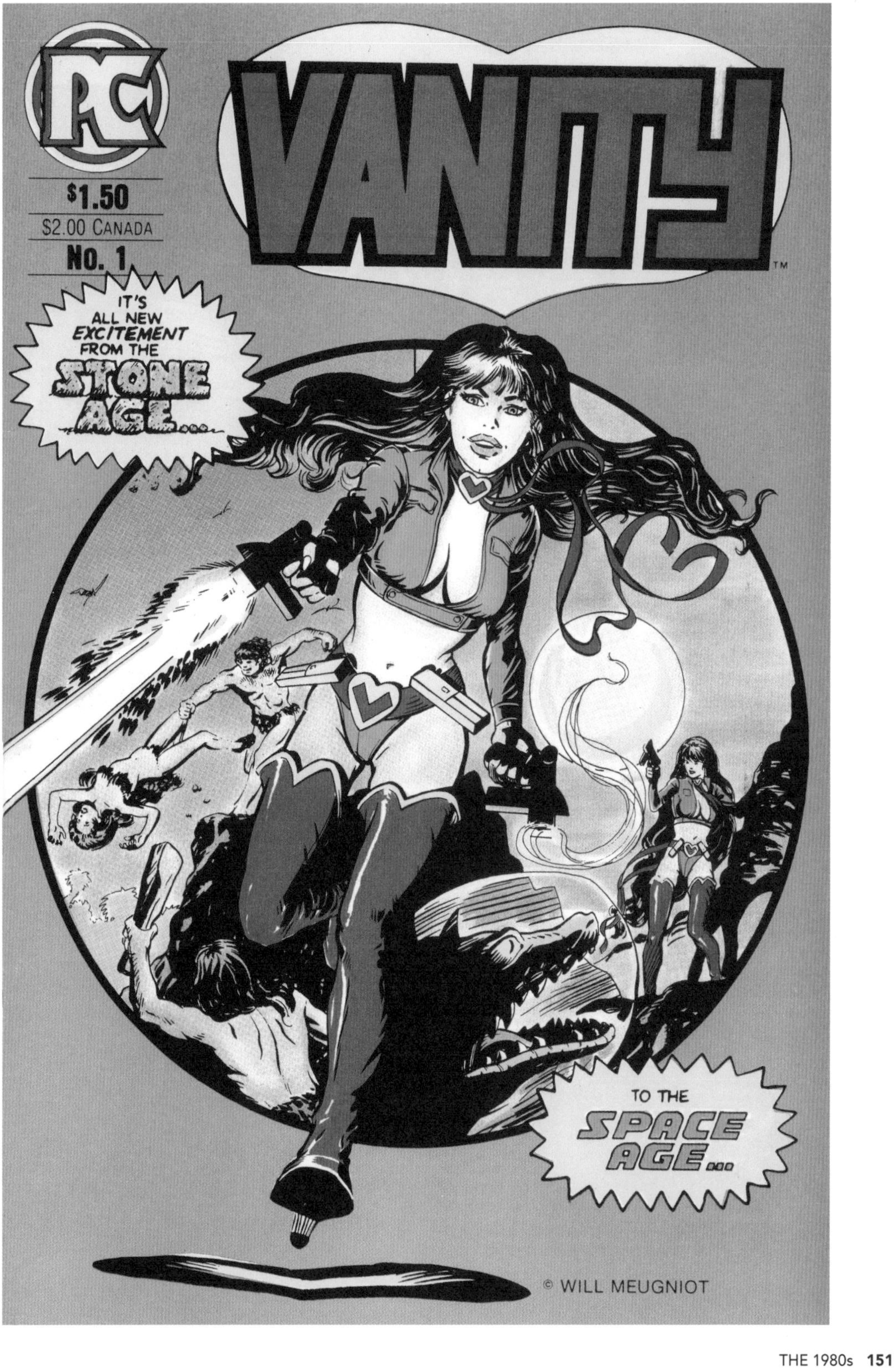
PC
VANITY
$1.50
$2.00 CANADA
No. 1
IT'S ALL NEW EXCITEMENT FROM THE STONE AGE...
TO THE SPACE AGE...
© WILL MEUGNIOT

SILK SPECTRE	A former teenage superheroine who returns to crime-fighting in one of comics' most popular stories	"I don't know anybody but god damned superheroes!"
		Created by: Alan Moore and Dave Gibbons
		First appearance: *Watchmen* #1 (DC Comics, 1986)

You don't have to like *Watchmen* to appreciate the impact that the famed series had on the comics medium, for better or for worse. For better: encouraging and promoting new ways of looking at old stories; pushing the superhero genre to new boundaries. For worse: so many comics that were published afterward stayed in the place of darkness that *Watchmen* explored, without taking its creativity and fresh approach as an example. Instead, these comics turned *Watchmen*'s very freshness into a new cliché.

Heavily promoted before its release by DC Comics, *Watchmen* was a self-contained story, told monthly, that ended after a dozen issues. The premise is fairly simple: Superheroes grown up. Superheroes with immense intellect, who have different views of morality and righteousness. Superheroes who use their power to get what they want in their personal lives, even if their public persona is that of a savior. Superheroes who grow bitter and tired, old and out of shape. The series presented new explorations of these characters and gave them space to become actual people. All in a format that allowed the creators to do whatever they wanted because it was a limited, contained story that didn't have to continue year after year.

That's a powerful combination, and *Watchmen* is still regarded as a highly influential work. Few other comics, and certainly no other superhero comics, are treated with as much academic respect.

Silk Spectre was the sole female lead in the story, and predictably she begins the series as girlfriend to the massively overpowered Dr. Manhattan, aka Jon Osterman. Her real name is Laurel Jane Jupiter (Juspeczyk), and she's the daughter of Sally, a golden age heroine who looks a bit like the 1940s "good girl art" character Phantom Lady. The two don't get along, mostly because Mom pushed Laurie to be a superheroine when she didn't really want to.

Sally is an ex-superhero whose sole plot points consist of being sexually assaulted by another hero, shamed by her rescuer, and written about by her fans in Tijuana bibles (your grandparents' X-rated fanfiction). We find out eventually that Sally had consensual sex with her almost rapist later on, during which she became pregnant with Laurie. Shocked and appalled that Sally could do that? Being friendly and accommodating to preserve social relations is a common reaction to assault, a way to try to wipe the slate clean mentally. That said, Moore doesn't exactly handle this phenomenon in the best or most delicate way. *Watchmen* is a comic in which motivations aren't spelled out explicitly on the page, though I'd argue that maybe sometimes they should be.

After a career as a silver age superheroine, following in her mother's footsteps, Laurie quickly becomes attached romantically to the mysterious superhero Dr. Manhattan. She's encouraged by the government to stay with him, despite his increasing detachment from humanity, in order to keep him content and pliable. Eventually their relationship ends, as relationships do, and Silk Spectre falls in with another, milder, masked man. Together they start superheroing again, which awakens feelings of excitement and power in Laurie that she thought had long gone away.

So what is Silk Spectre? An important part of a comic book that defined an era? A throwaway token female character given a bare amount of heroism and the most amount of girlfriending? Maybe she's a reminder that even books that expand our knowledge of the comics form and genre can fail at giving us a human connection. They may still contain characters who are only extensions of the men in their lives.

CHAPTER

7

The 19

90s

"COMICS AREN'T JUST FOR KIDS"

→

THE 1990s

In the early 1990s, a new art style was becoming popular at Marvel Comics: Todd McFarlane's energetic, highly detailed renderings in the pages of *Spider-Man*. Those issues, along with the much-hyped "Death of Superman" story arc at DC, spurred comic-collector mania. As fans bought multiple copies with variant covers, speculating on their value as if they were stock shares, artists and writers became dissatisfied with the traditional work-for-hire scenario. If their work was making the publishers scads of money, why were they giving up all claims to the original characters they invented? This thinking was front and center when Image Comics was formed by a group of (justifiably) emotionally distraught (male) artists.

Some call this a revolution in the comics industry. I call it a group of men who made enough cash to form their own company and saw that it was to their advantage to do so. The content of the books was usually high action, with throbbing muscles, painted-on suits, and proportionally distorted women. Even if the company was presenting an exciting new model that let creators own their creations, Image wasn't exactly friendly to female creators or fans. Fortunately, that would change (see, for example, *Bitch Planet*, page 228, and *Pretty Deadly*, page 219).

Marvel had been publishing creator-owned comics under its Epic Comics imprint since 1982. DC formed its Vertigo imprint in 1993, publishing a mix of non-comics-code books, some work-for-hire, and some creator-owned titles. Vertigo was headed by Karen Berger, an ambitious editor of the female-led titles *Amethyst: Princess of Gemworld* and *Wonder Woman*; she was responsible for head-hunting top British talent for DC (notably Neil Gaiman, Peter Milligan, and Grant Morrison). Berger wanted Vertigo to be a space where comics could grow up to their adult readership. Innovative titles such as *Enigma* and *The Sandman* proved the initiative a success.

As the market tightened—superhero books by the big two publishers dominated the shelves—three formats became rivals to the traditional single-issue comic. Namely, trade collections (previously serialized stories bound together in a single book), graphic novels (new book-length comic stories released in book stores), and manga (comics from Japan). Trade paperback collections allowed new readers to catch up on nonmainstream titles like *Love & Rockets* and *Elfquest* without having to hunt for hard-to-find back issues. Creators—especially female creators—gravitated toward the self-contained format of the graphic novel as an ideal space for memoirs and more serious stories. And from the start, manga had a strong following among women, possibly because they were available in bookstores. Manga stories were often heavily romance themed. So in a sense, the massive popularity of manga was the full-force return of comics' romance genre!

In the 1990s women were working as editors (Karen Berger, Alisa Kwitney, Joan Hilty), colorists (Adrienne Roy, Laura Martin, Marie Javins, Noelle Giddings, Patricia Mulvihill), letterers (Elitta Fell, Susan Crespi, Tracy Munsey, Saida Temofonte), writers (Devin Grayson, Kim Yale, Mindy Newell, Rachel Pollack), and pencilers/inkers (Jill Thompson, Julie Bell, June Brigman, Sandra Hope). But there's not enough room here to name the men who still dominated the industry. As in every other decade, women were there, working hard, but not in the same numbers as men.

Female creators were better represented in the art-house comics. Jessica Abel self-published *Artbabe* and contributed to numerous anthologies; Julie Doucet was publishing unrestrained comics about bodies and sexuality in *Dirty Plotte*, from Canadian comics publisher Drawn & Quarterly; Roberta Gregory was doing more work with Fantagraphics; Trina Robbins was creating extensive histories of female cartoonists and creators (much more extensively than in this volume, so check out her work!); Linda Medley was creating the successful all-ages comic *Castle Waiting*; and Carla Speed McNeil was publishing the Indigenous sci-fi epic *Finder*.

By the end of the 1990s, comics were considered real literature (well, at least the graphic-novel format was). The medium was being taught in schools and universities. The burgeoning webcomic world had just begun . . . all trends that would grow even bigger in the 2000s. ⚡

AMERICAN WOMAN	The spirit of America, who fights monsters while adorned in the stars and stripes	66As a nation, we can only move forward when everyone is going in the same direction!99
		Created by: Brian Denham, Richard Stockton, and Jochen Weltjens
		First appearance: *American Woman* #1 (Antarctic Press, 1998)

I know Wonder Woman has those stars on her red-white-and-blue outfit, but do you ever feel she's just not patriotic enough? Enter American Woman, a mysterious superhero who wears her U.S. citizenship proudly all over her body (including on her leggings, arms, and chest).

American Woman falls under the aesthetics of the bad-girl style of 1990s comic books, though it isn't the worst of the bunch. That's not to say it's one of the best, either. Glassy eyes, a vacuum-packed suit with a thong back, and revealing cut-outs up and down her costume make this a character created for a specific (i.e., hetero male) audience.

But back to business: American Woman wears a costume and a cape and fits firmly in the superhero genre, so what are her powers? Well, she can fly through the air, she's telepathic, and she has a magical staff. And she faces off against an adversary who's just as powerful (and as sexually provocative) as she is: the demon goddess Maxilla Maw.

In her first adventure, American Woman battles a demon riding a dragon, which results in the destruction of the Brooklyn Bridge and the death of at least twenty civilians (not to mention the dismemberment of the dragon). After a brief lovemaking scene in her civilian identity as Victoria Strauss with her bland boyfriend Eric Knight, she's whisked away to experience a warning of the dangers ahead—you know, by seeing what it would be like to be bound and naked in hell. She's held just long enough for a full-page pinup, of course. Then she's let loose and regains her supernatural powers. She's now clothed in the faith of the people who believe in her, which manifests as armor. It's this faith that Maxilla Maw is trying her best to shake in order to destroy American Woman.

But wait, if that's her origin story, then how did she already have powers? Or was all that just an awkward way of saying that she has a new suit?

Maybe we'll find out what's going on in the next issue, which also happens to be her last. The story quickly shifts from an attack of energy blobs on a skyrise to the dissolution of our heroine's relationship with her completely generic boyfriend. Then it's on to a new adversary: a mime who possesses a connection to the power of darkness. As American Woman stands on a podium giving a heartfelt speech about how we, as a nation, must acknowledge and celebrate our differences while moving forward, the mime decides to explode, killing an indeterminate number of people and causing massive destruction that can be seen from space. Here the story ends, with Maxilla Maw laughing maniacally.

It's hard to really know what this comic is all about. To be honest, it feels like when you're playing a video game and you get killed by a boss early on and see your mission failed and the Earth destroyed. The common interpretation might be that the story was meant to be continued, and this was just a cliff-hanger. But we can think of it instead as a commentary on the American Dream, and how struggles and valiant effort aren't always enough when carried out with brute force . . . which can often lead to powerful enemies.

Could this T&A comic be a biting social commentary and work of dystopian fiction? Why not? It's certainly able to be considered as more than just a story of a sexy lady-girl with superpowers.

ESSENTIAL READING: Check the usual sources for back issues of American Woman nos. 1 and 2 (1998) by Antarctic Press/Barrage Studios.

<table>
<tr><td>

BITCHY
BITCH
(AND BITCHY
BUTCH)

</td><td>

**The bitchiest bitch that
ever bitched**

</td><td>

❝If I had my way this book would be a
wimyn-only space but welcome to the patriarchal
economic system.❞

Created by: Roberta Gregory

First appearance: *Graphic Story Monthly #6*
(Fantagraphics Books, 1990)

</td></tr>
</table>

From 1991 to 2004, Bitchy Bitch was the voice of her generation, putting into words the uncomfortable anger and confusion that women struggle with in a male-dominated world. An exaggeration of feminist anger that's not meant to be taken literally or as the author's true feelings, Bitchy Bitch navigates her world fueled by pure, righteous rage.

From screaming at unfair deadlines while a tampon protrudes from her dress, to sexual frustration that leads her to buy all phallic-shaped groceries, to unsatisfactory sex with a man from a personal ad, Bitchy Bitch's first appearance in her own comic book is a breath of fresh air. Well, maybe not fresh. More like hilariously, amazingly filthy air. Bitchy Bitch apologizes to no one; she's a neurotic, anxious wreck who imagines stomping her enemies (new-age and hyper-religious coworkers alike) while worrying that she might be missing out on something special, something real. On the inside, she's just a big old softie, right?

Spun out of comics written as strips for *Seattle Weekly*, Bitchy Bitch became the star of Roberta Gregory's new series *Naughty Bits* once it premiered. This raucous collection of bawdy strips, geared toward women, addressed serious topics in an over-the-top manner. Soon Gregory created a lesbian version of the character deemed, appropriately, "Bitchy Butch"—a parody of all the worst extremes boiled down into the stereotype of the angry lesbian. Bitchy Butch, like her sister character Bitchy Bitch, explodes in fits of rage at the slightest hint of any wrong, especially if directed at anyone who doesn't fit her idea of a "perfect lesbian" (which excludes men, bisexuals, femme lesbians, lesbians who've been with men, and transgender lesbians).

Fortunately, Butch does evolve over time, becoming more comfortable with people who don't fit her standard of perfection. We're eventually given a look into where her anger comes from as we delve into her history and meet her softer side. Her fury stems from when she was a baby lesbian and feeling outcast from both the gay rights and women's rights movement.

Does Bitchy Butch give lesbians a bad name? Is she a reasonable exaggeration of a TERF (Trans-Exclusionary Radical Feminist) lesbian? Or is she a parody of all the opinions put onto the lesbian community by jealous heterosexuals?

Don't think of these characters as adult versions of the *Cathy* newspaper strip just because they show frustrated women dealing with daily life. The comics include frequent flashbacks to both characters' youth, before they became the bitches we know today (these storylines feature overbearing mothers trying to force their daughters into a perfect feminine mold). They're the bitches in whom we see parts of ourselves, but who are so over-the-top that we're relieved we aren't quite that bad. Bitchy Bitch and Bitchy Butch may not be heroines in the conventional sense, but damn if they aren't interesting women.

ESSENTIAL READING: *Life's a Bitch: The Complete Bitchy Bitch Stories* (Fantagraphics, 2005).

THE GIRL

An anarchistic girl on a path of violence and destruction

❝I'm a page three girl. I'm a Warhol superstar. I'm a dyke. I'm a riot grrrl. I'm the queen of sex. I'm a housewife with a jar of rat poison.❞

Created by: Grant Morrison and Philip Bond

First appearance: *Kill Your Boyfriend* (DC Comics, 1995)

What else are you going to do when you're young and bored in England, other than kill your geeky boyfriend and go on a spree with a group of Warhol-esque terrorists and your new psychopathic beau?

To "The Girl" of this story—her name is never given—life seems like a rat race: The schools are a system to feed you to work. You marry your high school boyfriend and live with him and nothing ever changes. So the Girl, hating her life and her family, and desperately fueled by sex hormones, rage, and boredom, decides to hook up with the local bad boy. But this bad boy is very, very bad indeed. Out of curiosity, he decides to kill the Girl's bible-loving, anime-masturbating boyfriend just to see what it's like.

Instead of being horrified, the Girl is relieved. Together they head out on the road, discovering the joys of sexual pleasure and living on their own. Teaming up with an avant-garde group of revolutionary artists, the two become the token murderers of the group. It turns out that the artists are too frightened of losing their grant applications to use those hand grenades they're hoarding.

So the duo ditches the artists and takes refuge in Blackpool, where every day is a holiday until the boy dies in a gruesome shoot-out with cops. Heartbroken (or something similar), the Girl tries to kill her disappointment of a father. But since the gun is empty, she sighs and submits to her inevitable life. Flash-forward a few years later and she's the perfect picture of a devoted wife, or at least one who's armed with a box of rat poison and has no moral qualms about using it . . .

Kill Your Boyfriend is pretty much exactly what you'd imagine a book with that title, from DC's mature-reader Vertigo imprint, would be. Writer Grant Morrison claims that his only influence was a movie called *Heartlands*, plus his own experiences as a youth doing ecstasy and being in love. That said, there is more than a little similarity between the book and violent-girl films like *Heathers* and *Natural Born Killers*, mixed with the general, universal alienated-youth-type feelings of inertia and restlessness. The main character's inherent, unbridled sexuality gets kick-started into full fury by a dose of ultraviolence. She's utterly repulsive by virtue of her ennui and lack of morality, and there's something chilling about her surface-level perfect homemaker life at the end. The comic showcases the brutality that could be hidden in any citizen; the Girl is just able to use her wits to hide her inherent violence from the rest of the world.

This is a comic for people who love stories about madness and violence, and the disaffection at the source of it all. It's a twisted tale, but one with surprising turns around every corner. You might not like the Girl, but you're not supposed to. Sometimes horrifying people are interesting to watch.

ESSENTIAL READING: *Kill Your Boyfriend/Vinamarama Deluxe* (DC Comics, 2016) pairs the story with another of Bond and Morrison's comics for a satisfying double feature.

THE JAGUAR

A sweet-natured transfer student discovers that she possesses an ancient mystical force

"I am the Jaguar, always hunted, always triumphant . . . engaged in a desperate, endless battle with the blackest EVIL . . ."

Created by: William Messner-Loebs, David Antoine Williams, and Jose Marzan Jr.

First appearance: *The Jaguar* #1 (DC Comics, 1991)

Maria De Guzman, a university student from Brazil newly transferred to Ann Arbor, Michigan, is plagued by dreams in which she is a supernatural heroine called "The Jaguar," a nemesis to all evildoers. Well, turns out they're not just dreams! Eventually Maria remembers her traumatic past—how her aunt Luiza, using the powers of the Jaguar, stopped a greedy corporation trying to destroy her community and their rainforest. Scarred by her aunt's savage murder of the corporate infiltrators, Maria repressed the memory for decades, until her aunt's own unexpected and suspicious death. Inheriting Luiza's supernatural legacy, Maria is transformed into a supernaturally strong and skilled hunter. She has the eyes of a cat, wears an enchanted costume that appears when she transforms, and is forced to come to terms with her newfound responsibilities and power.

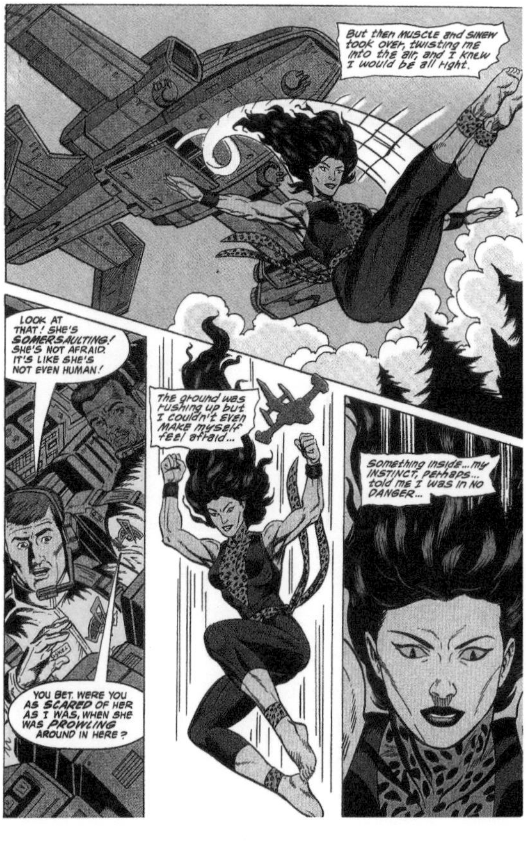
But then MUSCLE and SINEW took over, twisting me into the air, and I knew I would be all right.
LOOK AT THAT! SHE'S SOMERSAULTING! SHE'S NOT AFRAID. IT'S LIKE SHE'S NOT EVEN HUMAN!
YOU BET. WERE YOU AS SCARED OF HER AS I WAS, WHEN SHE WAS PROWLING AROUND IN HERE?
The ground was rushing up but I couldn't even MAKE myself feel afraid...
Something inside...my INSTINCT, perhaps... told me I was in NO DANGER...

But wait, there's more. Maria's school hides its own secrets, in the form of an underground facility tied to a mysterious government agency; it produces murderous cyborgs and is led by her academic mentor Dr. Ruiz. Or so Maria thinks. In reality, the "cyborg" patrols the grounds protecting innocent wanderers from local gangs prowling the campus. And he's not a cyborg at all, but rather a supersoldier tricked into thinking his unstable, black-hole-powered supersuit is a permanent robot body.

The Jaguar is a modern take on the classic jungle girl story, showcasing a heroine who derives her strength from the forests and wears animal skins as her costume. Like Miss Fury (see page 37), Maria receives her cat outfit as a gift; her powers are tied to her blood and not the costume. The comic was populated by a cast from varied backgrounds, and issues of class, race, and privilege pervade the series. Not only is the protagonist Brazilian, but nonwhite secondary characters are also well represented. Most are women, and they even have distinct personalities and appearances (a super-duper rarity in comics of the 1990s).

The story is the best type of superhero soap opera, mixing Maria's adjustment to a new school and Midwestern American culture with the burden of being the chosen one in a long line of superpowered women. The villains aren't flatly evil, and miscommunication abounds. Essentially, it's *Buffy the Vampire Slayer*, six years before that show aired.

The Jaguar was based on a 1960s Archie Comics superhero of the same name. That Jaguar was, well, pretty dull; the best thing anybody could've done was reinvent him. Which DC Comics did, licensing the character (and several others from Archie) for its new Impact comics line. The new Jaguar was a worthy successor, exploring explicit themes of social justice in her book.

You might think a story led by a teenage girl would be a tough sell in the hyper-masculine era of 1990s comics . . . and you'd be right. As Mark Waid, a writer on another Impact title, *The Comet*, writes in the letter column of *The Jaguar* #5: "They warned us that a comic book starring a teenage girl would never catch on in today's marketplace. Ha Ha. 'They' were wrong. Sales are strong, mail response is astounding, and the critics have given their thumbs up."

Unfortunately, success didn't last. After fourteen issues, *The Jaguar*—and DC Comics' entire Impact imprint, a laudable attempt to provide younger readers with an alternative to grim and violent superheroes—came to an end.

ESSENTIAL READING: No reprints exist, so tracking down back issues of the Jaguar's fourteen-issue run is your only option.

JAIN	A mysterious pregnant girl who discovers a hidden refuge of fairy-tale creatures	**"I'll be the best librarian in the whole world!"**
		Created by: Linda Medley
		First appearance: *Castle Waiting* #1 (Olio Press, 1997)

Eugh, I thought. A fairy-tale reimagining. How done! How tiresome! How hard to slog through! I stamped my feet at the very idea of reading *Castle Waiting*. But the book was an Eisner Award winner, so I had to try.

And how happy I am that I did! The series starts as an irreverent, fun reimagining of Sleeping Beauty, with a princess given all the gifts of an ideal ruler except one: wisdom. The story begins with a focus on the family of witches, who present the princess with gifts to help her through life, and the jealous cast-off

relative who resents that she wasn't asked to help. We all know the tale from here: the bitter witch curses the princess with death, but the last witch manages to lighten the spell to merely a hundred years of sleep. The princess awakens to true love's kiss and promptly marries and runs away with the strange prince who just happened to wander past at the right time (remember, they didn't give her wisdom).

But that's fine, because *Castle Waiting* isn't really Sleeping Beauty's story anyway.

With the castle abandoned by its rulers, the younger witches take over, and the structure, now termed Castle Waiting, becomes a refuge for all who need safety. Which is how we meet Jain, a pregnant and abused woman who takes off with what money she can gather to find the castle and some measure of protection. After various misadventures along the road, during which she is protected by her magic amulet and a healthy dose of good luck, Jain finally arrives at her destination.

But the castle isn't quite what she expects—it's infested with various sprites and poltergeists, and she finds herself overly waited on by the former witches eager to bring new life into their home. While anticipating the birth of her child, Jain discovers a massive library (shades of Belle from *Beauty and the Beast*, perhaps?) thanks to the generosity of the good-natured handyman Simon, whom in return she teaches to read.

At last Jain gives birth to a son. The child is a surprise to the household, emerging green skinned and be-tailed. Jain names him Pindar in honor of her father. We learn that the child's father, despite looking like a demon, was the kindest, sweetest man you could ask for. Jain's husband, on the other hand, was not.

The first volume of *Castle Waiting* adventures center on the comings and goings of the eccentric community members. Woven in and out is the story of Jain, a wealthy merchant's daughter with a tragic and complicated past. She's sweet and kind, but she also has a furiously strong will to survive. In addition to her story, creator Linda Medley works in an epic tale about a mysterious order of bearded nuns formed by a group of unhappily married sisters, who are joined by two young women running away from their own cruel men. Taken together,

Castle Waiting is a satisfying, multilayered saga.

Indeed, the series is incredibly engaging, and its characters are charming and entertaining. It's a reminder that although the comic books of the 1990s might be known for oversexualization and violence (see American Woman, page 158), the decade also saw the rebirth of the all-ages comics market, as evidenced by such titles as Jeff Smith's *Bone*, which garnered critical acclaim. Suddenly, comics were for kids again, and there was something beautiful and fresh in these books that appealed to adults, too. *Castle Waiting* is a great example of this trend, winning several Eisner Awards; it's been collected in two massive volumes of 400-plus pages each. The series went on hiatus in 2013, but Medley is currently at work on more stories, so catch up quick!

ESSENTIAL READING: *Castle Waiting*, vol. 1 (Fantagraphics, 2006) and *Castle Waiting*, vol. 2: *The Definitive Edition* (Fantagraphics, 2013). Avoid the 2010 edition of volume two, which doesn't have Linda Medley's name on the cover; that collection is incomplete and ends midchapter.

JINK	Silver-haired sexy rogue searching for trouble and treasure in the far future	*"It's an obvious trap. But he is really really cute and he's such a virgin and it's been so long!"*
		Created by: John Ostrander, David Boller, Terry Beatty, David Hillman, and Wendy Pini
		First appearance: *Jink* #1 (Warp Graphics, 1994)

Is it cheating to have two *Elfquest* characters in this book? I think not, since the series became so expansive that it produced a few hundred issues over several decades, introducing dozens of characters (for more background on *Elfquest*, read about Leetah on page 107). Jink is the star of one of two *Elfquest* spinoff titles that ventured into the world of science fiction (the other being the Star Wars–esque comic *The Rebels*).

When we first meet her, Jink is a rogue treasure hunter (she'd prefer "libera-

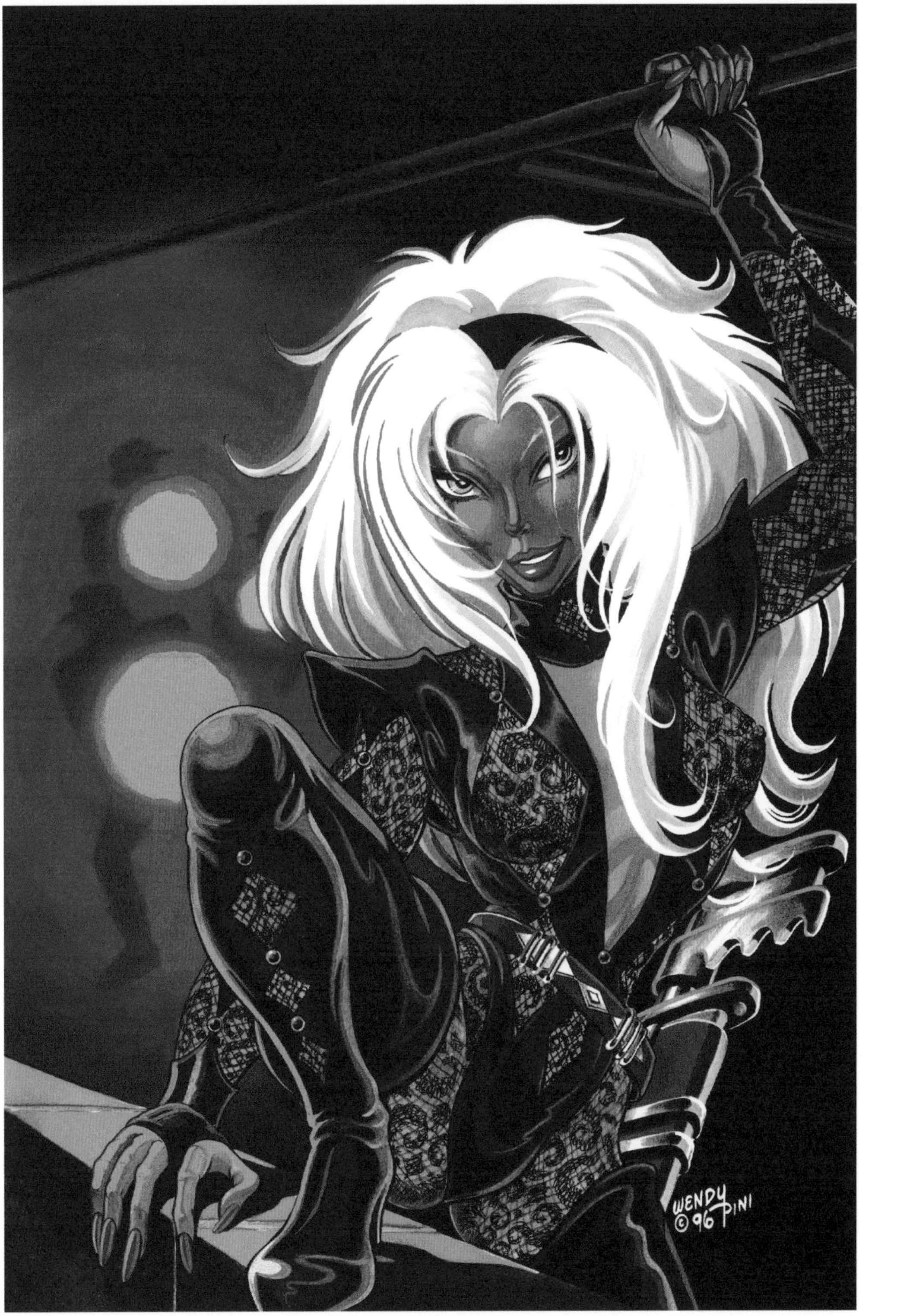
WENDY PINI
© 96

tor") who is looking for any and all artifacts related to the mysterious elves that, legends say, once populated her planet. We're given hints to Jink's parentage, and eventually we learn that she's an elf—but one who can change her shape at will. In addition, Jink can communicate telepathically and move incredibly fast. She's also astonishingly forgetful, the result of her habit of mind-wiping anything potentially sensitive from her brain (kind of like when, after an exciting night out, the next morning you delete the texts you sent). In fact, Jink forgot that she brokered an international peace treaty with an alien race, who are now about to throw her entire world into war! Uh-oh . . .

Though very much in tune with her organic, magical side, Jink is also skilled and comfortable with technology. This is a world set far in the future, with spaceships and ray blasters—the latter of which Jink really, really doesn't like. She's the type who likes to make love, not war.

In fact, she *really* likes to make love.

A lot.

In her early adventures, Jink seduces a young adventurer named Kullyn, who develops quite a crush on her. The only problem is that he has a girlfriend, Tamia, back home. In most comics this would be a problem, but Jink merely shrugs and seduces Tamia as well, forming a triad relationship with them and providing a much-needed fun balance to the serious humans. This development is a far cry from the relationship of the antagonists in the series, two men faced with homophobia within their culture. The play of sexualities in Jink's series, presented as fluid in a world with prejudice against it, provides important real-world context that was often lacking from the main *Elfquest* storyline.

Jink is a character who's sexy and who enjoys her pleasures, living for the moment but with some sense of morality that leads her to do the right thing to protect her friends and her people. Her open acceptance of her pansexuality was refreshing to read at a time in comics when most women's sexuality was dictated by the male readership. Here was a character who was sexual, but in a way that felt natural and normal, not forced to adhere to the gaze of certain readers.

Premiering in her own twelve-issue series, Jink spun off into a backup feature in the *Elfquest* anthology that lasted for thirty-one issues. Twenty years later, we still don't know the full mystery of her parentage or her history. But with the final issues of *Elfquest* wrapping up, it's almost guaranteed that her mystery will be a major reveal.

ESSENTIAL READING: *Elfquest Reader's Collection #14: Jink!* (Wolfrider Books, 1999).

A bisexual woman who grows from a naive student into accomplished mother

❝You know, I just don't get the rainbow thing . . . gays are supposed to have taste and fashion sense.❞

Created by: Leanne Franson

First appearance: *Liliane* #1 (Self-published zine, 1992)

In Liliane's first appearance in Leanne Rae Franson's self-published comic zine, we're introduced to a bisexual massage therapist exhausted by clients who hit on her for sexual release when she's just trying to book appointments. She retreats to the local gay men's bar, where she knows she won't get picked up. But she worries that doing so means she must really be giving up on love. Then a sexy Quebecois unmistakably starts cruising her.

What does he want? Is he straight, trying to pick off gay girls at the bar when they feel comfortable? Does he think she's a man? Is he just looking for a friend? The excitement of the unknown (and the man's handsome looks) invigorates our Liliane, and she decides to go for it. After a bit of language confusion and some identity discussion, she discovers that her cruiser is a gay man who is bicurious and wants to see what it would be like to be with a woman. After making out with Liliane, much to his surprise he discovers that he's very attracted to her.

Alas, his boyfriend is waiting at home, and he's a good man, so he turns off his curiosity and abandons Liliane at the bar.

Now that's a story you don't often see in comics, or in most media for that matter.

Liliane is rendered in a simple, single-line style, similar to the feminist underground comics that began surfacing in the 1970s. She appeared in self-published zines before moving into the digital world and a long-running webcomic. Though the adventures are at times based on real events, Liliane is a fully separate character from her creator.

As her story progresses across various formats, we watch Liliane's adventures in sexual identity, starting as the best friend to a revolving door of gay men when she lived in the desolate fields of Saskatchewan. Back then, Liliane disdained the company of women. But after some introduction to the comfort of female friendship while at university in Montreal—and being abandoned by her gay male friends—Liliane grows out of her "men-only" shell. She promptly falls into a hearts-in-her-eyes crush on a hot butch girl, who eventually breaks Liliane's heart.

We watch Liliane gain crushes on men and women, have her heart broken, visit leather bars and fetish clubs, and eventually start a family as a single mom and settle down (though "settling down" with an active kid to watch over isn't exactly an accurate description). Liliane changes and grows over time, just like a real, non-comic-strip human.

ESSENTIAL READING: Check out the webcomic online at liliane.comicgenesis.com. Be warned: there's a ten-year gap, but Leanne Franson has recently returned to posting.

MARTHA WASHINGTON	Not the wife of a Founding Father, but a survivor against all odds in a dystopian future	**❝I've got a whole lot of work to do. I've got to save the president and a crew of eighty on a space cannon.❞**
		Created by: Frank Miller and Dave Gibbons
		First appearance: *Give Me Liberty* #1 (Dark Horse Comics, 1990)

Martha Washington lives in a future that could be called dystopian, though when you look at its individual elements, there's shockingly little that differentiates her world from modern society.

A young girl born to a freedom-fighter father who was murdered when she was a baby, Martha is thrown into "The Green," a ghetto in the middle of an unknown city. There, all children live in locked cages stacked on top of one another and sleep on hard metal cots. Martha learns early on how to stay quiet to survive, and as a protection mechanism she dresses like a boy. She has an innate skill with computer engineering, a talent that will prove invaluable. But her difficult life descends into horror early on, beginning when she witnesses the murder of her favorite teacher. Martha instinctively takes the offensive and stabs the murderer in the neck, killing him. This experience sends her into a catatonic state and she's shipped to a mental hospital, where she discovers experiments that are turning children into telepaths.

When cast out from the asylum, Martha eventually steals a debit card and hacks an ATM to get enough cash to survive. When we next meet her, the country's government has changed (through some judicious use of firebombs) and

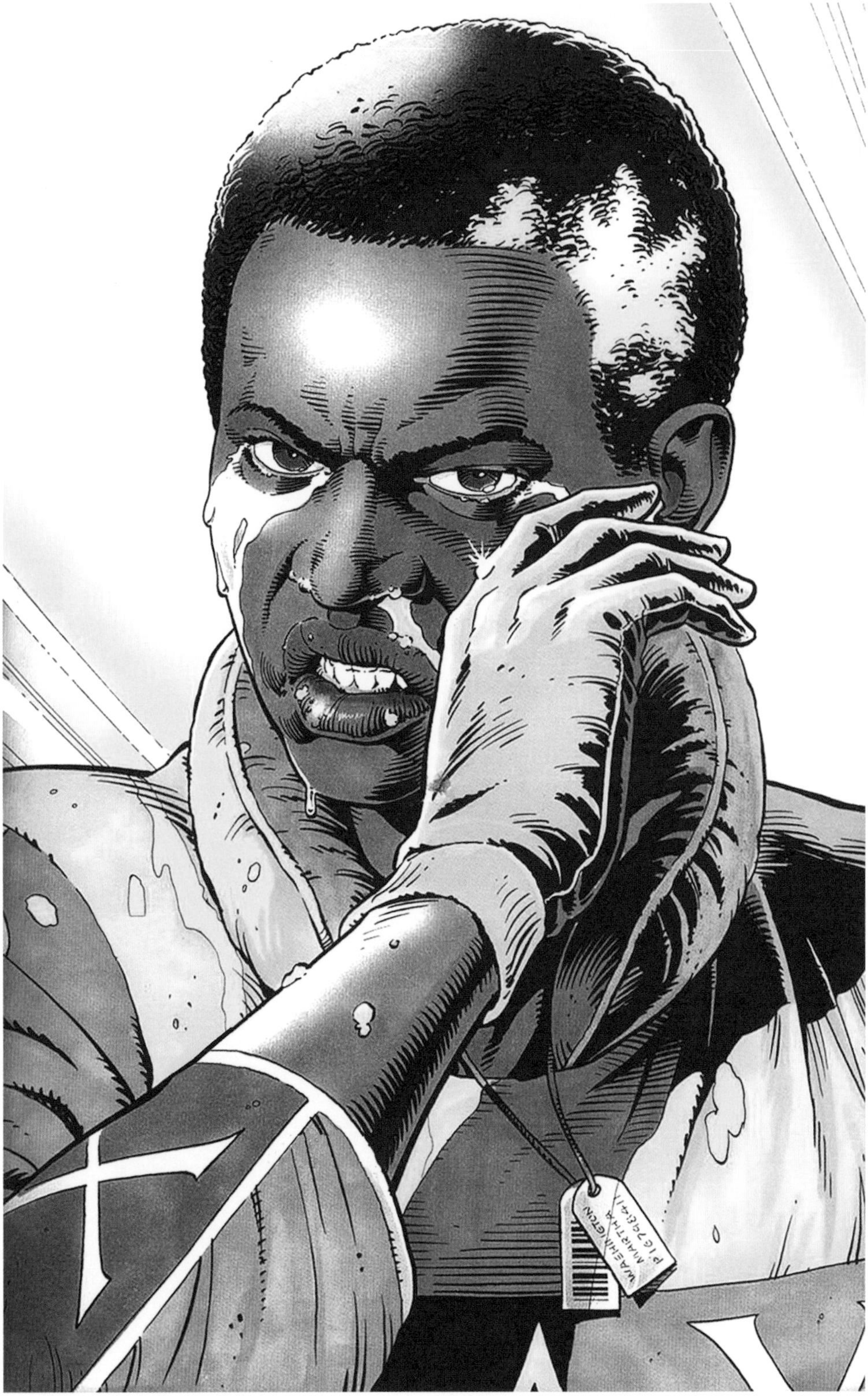
WASHINGTON
MARTHA
P1672641

the current leader is a militant environmentalist who is benevolent, kind, even Trudeau-like (Justin, not Pierre!). That doesn't mean everything is right in the world, though. To clear her record, Martha joins the army and becomes a war hero, but only after withstanding trials that make her previous experiences look pleasant by comparison.

Winning her way back to her world, Martha meets the president, telling him about the Green and the horrors there. In the end, she's reunited with her family as the Green is torn down. Just when you think she might be due for a happy ending, well . . . this is only halfway through the series. Sixteen-year-old Martha still has a lot of adventures ahead, and none of them are kind. But at least she eventually gets some friends, including an Apache leader who thinks she's pretty great and a telepathic mutant child she met in the hospital.

Give Me Liberty presents a dystopian world that's Margaret Atwood–esque, featuring a tyrannical ruler who disguises the strict reign of his administration with news segments showing that the country has never been more prosperous. We should applaud such sharp political satire, right? Well, sure, if you can get past the rampant homophobia layered throughout the saga. It's ridiculous that the only characters who are gay turn out to be rapists and villains. That's not only gross and disturbing, it's also unfortunate, because otherwise this book would be a classic. It's a cutting and angry satire of race relations, black and Indigenous, in America.

Martha is a survivor against all odds, and despite her harsh upbringing (or maybe because of it) she becomes a heroine who's anything but reluctant. With an incredibly sharp mind and a body at the peak of physical strength, she's pretty much a perfect superhero. And though she's had to do horrible things to perservere, the story shows the psychological effects that those actions exerted on her over time, as well as the real effects of poverty and war. The focus throughout is on her survival, yet still being able to save the world and everyone she cares about.

Compared to Frank Miller's and Dave Gibbons's more high-profile works (*The Dark Knight Returns* and *Watchmen*, respectively), you might be tempted to call *Give Me Liberty* a hidden gem. Which is funny, because at the time it was published, this was one of the best-selling independent comic books on the market. Strange what we forget.

ESSENTIAL READING: Delve into *The Life and Times of Martha Washington in the Twenty-First Century* (Dark Horse Comics, 2009).

SCARY GODMOTHER

A witch who makes the perfect babysitter for inquisitive young children

> **"** Have you ever been walking home from school late on a winter's afternoon and the shadows creep up on you and chase you all the way to your front door? **"**

Created by: Jill Thompson

First appearance: *Scary Godmother and Friends* #1
(Sirius Entertainment, 1997)

With long, curly red hair, which looks suspiciously like that of her creator Jill Thompson, Scary Godmother is your typical broomstick-riding, pointy-hat-wearing witch except ... she's not scary in the slightest. And that's a good thing! She just likes to play occasional tricks on mortals who try to dabble in the magical realm.

The *Scary Godmother* series features the adventures of Hannah Marie, an adorable little girl who every so often gets up on the "fright side" of the bed and enters a magical world of Halloween monsters. Besides our title character, we meet vampires in love, pop-culture-obsessed werewolves, ghostly cats, fashion-conscious skeletons, and a giant multieyed blob beast (aka Bug-a-Boo).

Despite their looks, the monsters in *Scary Godmother* are really the friendly sort, and they're pretty sweet to dear Hannah. Sometimes they even teach practical skills, like how to make dessert spiders out of chocolate chips and chow mein! As in any good horror comic, each issue includes more than a few horrible puns, like the big-screen "skel-a-vision" and "scare-e-o" set mentioned in the Valentine's Day issue (which the monsters of course celebrate, or at least the massacre part of the holiday).

Scary Godmother began as a black-and-white comic feature, and eventually became a series from Sirius Comics, before branching off into color comics from Dark Horse and even some animated films. Through all its iterations, the adventures usually revolve around Hannah, the little mortal girl, more so than the title character. Hannah's experiences in the Fright Side are cute, with just the right amount of monster madness to keep readers entertained. For example, Hannah learns about the solstice from her vampire best friend Orson, and in turn she teaches him about

Christmas. Together they show great kindness toward a poor lonely dragon, offering to have him over, babysit his treasure, or scare him from under his bed when he's feeling lonely.

Yes, *Scary Godmother* is a children's comic. But like the best children's media, there's more than enough plot and excitement to keep adults interested, too. Besides, who wouldn't want to visit the Fright Side and hang out with Scary Godmother and all her friends? So indulge your inner child, or pretend you're buying a copy for a younger relative, if you must.

ESSENTIAL READING: The deluxe edition *Scary Godmother* (Dark Horse, 2010) introduces the beautifully painted and fantastically eerie world of Scary Godmother and her friends.

SIMONE CUNDY	A dreamer trying to flee small-town nightmares	**❝I believe in the holy trinity. My head, my heart, and my hymen.❞**
		Created by: Peter Milligan and Duncan Fegredo
		First appearance: *Girl* #1 (DC Comics/Vertigo, 1996)

Simone Cundy is a fifteen-year-old in girl in Bollockstown, England, who is prone to daydreams. Which include committing suicide by rat poison, having her dead body urinated on by her pet dog, exploding her family's lottery-winning ticket, and sewage workers converting sanitation systems to pay toilets. That's definitely an active imagination!

Disaffected and angry, Simone hates the town she feels stuck in. In her free time she enacts elaborate hanging tableaus with her Barbie and Ken dolls and passes out in abandoned buildings. She lives in a household with two older and useless brothers; rounding out the happy household is an abusive father who doesn't hesitate to kill the family dog when he thinks it wrecked his television and who assaults his wife if she speaks out of line. Simone can't go to school because she's bullied by mean-girl gangs, so she spends her time trading quips with other class cutters who ride the elevators for fun. It's not a good life, and Simone has definite cause to be miserable (not that '90s youth culture needed a reason to indulge in angst).

As these stories tend to go, the tortured status quo of Simone's life changes with one memorable action: Seeing her blonde near-doppelgänger being raped by the sewer guy from her dreams, Simone engages in real violence and knocks him out. The next night she wakes to find her father impaled on the fence outside, near death, and is told a few days later that the sewage worker has been murdered. She delivers her sister's baby, only for it to end up dead, too. How is this all connected?

To find out, Simone tracks down her twin. Who, as coincidence has it, is tracking her down as well. Why? Well because they are, in fact, really twins. And Simone's twin, named Polly, is so embarrassed by how awful Simone's life is that she begins to make her over in her own image. Strong, aggressive, devirginized.

Girl is a little bit *Fight Club*, a little bit *Heathers*; it's about social engineering, teenage disassociation, awful English small towns, and the spread of urban blight. It's kind of wonderful.

Collaborations between writer Peter Milligan and artist Duncan Fegredo are always intense. Fegredo's artwork is effective and unglamorized, with a strong sense of movement and power, both in the individual scenes and in the way the panels flow together. And the art melds perfectly with Peter's off-the-wall surreal scripts, which comment on the bizarreness of the mundane.

Simone just sort of floats through the really bad hand she's been dealt by the universe, using the strength of her imagination to survive. Pretty much all of us who have used a comic to escape reality can probably relate to that. Every so often you need a story that's gritty and dark and disconcerting, and the three issues of *Girl* fit the mold perfectly without being exploitative. Simone is a perfect symbol of disgruntled, authentic teenage rage against the establishment.

ESSENTIAL READING: Can you believe a comic as good as this one has never been collected? What justice is there in the world? Well, you'll just have to track down the original Vertigo comics.

SQUIRREL GIRL	A spunky superhero who triumphs against the biggest foes with the power of petite rodents	*"I don't need luck. I eat nuts."*
		Created by: Steve Ditko and Will Murray
		First appearance: *Marvel Super-Heroes* #8 (Marvel Comics, 1992)

As with Dazzler (see page 135), I didn't need to refresh my knowledge of Squirrel Girl before writing about her. I can take a bit of hipster pride about this Marvel Comics character, given that I was fond of her before her recent surge in popularity.

Many readers first noticed Squirrel Girl in the pages of the 2000s *Great Lakes Avengers*, which spun out of the *West Coast Avengers* series of the 1980s and '90s, a superhero book more embroiled in melodrama and telenovela/soap-operatic-type plot devices than most. If you don't believe me, go back to the arc where Scarlet Witch, a mutant who married a robot, has magic children, only to have them disappear when she's not around; she eventually discovers they're the splinter souls of a demon. All of which sends her into a psychotic rage as her husband's robotic memory is reset to factory defaults . . .

But I digress. Our focus is the mellow and bubbly Avenger with the abilities of a giant squirrel, bearing a large fluffy tail and facial markings as evidence of this connection. This results in her having increased speed and agility as well as the power to command (or at least to request nicely) that her squirrel friends help her out.

Squirrel Girl has one more important skill: the ability to be incredibly cute and charming. In recent history, that has enabled her to fool her way into Iron Man's base and commandeer a customized squirrel battle suit. And after she spent years of freelance superheroing, it also got her a stable job as a babysitter for Luke Cage and Jessica Jones's child (before she decided to go back to school).

But before going solo, Squirrel Girl was part of a ragtag group of misfit superheroes. If New York and California can have their own teams, you have to figure that supergroups exist all over America (heck, *even Canada maybe*). Sure enough, there was a team called the Great Lakes Avengers. Pretty much intended as a lighthearted group of superheroes, they became some of those brought-up-every-few-years jokey characters that resonate with die-hard fans. Squirrel Girl in particular was a character who, upon first glance, appeared to have few practical powers, certainly nothing of much consequence. But she faces off—and wins—against the likes of Doctor Doom and Galactus.

After appearing off and on in various roles throughout the Marvel Universe, in the 2010s Squirrel Girl got her own series, which launched to great popularity. The character was a bit like a more innocent, carefree version of Deadpool, constantly breaking the fourth wall and addressing viewers directly. Added to that, writer Ryan North made sure to pepper the comic with groan-worthy puns and jokes. Artist Erica Henderson updated Squirrel Girl's looks to make her more distinctive than most heroines in mainstream comics, endowing her with a muscular and curvy frame and a most noteworthy butt (well, that was due to her tail, which she carefully tucked into her pants to grant the appearance of a larger tush).

The character proved popular with fans as a comedy comic, and she even had a crossover with Howard the Duck (possibly because both Ryan North and Howard the Duck writer Chip Zdarsky hail from the same city in Canada, in addition to being obsessed with animal-like superheroes). It remains to be seen what role Squirrel Girl will have in the future, but right now she's in a good place to kick butts and eat nuts.

ESSENTIAL READING: You know, you could buy one of the reprints, but why not skip straight to her solo adventures and pick up one of the more recent collections: *Squirrel Power*; *Squirrel You Know It's True*; *Squirrel, You Really Got Me*, Now; or *I Kissed a Squirrel and I Liked It*. Ryan North notes, "I'm not saying I started writing Squirrel Girl just so I could give the collections 'girl/squirrel' themed titles, but I am saying . . . it doesn't hurt."

WITCHBLADE	Homicide detective who wields an ultra-powerful tool of supernatural origin	"I am the light. I am an angel of death. I am power."
		Created by: Marc Silvestri, David Wohl, Brian Haberlin, and Michael Turner
		First appearance: *Cyblade/Shi: The Battle for Independents* #1 (Image Comics, 1995)

In the 1990s the bad girl reigned supreme. Of course, pinup girls in scandalous clothing weren't exactly new to comics. In fact, as we saw from Sally the Sleuth (page 17), they've been with us since the very beginning. But girls who were on the ambiguous side of good and evil, who fought monsters viciously and with a savage joy, those characters are particular to the '90s.

Also unique to the decade were the particular aesthetics of the bad girl character, all of whom were fairly interchangeable. Big boobs, big butts, long, long slender legs, pouty lips, tiny noses, and catlike eyes with arched brows were the hallmarks. Along with clothing that somehow always managed to just cover the nipple and vulva, though rarely much more. *Witchblade* artist Michael Turner was considered the expert of this aesthetic, and his art was consistent, stylized, and sexualized.

Sara Pezzini is a homicide detective who does anything to solve a case, including dressing up in revealing skintight outfits to lure out bad guys (just like Sally the Sleuth!). In one such adventure, she throws herself in front of her partner Detective Yee to save his life and succeeds in getting riddled with bullets. That's when the Witchblade, a powerful ancient artifact destined to bond with only one wearer in any generation, reaches out to Sara and heals her. It instantly bonds to her skin, traveling in tendrils across her body, which I admit that as a preteen girl I thought looked wicked cool. As an adult, however, I find the way the fingerlike wisps curl across her body as she sleeps to be über-creepy. Soon Sara's identity is interchangeable with the weapon. They are the Witchblade.

Not only does Sara have to deal with a mysterious demonic weapon that's decided they're best buds, but she's also looking after a teenager named Lisa, the daughter of Sara's viciously murdered best friend.

As the series progressed, Sara got into more and more adventures, becoming very soap operatic in style. Eventually she gets impregnated after being raped by another magical-force-possessed superhero (there ends up being a bunch of them) and has to give up the Witchblade. She gets it back later, along with a mysterious superpowered daughter named Hope (not the last time this plot line is used in a comic; check out the past five years of *X-Men*).

Witchblade wasn't just the defining comic of the bad-girl style in the 1990s, it also successfully branched off into other mediums, including television, anime, and manga. For a long period during the decade, Sara Pezzini was the most prominent female character in comics. There are more than a few women who adore this character, despite that she was marketed to male readers. As comics writer Tini Howard said in an interview: "She's ripped up rock T-shirts and she swears too much. She makes bad decisions and frustrates those close to her. She's not afraid of anything she can punch. She's pure '90s rock and roll, and that's a beautiful thing."

Witchblade has changed somewhat over the years, though she's never lost her tough and sexy edge. Howard says of her favorite run: "While she may have cheesecakey origins, writers like Tim Seeley made her into someone I could really relate to and love."

Über-strong, determined, tenacious. Sara is the epitome of the "strong female character" archetype. In other words, she's drop-dead gorgeous and imbued with magic-enhanced strength (because god forbid a woman should have bulky muscles) whose sole defining quality is: she's tough. Though that's a definite improvement from a fainting damsel in distress, it's still not very nuanced.

CHAPTER

8

The

20

00s

WEBCOMICS AND COMIC-CONS

→

THE 2000s

The release of movie trailers for *The Phantom Menace*, *Blade*, and *The Matrix* at the 1998 San Diego Comic-Con (SDCC) made it bigger than just a comic book event. The comic con was becoming the center of all nerd pop culture, which itself was rapidly becoming just regular pop culture.

And as conventions opened up to more general pop-culture enthusiasts, women and girls who'd previously felt uncomfortable in the boys' club of comics fandom found like-minded female fans with whom they could connect. Convention attendance surged with women present in increasing numbers.

The rise of cartoons and live-action films showcasing Marvel and DC characters also contributed to an increase in female readership as did internet forums, message boards, and LiveJournal hubs, which allowed fans to share their interests. The increasing accessibility led to a change in readership demographics. Though traditional "floppies" (single issues, as opposed to trade collections or graphic novels) were still not at parity in terms of female vs. male readers—as they'd been, say, in the 1940s—they were closer than ever before. And for some graphic novels, manga, and webcomics, female readership was even higher than its male counterpart.

Along with the rise of the traditional comic book convention (or "pop culture expo," as many were renaming themselves) came the rise of the indie-comics festivals like TCAF (the Toronto Comic Arts Festival) and the Small Press Expo in Bethesda, Maryland. These events were usually free, or cheap, to attend. The independent, underground, and self-published comics projects featured at these cons lacked the old-boys'-club mentality of many traditional comics publishers.

Graphic novels, such as Alison Bechdel's *Fun Home*, Marjane Satrapi's *Persepolis*, Jessica Abel's *La Perdida*, *Diary of a Teenage Girl* by Phoebe Gloeckner, and *Goodbye Marianne* by Irene N. Watts, became critically acclaimed hits outside the usual comics audience. They turned up on the syllabi of a wide range of college courses, from queer studies to cultural studies to women's studies. *Persepolis* and *Diary of a Teenage Girl* have since been picked up for feature film adaptations, while *Fun Home* went on to become a Broadway musical. Comics, or at least graphic novels, by women had become Big Business.

The era's most significant industry change was the growth of webcomics, a part of comics history that tends to be overlooked. Early examples date to the 1980s, with the first rush of content beginning in the late 1990s. In the 2000s, webcomics, like other online content, proliferated as faster internet access became more widely available. Genres ranged across the board, with fantasy, slice-of-life, and computer/tech humor being the most numerous.

Before 1999, few webcomics creators were women (for the same reasons that women aren't well-represented in the STEM fields; they required specialized knowledge that young girls were often discouraged from learning). But when webcomics suddenly surged in popularity at the turn of the decade, many women were on board, including Nitrozac (*Joy of Tech, After Y2K*), Maritza Campos (*College Roomies from Hell!!!*), Dorothy Gambrell (*Cat and Girl*), Gisèle Lagacé (*Cool Cat Studio*), K. Sandra Stanley (*Boy Meets Boy*), Shaenon K. Garrity (*Narbonic*), Jennie Breeden (*The Devil's Panties*), Justine Shaw (*Nowhere Girl*), and Faith Erin Hicks (*Demonology 101*).

The first almost fully accessible comics format had finally been created. Webcomics could be made by anyone with basic computer hardware (or access to it), and the stories could be viewed free of charge by anyone anywhere with access to the internet and a device. Comics were no longer dependent on interstate shipping or sequestered in dingy comic-book dungeons. They had no authority governing their content. And they didn't need steady sales to survive (though that definitely helped). This was the biggest evolution in comics history. ⚡

ANNABELLE	A creepy sentient doll immersed in endless modern-day gothic tales!	❝How can something like myself, created by someone with so much sadness, pain, and suffering, be anything but an instrument for the same?❞
		Created by: Serena Valentino and FSc (Foo Swee Chin)
		First appearance: *Nightmares & Fairy Tales* #1 (Slave Labor Graphics, 2002)

Annabelle, the protagonist of the series *Nightmares & Fairytales*, is a sweet and deeply insightful storyteller. She has the remarkable ability to go unnoticed in any situation, observing and learning quietly without anyone remarking on her presence . . .

Well, that's probably because she's a rag doll.

She's also a fine example of the creepy goth-girl hero, a fiction archetype passed down through the generations, and one that has always entranced readers. Though this particular character is unusual in being a narrating, inanimate doll, Annabelle's character type has a long history.

A neglected wave of the comics movement, especially by those who write "best of the decade" overviews, was the surge of interest in goth-girl titles that appeared at the end of the 1990s. As comic writer/artist Megan Kearney, whose *Beauty and the Beast* webcomic has been running since 2012, notes: "The goth wave of the late '90s and early 2000s featured a lot of girl-led titles, like Roman Dirge's *Lenore*, Serena Valentino's *Nightmares and Fairytales*, Ted Naifeh's *Courtney Crumrin*, and Junko Mizuno's *Cinderalla*, that the mainstream comics media resolutely ignored." Maybe that's because the writers of top-ten comics lists are primarily adult males, who don't have much knowledge about comics aimed at preteen girls.

Leading the way in the '90s gothic-girl trend was *Lenore the Cute Little Dead Girl*, first published by independent comics publishing house Slave Labor Graphics. But little girls have always had a fasciation with dark and macabre characters. There's a reason why every girl wants to be Wednesday Addams and Neil Gaiman books are on most fangirls' shelves. The dead/goth child movement of the late 1990s and early 2000s has its roots in a much older and equally fangirl obsessive movement: the gothic romance. (Remember Laura Chandler way back in the 1970s section?)

Annabelle's story in particular hearkens as much to these melodramatic gothic romance tales as it does to the modern goth-girl archetype she represents. Time and again, her owners fall into madness, despair, and tragedy. Whether it's Annabelle's curse that causes these tragedies, or it's her curse to witness them, we never know.

Whatever the reason, the tales that Annabelle recounts delve into a world full of vindictive lovers, murderous nuns, kidnapped babies, disembowelment, human sacrifice, and all sorts of ghoulish and awful things. Yet the skill of the artists, including the main series artist FSc, make all this horror look, well, fairly charming! Even with the horror, the odd story has a happy ending and the series is filled with a range of female characters: ambitious ladies, malevolent villains, and the occasional fainting violet.

Similar to the Old Witch (page 63) from EC Comics, Annabelle's personality frames the stories in her comic, but for the most part she takes a backseat to the adventures she presents. Even though this story stars a doll, and it might look innocent on the surface, these grisly tales are definitely not for children. Though the teens in your life will get a gruesome kick out of it.

ESSENTIAL READING: *Once Upon a Time (Nightmares & Fairy Tales, Volume 1)* (Slave Labor Graphics, 2004). In this volume you're introduced to the twisted fairy tales that Annabelle retells, as well as the origin of the doomed lovers who were once her owners.

DIDI (DÉSIRÉE CHASTEL)	A sweet-natured Montreal waitress, probably best known for having the biggest heart in webcomics	66 I was first of my school to get breasts. 99
		Created by: Gisèle Lagacé and David Lumsdon
		First appearance: *Ménage à 3* (webcomic, 2008)

DiDi is one of a trio of Montreal roommates navigating their way through love, lust, and friendship in the adult-humor webcomic strip *Ménage à 3* (aka *MA3*).

R... Are you Power Girl?

So what do you say, Jung? Help a brother out?

Well, the boss *did* want to hire a new girl since our last one ran out of here screaming and pulling her hair.

Did you *hear* that, Zii? You're *in!*

A Quebecois waitress, DiDi is the frequent object of adoration by male and female characters alike. But she holds a secret that is slowly revealed through the course of the online strip—despite being very sexually active, she has never had a satisfying experience. In many comics it would be an easy setup to have the man-child protagonist "take care" of her; instead, DiDi attends sexual therapy and learns that she requires an intense emotional connection before she can have a physical response.

By turns stubborn, naive, sweet natured, and competitive, DiDi is a complex character who changes significantly during the series—just like a real person. Questioning her sexuality and experimenting with different lovers and friendships, she seeks to understand herself in a way that is, at times, highly sensitive. But the atmosphere is always lightened with a punchline at the end of each three- or four-panel strip.

Often lazily summarized as "an R-rated Archie strip," *MA3* showcases that stories can have sexy characters, and penis jokes, and not lack for a sophisticated storyline that delves into questions of sexual identity and maintaining relationships. Being created by a female artist and a male cowriter no doubt had much to do with the nuance of the strip and its appeal to both male and female readers.

ESSENTIAL READING: All of *MA3*'s strips are available online, as well as in trade paperbacks self-published through Pixie Trix Comix.

EMPOWERED	A damsel in distress, trying desperately to make it as a big-name superhero	"Okay, so I'm Lame-o-Tron 3000 from Loseria, planet of the wankers!"
		Created by: Adam Warren
		First appearance: *Empowered* #1 (Dark Horse Comics, 2007)

Elissa Megan Powers's superheroine codename, Empowered ("Emp," for short), is tongue-in-cheek, for her outfit and adventures suggest anything but a female empowerment story. Her powers come from her super-thin supersuit membrane, which grants Emp the strength of ten men and the ability to forceblast at her foes . . . as long as the fabric isn't snagged or ripped. Which happens frequently, and at a moment's notice, causing Emp's strength and superpowers to deflate. And as the fragile cloth tatters further, she's eventually left helpless. (I'm not sure how a ball gag affects her powers, but by the end of each of her adventures that usually comes into play as well.)

In addition, the suit increases her sexual responses, and its durability is affected by her mood. In other words, Emp's low self-esteem causes the suit to rip more easily, and the suit turns her on while it's on her body.

Empowered started off as a way for creator Adam Warren to have some fun with the traditional "damsel in distress" pinups that were requested from him at comics conventions. He decided to make the best of a bad situation and incorporate plot points and create a character who is self-aware of her role. As a result, Empowered is meek and distinctly lacking in self-confidence because of her unreliable powerset and her recurring state of humiliation. A member of the Superhomeys superteam, Emp is aware that her teammates consider her a token diversity hire, needed to fill their mixed-gender quota. Also on the team is the ambitious Sistah Spooky, who plays the role of the feminist reader, exasperated by Empowered's constant state of distress and undress.

Supporting characters include Empowered's boyfriend Thugboy, a former villain's minion turned ego booster and occasional rescuer. He points out that Empowered's vulnerabilities make her a more genuine hero than her mocking teammates, since they don't face as much risk as she does. Emp's best friend is Ninjette, a sexually frustrated young woman who has become a self-practiced master of the ninja arts. She also sees beyond Empowered's insecurities to the heroine within.

So, is *Empowered* a satirical look at bad girl comics? Is it a straightforward T&A sex comedy? Is it the tale of a naive and self-conscious girl working to do the right thing and be a hero despite the limitations she faces?

I can't tell you that, because I don't know! It is a fun read, but the art definitely includes an overwhelming amount of male gaze. If you like your porn with a side of wink and character building, then this comic might be for you. After all, there's nothing wrong with getting a bit turned on while you read a story.

ESSENTIAL READING: *Empowered*, vol. 1 (Dark Horse Comics, 2007). All of the *Empow-*

ered comics are available in affordable paperback collections from Dark Horse, so you can catch up handily.

JALISCO	An unassuming private eye in a corrupt city	66 If there's something I'm good at, it's disappearing without leaving any traces. 99
		Created by: Carlos Trillo and Eduardo Risso
		First appearance: *Chicanos* #1 (IDW Publications, 2005)

Chicanos is a *Sin City*–esque pulpy noir crime comic with a stark black-and-white palette. Our heroine Jalisco is short, not very lucky in love, a little odd looking, and ... pretty good at her job. Even though it always gets her in trouble.

We start off the story meeting Mr. Walken, a crime boss who cuts an ear off his employee Tarantino-style (Oh, I see what you did there with his name. Cute!), and then leaves as a tip after a less-than-adequate shave with benefits from two comely spa attendants. Yuck, right? How can I even mention this comic in a feminist book? Well, I'm coming to that. So, Mr. Walken tortured his minion because he heard that a private eye is on the premises, looking for a paper that could put his entire business under. And his goons were too dumb to bother stopping the intruder. Crashing into his office to catch the detective himself, Walken is startled to see no one but a short cleaning lady with skinny ankles throwing out the trash. He apologizes profusely and leaves.

Of course, that cleaning lady is our heroine, the private eye Alejandrina Yolanda Jalisco. A former cop who quit when she couldn't pursue her leads, Jalisco kept her cases going by becoming a private investigator and dedicating herself to good cases (and those that'll pay the bills). Though rarely taken seriously because of her stature, she is damn good at her job. She isn't very good at attracting men, however, which she badly wishes she was, especially after a long dry spell. Jalisco isn't exactly a perfect beauty, and it's great to see a female character who doesn't need to be gorgeous to also be a superspy. Who cares about being beautiful when you're so proficient at what you do?

Her encounters with the Walken crew start to catch up to Jalisco and the mobsters attempt to murder her, bribing a racist cop to look the other way. Fortunately, some of Jalisco's many neighborhood friends intervene, hurling their belongings at the mobsters and the cop, letting her escape. Phew, friendship is magic, indeed. Jalisco spends a few days hiding, then finally gets impatient and blasts the crime lord away (by accident, but still).

From here on in, she gets embroiled with all the traditional crime tropes (oh,

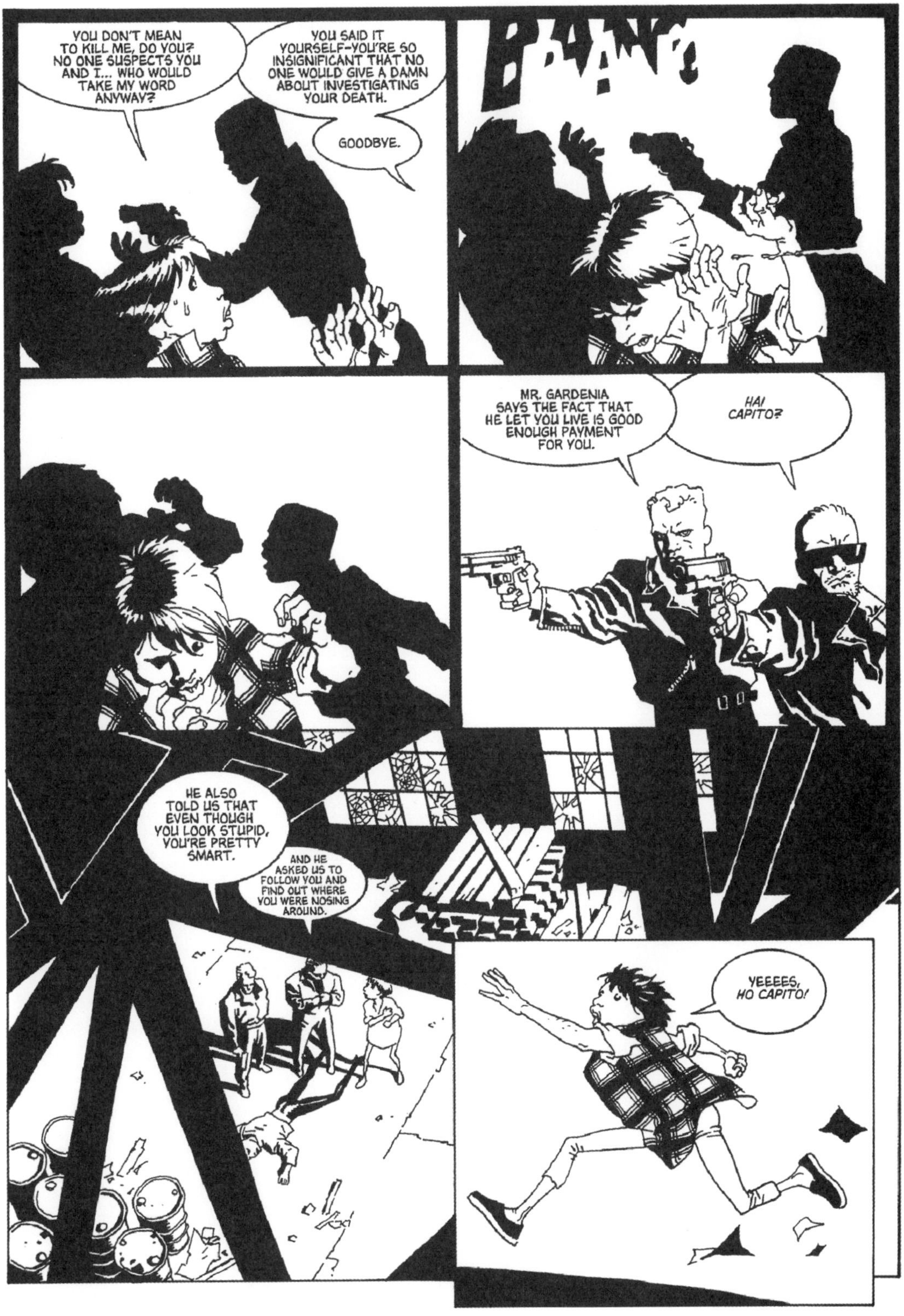
YOU DON'T MEAN TO KILL ME, DO YOU? NO ONE SUSPECTS YOU AND I... WHO WOULD TAKE MY WORD ANYWAY?
YOU SAID IT YOURSELF—YOU'RE SO INSIGNIFICANT THAT NO ONE WOULD GIVE A DAMN ABOUT INVESTIGATING YOUR DEATH.
GOODBYE.
MR. GARDENIA SAYS THE FACT THAT HE LET YOU LIVE IS GOOD ENOUGH PAYMENT FOR YOU.
HAI CAPITO?
HE ALSO TOLD US THAT EVEN THOUGH YOU LOOK STUPID, YOU'RE PRETTY SMART.
AND HE ASKED US TO FOLLOW YOU AND FIND OUT WHERE YOU WERE NOSING AROUND.
YEEEES, HO CAPITO!

and I love them so!). Like being framed for the murder of her client and going undercover to catch an extortionist. Along the way we learn about Jalisco's tragic past (every P.I.'s gotta have one): her first case led to the crippling of her father by her mother, the result of an adulterous affair that Jalisco witnessed and tattled on. But Jalisco's got problems even outside private-eyeing. Her vivacious best friend Marita has become friends with a sporty policewoman named Maggie, who belittles Jalisco's detective skills. Again, it's pretty remarkable that Jalisco's problems revolve around something other than a guy. You know, almost as if women have developed and complex emotional relationships beyond their romances.

It's not just her physical appearance that makes Jalisco unlike most other private eyes. The series deals honestly and frankly with racism against Latino communities in the United States. A frequent subplot is that cabs refuse to stop for her, racists accost her on the street and threaten to kill her, and she's frequently mistaken for a servant instead of a detective (which she uses on occasion to her advantage to infiltrate classified areas).

I can't say that the comic doesn't make me cringe at times. It's a crime comic, pretty heavy on the rough-and-tumble-ness of sex and violence. But Jalisco is an incredibly compelling character. It takes guts to be a private eye when you're short, average looking, and not white. She comes off as more than just the sum of her parts. Jalisco is fully complex, subject to her own whims and pettiness but without letting them distract her from her mission.

ESSENTIAL READING: If you can read Spanish, opt for the original volumes of *Chicanos* published in a collected edition by Public Square Books (2006). Otherwise, sample the English translations by IDW (2006); not all the stories have been translated.

JAMIE McJACK	Curvy sidekick turned romance detective!	66*Is it more selfish to have multiple lovers who fulfill you in different ways . . . or have one lover and expect them to fulfill you in every way?*99
		Created by: Danielle Corsetto
		First appearance: *Girls with Slingshots* #1 (webcomic, 2004)

Jamie McJack isn't the main character of *Girls with Slingshots*, the triweekly webcomic that ran from 2004 to 2014. That honor belongs to Hazel Tellington, Jamie's best friend, a struggling writer with a tendency to drink too much and make poor decisions. In comparison to the often negative Hazel, Jamie has a bouncy, energetic personality and is always able to look on the bright side. A short, curvy girl, Jamie is looked upon with attraction by most men in the series, though she starts off with a surprising secret: she's a virgin.

Throughout *Girls with Slingshots*, Jamie experiences the most changes of any character. Discovering her sexuality and dating various men, she realizes after a few years that she is attracted to Erin, a quiet, shy young woman. The only problem? Erin is going through some sexual discoveries of her own, and she determines soon after falling in love with Jamie that she's asexual. Luckily that's no deal-breaker when you love someone, and together she and Jamie make it work. Knowing that Jamie needs sex in addition to love, the two decide to open up their pairing, and by the end of the saga they're happily committed in a polyamorous relationship.

Jamie isn't afraid to have fun and go on ridiculous adventures. A self-declared "romance detective," she's often found in the midst of her friend's romantic lives, aiding—or interfering with—their dating trials. And through it all, she remains best friends with the cranky and difficult Hazel.

Jamie is a perfect example of the power of serial storytelling. Following along on her journey over the years, throughout the changes in her life, the reader becomes invested in her character. And the changes she goes through lead us to realize how complex the world of love, dating, and sex really is.

ESSENTIAL READING: Danielle Corsetto is rereleasing each strip online in color, hooray! A self-published print series is also available; check girlswithslingshots.com.

JESSICA JONES	Former superhero turned private eye with a traumatic past	**❝I didn't kill this girl. And you're sitting here with me while whoever did do it is out there doing a pee-pee dance.❞**
		Created by: Brian Michael Bendis and Michael Gaydos
		First appearance: *Alias* #1 (Marvel Comics, 2001)

Jessica Jones: Private investigator. Failed superheroine. Trauma survivor. Journalist. Mother. Avenger. The star of the dark, not-quite-a-superhero comic book *Alias* (in addition to spin-off comics such as *New Avengers* and *The Pulse*, and the eventual Netflix adaptation *Jessica Jones*), Jessica has worn a lot of hats during her time in the Marvel Comics universe. She's perhaps best known as a

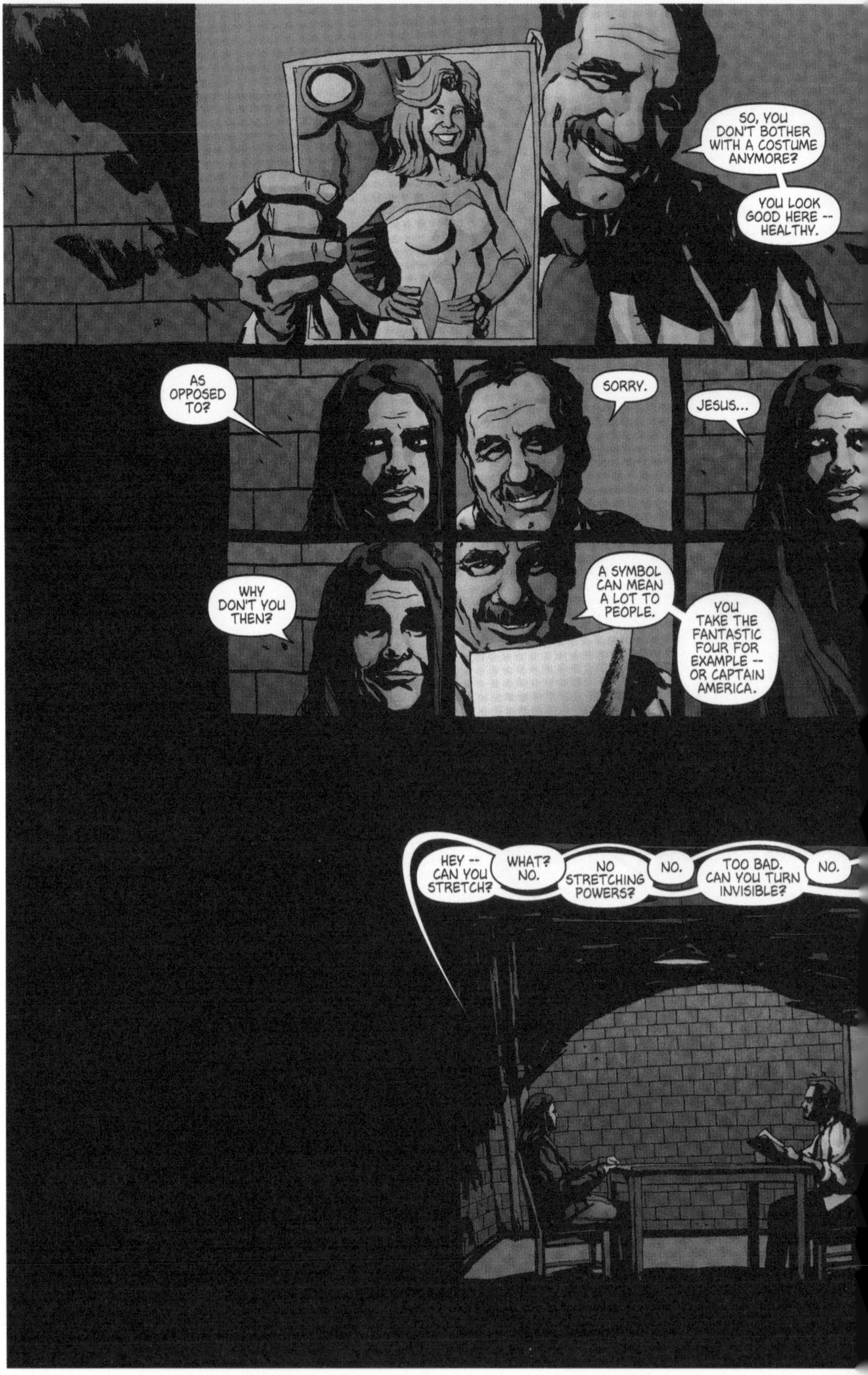
SO, YOU DON'T BOTHER WITH A COSTUME ANYMORE?
YOU LOOK GOOD HERE -- HEALTHY.
AS OPPOSED TO?
SORRY.
JESUS...
WHY DON'T YOU THEN?
A SYMBOL CAN MEAN A LOT TO PEOPLE.
YOU TAKE THE FANTASTIC FOUR FOR EXAMPLE -- OR CAPTAIN AMERICA.
HEY -- CAN YOU STRETCH?
WHAT? NO.
NO STRETCHING POWERS?
NO.
TOO BAD. CAN YOU TURN INVISIBLE?
NO.

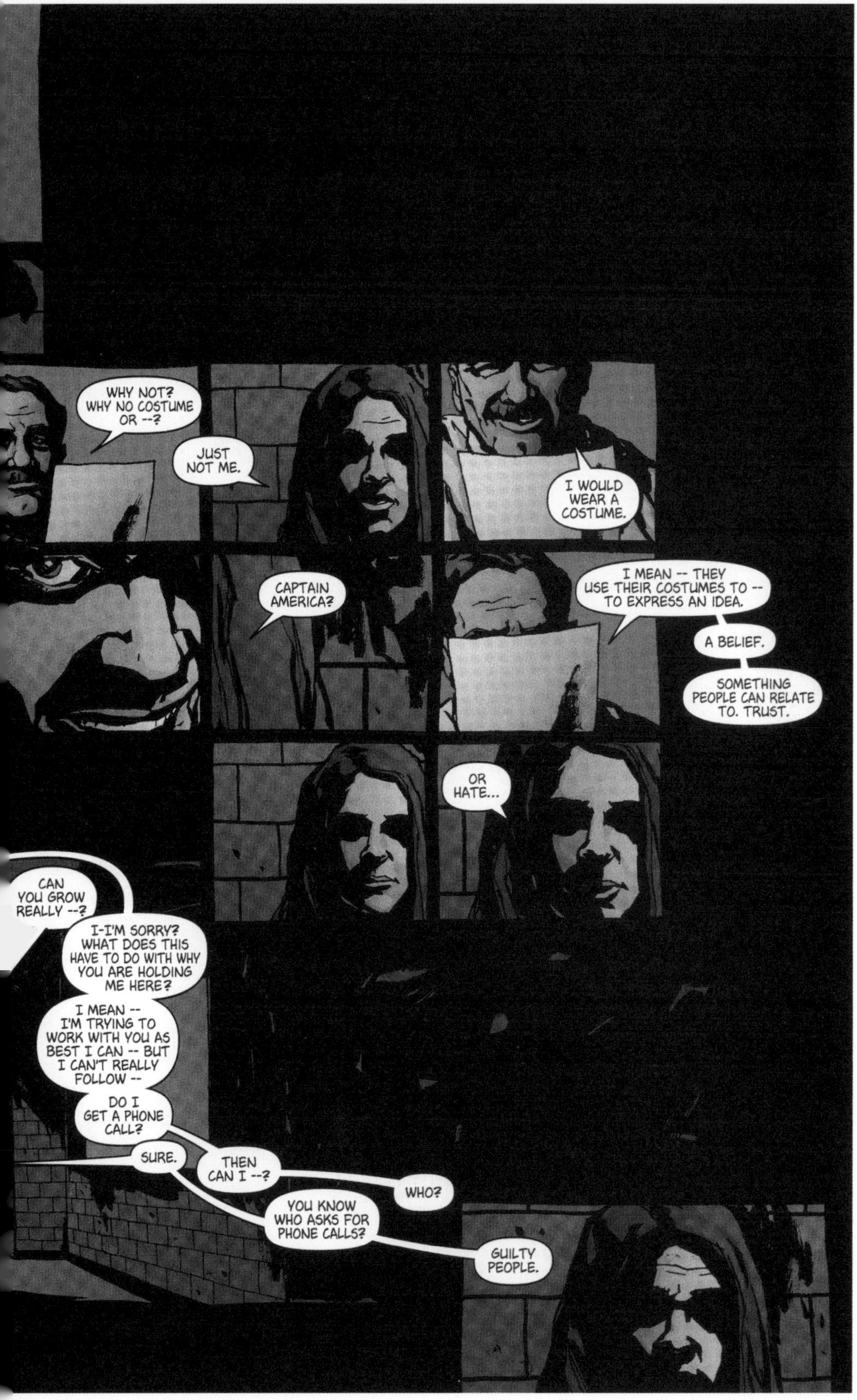
WHY NOT? WHY NO COSTUME OR --?
JUST NOT ME.
I WOULD WEAR A COSTUME.
CAPTAIN AMERICA?
I MEAN -- THEY USE THEIR COSTUMES TO -- TO EXPRESS AN IDEA.
A BELIEF.
SOMETHING PEOPLE CAN RELATE TO. TRUST.
OR HATE...
CAN YOU GROW REALLY --?
I-I'M SORRY? WHAT DOES THIS HAVE TO DO WITH WHY YOU ARE HOLDING ME HERE?
I MEAN -- I'M TRYING TO WORK WITH YOU AS BEST I CAN -- BUT I CAN'T REALLY FOLLOW --
DO I GET A PHONE CALL?
SURE.
THEN CAN I --?
WHO?
YOU KNOW WHO ASKS FOR PHONE CALLS?
GUILTY PEOPLE.

character who uses alcohol, sex, and drugs to numb herself to damage that she's caused, as well as the damage done to her by a maniac known as the Purple Man, a C-list supervillain who destroyed her life.

The story is powerful showing what one villain can do to a single person, instead of trying to destroy the universe or rule the world. And though *Alias* could have wallowed in the showcase of a broken woman, it instead highlights real trauma and survival. We get a character who might be currently defined by her past, but who is in the process of recovery and healing. And we are allowed to follow along as she survives day by day until she eventually finds closure.

Part of that closure involves having sex with the super-hot superhero Power Man (aka Luke Cage) and getting pregnant by him. So I'm not saying you won't come across a few tropes in the book that aren't disappointing to see. But what story is completely, 100 percent perfect?

In the course of her solo first series, Jessica Jones investigates the dark and seedier sides of the Marvel Universe, discovering people who are using Captain America's sex life to frame him for murder; the kidnapping and exploitation of the young and troubled Spider-Girl; and finding love and lust in the arms of Luke Cage, and then Scott Lang (Ant-Man), and then Luke Cage again. We learn about Jessica's character and personality through her adventures, long before we find out the defining moments of her life, with the Purple Man back-story emerging only after several issues pass. Throughout all this—and despite that Jessica has an abrupt and callous attitude toward her own life—we see the depths of her compassion for others time and again. And that compassion defines her character.

In addition to Jessica's jobs and romances, we delve into her complicated friendship with Carol Danvers, aka Ms. Marvel (see page 124). (FYI, that role was changed to Patsy Walker, aka Hellcat, in the Netflix series.) Carol doesn't understand why Jessica is pushing away all her old friends. As the story progresses we are told via flashbacks how Jessica, after surviving the traumatic death of her parents and brother, found a measure of purpose in the role of superheroine. And how the Purple Man decided to use her as his plaything, assaulting and manipulating her until he grew bored and sent a mind-controlled Jessica to be beaten up by her former friends the Avengers. As if that weren't bad enough, after she recovered from the beat-down, Jessica discovered that the Avengers didn't much care about her at all—at least not enough to stand by her side while she recovered.

The covers of *Alias* are atmospheric and dark; painted by David Mack, they reflect the overall tone of the story, if not exact scenes. The interior art, drawn by Michael Gaydos and colored by Matt Hollingsworth, is rough, and at times even purposefully ugly, which works well for the storytelling. Gaydos uses the volume of the panels to slow the pace during intense scenes, allowing us to focus on moments of greater emotional importance. Multiple small panels showcase the character's feelings as they change rapidly, while full-page artwork that stretches across panels helps us understand the fast-racing thoughts that happen during a flash of anxiety.

All in all, Jessica Jones in *Alias* is a great example of how to create a complex female character with past trauma, in which that trauma isn't her defining trait or used simply as a plot device. Fortunately, her story continues: after the end of Jessica's self-titled series, we follow her new career as a journalist in the series *The Pulse*, before she joins the New Avengers with Luke Cage.

ESSENTIAL READING: Dive into Jessica's adventures with *Alias Omnibus* (Marvel Comics, 2014), a full collection of her solo series.

NIBBIL	Tiny sex goddess and part-time conscience	"Oh no! I've been bondaged! GOSH, I'm so very helpless!"
		Created by: Colleen Coover
		First appearance: *Small Favors* #1 (Eros Comix, 2000)

The gist of the *Small Favors* series is that because she indulged in too much self-pleasure, 21-year-old Annie is punished by supernatural forces and given a conscience. That conscience is Nibbil, a diminutive spirit the size of Tinkerbell, equipped with fluffy hair and a liking for wearing a sailor uniform. Nibbil, to the ignorance of her higher-powered bosses, is equally as sexually voracious as Annie, and together they get along *very* well. I mean, they have a lot of sex. Every type, every position. But all very much enjoyed, and each woman is respectful of the other. The second volume focuses mostly on the introduction of a third party, and a fourth, and a fifth . . .

How to write about a porn comic without talking about porn is a challenge. And yet, porn made by women for women is pretty important to talk about. The genre is incredibly subjective, full of so many different nuances catering to people's likes and dislikes, all of which have been created through myriad life experiences, some powerful and some subtle. If a particular type of pornography is not to your taste, does that make it bad?

Small Favors is porn that is made with women readers in mind, featuring characters who authentically and joyfully enjoy having sex with each other. Enthusiasm and consent are definitely a good thing in porn (as they are in sex!).

Together, Nibbil and Annie go on adventures and role-play, with Nibbil sometimes in her Lilliputian size and sometimes using her supernatural powers to become full size, too. In their romantic escapades, the couple shows a bubbly

desire for each other, changing power positions at will and displaying an inventive curiosity about all the possibilities in their new relationship.

But technically Nibbil is failing at her job. When her adjudicator, the supremely chaste Janus, comes one day for a home-check visit, the girls are compelled to clean up their act in a hurry until they're gleaming paragons of virtue. Janus doesn't quite make it to their house, though, since she ends up in the bedroom of their very pretty neighbor by mistake and, ah, trades in her purity for curiosity.

The comic breaks the fourth wall a few times, addressing the reader directly as complicit in the women's adventures and treating the characters as exhibitionists who enjoy the readers' attention. One story features Nibbil engaging in balloon sex—that is, sex with word balloons. Which I for one think is a highly inventive use of the comics structure. Scott McCloud really should mention it in his next academic treatise on the medium.

Creator Colleen Coover states in her introduction to the first collected edition that the concept is a simple one: "Pretty girls make people happy. That's the joy of a pretty girl, you just never know when that smile is going to bloom, when that hair is going to blow in just that certain manner or when she will laugh that laugh. And no matter how you felt before, you'll feel better! The pretty girl will make you happy." You can't argue with that logic.

ESSENTIAL READING: In *Small Favors*, vol. 1 (Eros Comix, 2008), you can meet the girls and catch up on their sexy adventures. The second volume involves more group activities, so if you'd rather read that . . . you probably won't miss a lot of plot points from volume one anyhow.

ROSE HARVESTAR	A headstrong and naive princess with magical powers forced to grow up to protect her kingdom	*I'll go to the meditation... but I won't pay attention!*
		Created by: Jeff Smith and Charles Vess
		First appearance: *Rose* #1 (Cartoon Books, 2000)

Technically, Rose is introduced in the series *Bone*, which premiered in the 1990s. But in *Bone*, she's an old woman named Gran'ma Ben and bears little resemblance to the younger self featured in her own series.

Rose's comic reveals that she is the daughter of the king and queen in a magical fantasy land, trained to sense danger via a hereditary power called "The Dreaming." She has a sister, Briar, who isn't as lucky and who seemingly possesses no magic at all. Together they're sent to a faraway cave to endure a trial, called "The Turning," to determine their ability to lead their people.

Rose is an excitable, powerful seer, but she's unfocused, preferring to play with her dogs instead of working on her leadership skills. Her sister, meanwhile, is serious and somewhat bitter because she lacks the skills that Rose has. As their adventure progresses, it's clear that Rose has developed a crush on Lucius Down, the captain of the guard sent to protect them, though Briar believes Lucius likes her best instead. In fact, the guard does seem to like Briar—in an almost hypnotized fashion. Together the sisters enter the cave, where they begin their training for the final test.

Rose is set to rule a country on the verge of change. For many years, an evil god of locusts has been trapped inside the once-benevolent queen of dragons, who was turned to stone in order to keep him imprisoned. But the powers that bound the dragon are slowly weakening, and a prophecy foretells that someone powerful is coming to free the demon. During her training, Rose runs into trouble when—ignoring her lessons to play with her pooches—she accidentally frees a river dragon who's possessed by the foretold demon emancipator. Using her skills with a sword and her powerful fists, Rose manages to persuade the dragon to pick on an easier target—which he promptly does, attacking a nearby village. (But at least Rose and her dogs are okay, right?)

Soon it becomes clear that Rose's sister is hiding a deep secret, an evil secret, a—okay, *she* is the emancipator of the locust demon!

Not only that, but Briar manages to enlist the aid of "the hairy men," giant ratlike beasts desperate to stay in the security and abundance of the valley. Which

Briar promises they will be able to do, *after* they destroy Rose's entire army.

Rose is a princess and a warrior, with weaknesses that accompany her youth. She's natural and normal enough, and more interesting than an absolutely perfect heroine would be. She lacks concentration and is gullible, but she's also fiercely loyal and has a strong moral compass. Briar is her opposite; practical and guided, but prone to jealousy and bitterness at being passed over time and again in favor of her popular, more beloved sister.

Rose isn't a complex story; it's an adventure of princesses and dragons, of love, loyalty, and jealousy. And, eventually, of sacrifice and grief as well. I'd say it's a classic children's story for the ages, but the end might be a bit too heartbreaking (though if kids can handle everyone dying in the Narnia books, they can probably handle this).

ESSENTIAL READING: *Bone Prequel: Rose* (Scholastic Books, 2009) collects the entire adventure.

THE SAUCY MERMAID	A sexy mermaid who just wants love—and probably to drown you	66Do you like Michael Jackson?99
		Created by: Kate Beaton
		First appearance: *Hark! A Vagrant* #34 (harkavagrant.com, 2009)

By and large, most of Kate Beaton's popular *Hark! A Vagrant* webcomic strips deal with Canadian historical figures, literary fiction analysis, or superheroes/classic detectives being rude. But Kate has also created original characters. Some have starred in children's books (like "Fat Pony," a pony who is fat, and "King Baby," a baby who's a king). Others teach us lifelong important lessons about . . . how 1980s businesswomen have sex, how to protect yourself against straw feminists in your closet, and how boobs and butts make Strong Female Characters.

Kate Beaton's Saucy Mermaid appears in roughly eleven different strips, starting in 2009. At first a nod to the *Odyssey*, the strip begged the question, What if mermaids were actually really, really bad at seducing guys with their songs? The answer is, they get berated loudly by sea captains until they pledge to learn Michael Jackson instead.

The Saucy Mermaid appears again a few strips later as a "sexy omen" from the sea. Then, unusually for *Hark! A Vagrant*, she returns in a fairly serious multistrip storyline, in which she tries to seduce a handsome sailor but fails miserably. He claims that she is just not ladylike enough for him, despite her bewitching eyes.

Determined, the Saucy Mermaid somehow finds a pair of legs and puts on

a pretty dress, pulls up her hair, and goes to the sailor's home, where he is bewildered but charmed by this unexpected guest. He invites her in and tries to feed her hard biscuits and fish, while she sits primly quiet and asks nicely to go for a walk. Out to the sea. Later they head out to a tavern where the quiet lady-mermaid sees a young prostitute trying to seduce a drinker. The prostitute and lady-mermaid exchange strained glances. The sailor ushers his date out of the building, realizing that both she and the prostitute have the same hungry look in their eyes, and he abandons her.

Don't worry, he wasn't slut-shaming. He just figured out that she was a mermaid and probably would in fact lead him to the sea and murder him! And yeah, the apology she writes and leaves at his door the next day pretty much confirms that. But maybe the note means that she isn't all bad? So he goes down to the docks and sits with her and asks her to sing for him.

It's a strange love story, or friendship, to be sure. The ending is ambiguous; whether the sailor is prepared to be eventually drowned, or whether the mermaid has truly changed her ways, is unclear. That said, in the midst of jokes about Canadian confederacy and superpowered butts, this is a surprisingly moving short story born out of a joke about mermaids being bad at their jobs.

ESSENTIAL READING: You can read Kate Beaton's comics for free at harkavagrant.com. Also check out her books: *Hark! A Vagrant* and *Step Aside, Pops* are collections of her comic strips (both published by Drawn and Quarterly); *The Princess and the Pony* and *King Baby* (both by Arthur A. Levine Books) are kids' picture books.

STREET ANGEL

A tough skateboarding teenage punk, in a futuristic world fighting ninjas, pirates, and demons	66 *Still not dead, jerks!* 99
	Created by: Jim Rugg and Brian Maruca
	First appearance: *Street Angel* #01 (Slave Labor Graphics, 2004)

Street Angel is a product of a different time, a version of what our present day might be like if the styles and themes of the 1990s were still dominant. Super-scientists, ninjas, master criminals, demon worshippers, and time-traveling pirates all array themselves against a streetwise and smart-alecky 13-year-old named Jesse Sanchez, aka Street Angel. She's armed only with a skateboard and her self-taught martial arts, which are more than up to the task.

Street Angel is a throwback, and a very charming one at that. Her action-packed saga begins in the year 2006—an alternate 2006, with a distinctly nineties flavor. An elite police squad has recently overthrown the chaos of ninjas that had taken over Angel City. They bring Street Angel to meet the mayor, whose daughter has gone missing, having been kidnapped by the dastardly Dr. Pangea. Of course Street Angel saves the day, rescues the girl (who is far from grateful), and, like a classic loner hero, continues on her solo path.

Orphaned at a young age, Jesse is a typical teenager in her behavior and mannerisms, but possesses incredible fighting skills. Equipped with a mega-phone through which she loudly communicates her (never-filtered) thoughts, along with her ever-present skateboard, Street Angel sets out on missions to save the world. She's also homeless and must Dumpster-dive for food. Jesse may be the world's toughest skateboarder, but her biggest fear is that her classmates will find out about her secret living situation. Jesse Sanchez has been called "The World's Toughest Superhero" and "The Princess of Poverty"—she's both, and that's what makes her such a great character.

ESSENTIAL READING: The original Street Angel stories are available in an easy-to-find collection by AdHouse Books. Meanwhile, its creators have been making new stories, which you can find on Jim Rugg's website (jimrugg.com).

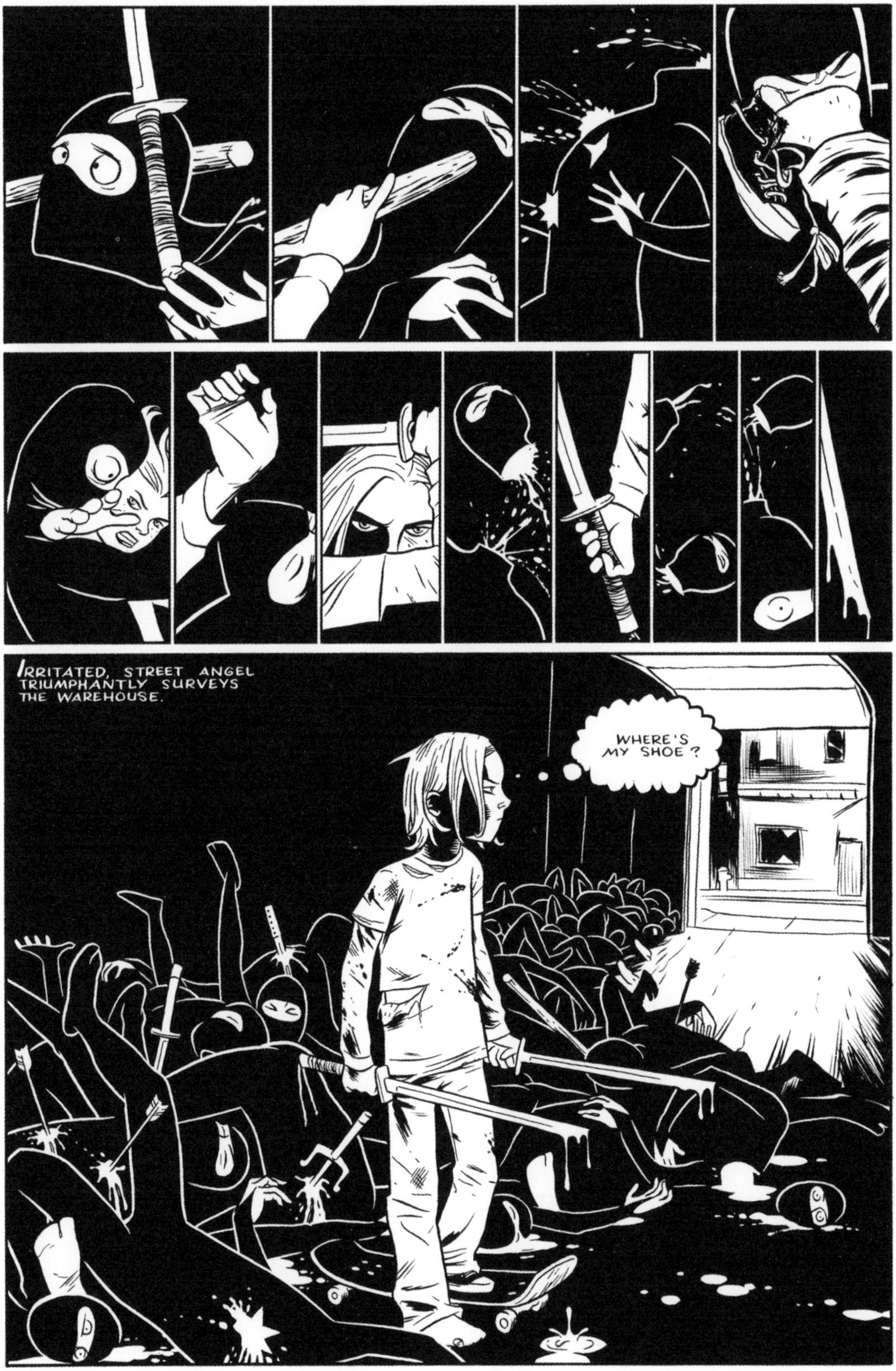
IRRITATED, STREET ANGEL TRIUMPHANTLY SURVEYS THE WAREHOUSE.
WHERE'S MY SHOE?

XAVIN

A super alien warrior and dedicated partner

"For us, changing gender is no different than changing hair color."

Created by: Brian K. Vaughan, Adrian Alphona, Takeshi Miyazawa, Craig Yeung, and Christina Strain

First appearance: *Runaways* vol. 2, #7 (Marvel Comics, 2005)

Most of the cast of the ensemble team group book *Runaways* are women, and they're a pretty eclectic batch. We're talking about an alien, a witch, a mutant, and a girl with a telepathic dinosaur, all of whom have evil parents and are on a mission to fix the problems caused by their parents. Along the way they encounter betrayals and deaths, and they struggle to survive on their own as a new family.

Xavin enters the equation partly through the comic's second series. Right after our resident alien, by the name of Karolina Dean, makes a romantic play (rejected) for our resident witch (Nico Minoru), Xavin drops out of the sky in the form of a handsome young man. But soon we see Xavin's true form: a super-Skrull from the planet Tarnax VII!

So, super-Skrulls are basically green, craggy-chinned aliens with the powers of each of the Fantastic Four, in addition to their natural shape-changing ability. In other words, all these aliens can turn rock solid, become invisible, stretch, and transform into flame. Pretty cool, eh? (Xavin, still in training, can use only a single power at a time.)

It turns out Xavin has arrived to marry Karolina! And . . . no one had told Karolina this news. You see, her parents had promised Karolina to Xavin's parents many years before, in exchange for starting a war with the planet that exiled the Dean family.

Having grown up as the child of two warlords, Xavin is unusually practical and forthright. When Karolina states that she'll never marry him—mostly because Xavin is a dude and Karolina only likes girls—Xavin simply and efficiently changes gender presentation to female. And off Xavin and Karolina go to Karolina's homeland to stop the war their parents created.

That could have easily been the end of a throwaway character, but both Xavin and Karolina return about ten issues later. Despite almost getting married, the pair failed in their mission to bring peace to their people. Now back with the Runaways, Xavin becomes a true member of the team, throwing themselves in the path of danger and protecting allies. Eventually Xavin becomes friends with people whom at first they merely tolerated.

Why refer to Xavin as *they* instead of *he*, as Xavin originally appeared, or as *she*, as Xavin appeared most often in the series? Because Xavin doesn't specifically identify as any particular gender, though they are usually female in appearance because that makes everyone in the Runaways more comfortable. They do state at one point that they're ill at ease at the thought of their girlfriend Karolina being completely dismissive of the potential for Xavin to present as male, which points to Xavin being fairly gender fluid.

It's good to see a character in a comic expressing this complexity. It's still rare in comics (especially mainstream superhero comics), outside of magical creatures or aliens such as the Skrulls. Comics certainly have a long way to go in presenting gender variance among human characters.

ESSENTIAL READING: In *Runaways: The Complete Collection* vols. 2 and 3 (Marvel, 2015), you can see Xavin's first appearances and how they integrate into the team.

ICON
OF THE
DECADE

The
2000ˢ

RAMONA FLOWERS	Superpowered and super-cool chick with seven deadly exes (and one giant hammer)	❝*Bread makes you fat.*❞
		Created by: Bryan Lee O'Malley
		First appearance: *Scott Pilgrim's Precious Little Life* #1 (Oni Press, 2004)

Ramona Flowers enters the world of Scott Pilgrim as the manic pixie dream girl he's always wanted—in fact, he literally dreams about her the day before they meet. Problem is, Scott's going through a little mental health crisis after a messy breakup and current rebound with a 17-year-old girl who worships him.

But enough of Scott (he's gotta be mentioned, though, because his name is on the cover). Ramona is the token American of the Toronto-based *Scott Pilgrim* series. Her hair color is ever changing, she wears platform shoes she got in England, and she rollerblades even in the Canadian winter. In other words, she's super cool and Scott is immediately infatuated with her. Ramona starts off the series with a maybe-boyfriend, but Scott doesn't let that stop him from hitting on her at a party (dude, stop being weird). Ramona seems to be okay with his strangeness, which is unfortunate because it presents a bad lesson. Then it turns out that the reason Ramona goes through Scott's head all the time is because she *literally* goes through his head. As a "ninja delivery girl," she uses his mind as a quickie subspace highway to deliver packages. So really, it's her fault that he's obsessed.

Ramona becomes charmed by Scott's nervousness, and the two start dating. Scott finds out that Ramona has a massive tea collection, as well as an equally massive collection of evil exes determined to fight Scott.

Okay, maybe not *massive*; more like a reasonable amount for a girl her age (the exes, that is; the tea is just too much). Ramona's evil ex-BFs range from a mystical anti-jock to a superstar actor to an omnipotent vegan to her former roommate. Among others.

But it's not just Scott who has exes to fight. Ramona, too, must face up against Scott's previous/concurrent girlfriend Knives Chau, and the two square off in an epic battle in the Toronto Reference Library. Added to that is Envy, Scott's powerful and super-rock-star ex, who forces Ramona to whip out her giant hammer during a fight.

Ramona is the epitome of the cool girl, but she's not terribly compelling, or really very nice. She seems to float through people's lives without exhibiting much passion for anything at all. Even though Scott is kind of obsessive and clingy, Ramona's not that great either, making fun of Scott's lameness whenever he's overly excited and telling him he smells after she gets annoyed. As the series progresses, we see Ramona start to grow up a little, eventually. She makes peace with her romantic history, and her feelings for Scott, after spending some time apart from him to regroup.

The *Scott Pilgrim* series was massively popular, much more so than most people expected a little indie Canadian comic would be. The stories were an affectionate nod to the west end of Toronto, and various landmarks became focal points, along with nods to the celebrities and artistic community who live there. Eventually Scott Pilgrim mania peaked when a feature film was released, with Mary Elizabeth Winstead in the role of Ramona. Soon girls at all the comics conventions were walking around with Ramona Flowers's iconic bag and chunky blue hair (she had other colors, but the blue seems to have caught on the most). It's funny to see a character who was just the girlfriend in a male-centric book get so much attention, becoming a persona fans could latch onto if only for the space of a con. Every girl wants to be a Ramona Flowers, but it doesn't seem like many guys wanted to be Scott Pilgrim.

CHAPTER

9

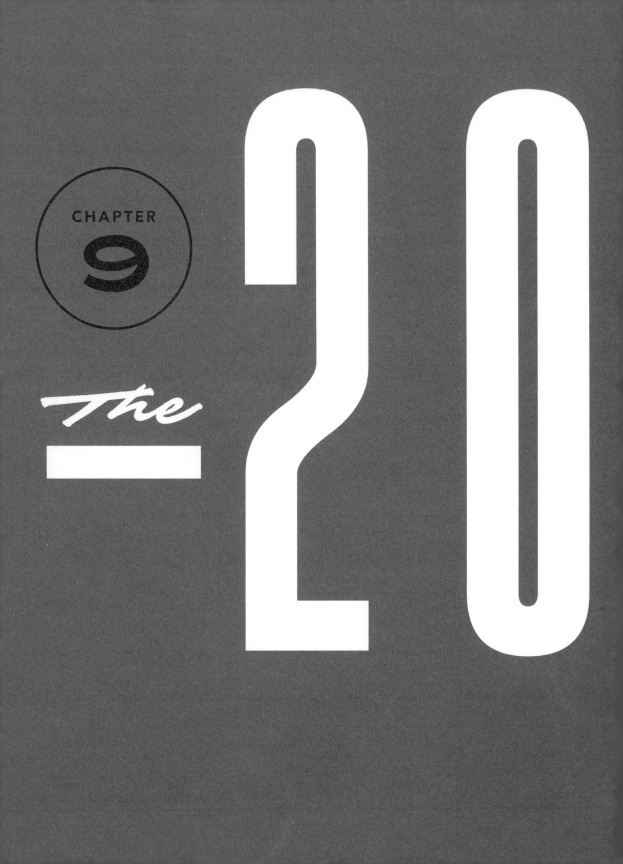

The 20

10s

DIGITAL AND DIVERSE

→

THE 2010s

In 2010 Raina Telgemeier, an up-and-coming cartoonist who'd had some success adapting Ann M. Martin's popular *Baby-Sitters Club* stories to comics form for Scholastic Books, released *Smile*, her first original full-length graphic novel. That book, and her follow-up graphic novels *Drama* and *Sisters*, was enormously popular. How popular? By 2015 Raina had spent three straight years on the *New York Times* best-seller list for graphic novels. Yet you won't find any of her books on the best-seller list from Diamond Comic Distributors, supplier of the continent's comic book shops. It's a clear signal of how the bookstore market, the educational market, and the rest of the market *outside* the comics shop/direct market are once again becoming healthy for comic book publishers.

And what about comics that are not sold in ink-on-paper form? Well, the popularity of webcomics has decreased significantly. With the rise of social media platforms fans no longer need to visit sites to connect with creators. Meanwhile, downloaded digital comics are becoming the electronic format of choice—primarily due to software apps like the ComiXology platform, which makes digital comics easy to read on portable devices.

Wherever they get their comics, this decade's readers—especially the younger generation—are clamoring for the pages to reflect the diversity they see in their lives, in their social media feeds, and in the mirror. Marvel and DC have made small steps, incorporating more characters of color, more transgender characters, and more queer characters into their comics. Buyers impatient with this slow—and unreliable—shift are turning instead to webcomics and small press publishers such as Northwest Press (a LGBT-focused publisher) and Iron Circus Comics (a sex-positive comics publisher, run by webcomic creator Spike Trotman). Sometimes readers find these publishers through Kickstarter, which has been a particularly helpful fundraising aid for webcomics creators such as Kaja Foglio (*Girl Genius*, with Phil Foglio), Emily Horne (*A Softer World*, with Joey Comeau), Michelle Czajkowski (*Ava's Demon*), Gisèle Lagacé, and Shouri (*Ménage à 3*, with David Lumsdon).

Today, some eighty years after comic books became a popular medium for storytelling, we have a multitude of women creating them. Women are drawing and writing and coloring and painting and editing and lettering, in a wide array of genres and formats, for fans who worship the characters and stories they develop. We have creators whose young-adult books skyrocket up best-seller lists (like Raina Telgemeier, Mariko Tamaki, Jillian Tamaki, Noelle Stevenson, Shannon Watters, Brooke A. Allen, and Hope Larson). We have women creating gritty crime dramas and suspense tales (Ming Doyle, *The Kitchen*; Becky Cloonan, *Southern Cross*), terrifying horror comics (Emily Carroll, *Through the Woods*; Marjorie Liu and Sana Takeda, *Monstress*), and long-running epics (Pia Guerra, *Y: The Last Man*; Fiona Staples, *Saga*; both written by Brian K Vaughan). Women are forming comics reading groups across the globe; female retailers are collaborating to recommend new and exciting reads. Women are prominent among the librarians who put graphic novels in readers' hands, and they are the journalists who analyze the impact and evolution of comics as an art form. Women who attend comic cons are convincing organizers to establish more stringent harassment policies and to bring on more female and nonbinary creators as panel speakers and guests.

Are we at a place where women who want to buy, read, create, and celebrate comics are treated equally, and not ignored or looked down on by male fans and industry decision-makers? Sadly, no. Not always, not yet. But it's clear that female readership is the strongest it's been since the 1940s. Graphic Policy, a website that examines the industry's demographics, currently estimates that over 53 percent of those who like comics are women (based on social media engagement).

In this history, we've shown that women are not storming the clubhouse built by male creators—we've been here, building the industry and fan community, from the very start. And we'll never fade away. ⚡

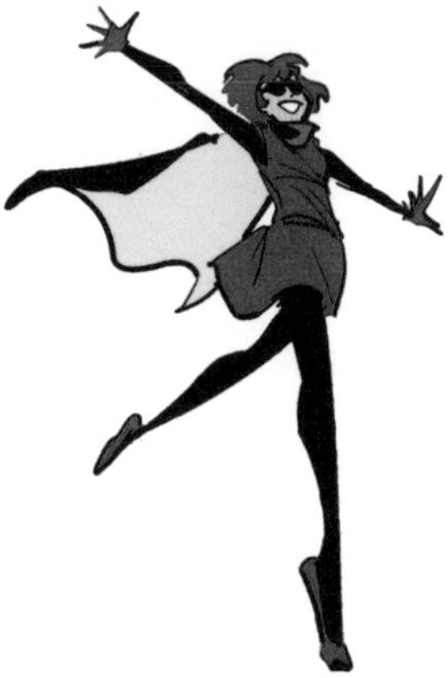

BANDETTE	Mysterious thief who liberates rich ne'er-do-wells from their possessions	***"This is called justice. Or larceny. One of the two."***
		Created by: Paul Tobin and Colleen Coover
		First appearance: *Bandette* #1 (Monkeybrain Comics, 2013)

Bandette mixes pop-art-stylized images with a type of French New Wave cinema aesthetic. And now you're yawning? Have you ever *watched* New Wave films? Then shush! This series is funny, quirky, and charming, with a bit of an alien nature to it.

Our teenaged heroine Bandette talks to herself constantly (or to little animals, or to her trusty steed, her ever-faithful chariot, her . . . scooter), and we soon learn that she's taken it as her self-appointed mission to liberate treasures from those who are profiting from immoral acts. The art is stunning, with lithe Bandette looking stylish in a bright red dress, gloves, and flats, plus a yellow-lined cape, over the traditional burglar's uniform of a black unitard and domino mask. Often she's shown in an environment of desaturated buildings, streets, and houses, which makes her pop off the page even more.

Bandette steals certain items purely for her own whims and pleasure, gravitating toward the literate and artistic rather than the merely shiny. But she also spreads her wealth generously. For example, she bestows priceless artifacts upon bakers who please her with their services. And our young and charismatic Parisian thief doesn't go it alone. At the touch of a button, Bandette's friends the "urchins" come to her aid, providing distractions (and firepower, when needed). Bandette is also a friend to those in (reluctant) need, switching from moralizing thief to superhero upon request from Inspector Belgique.

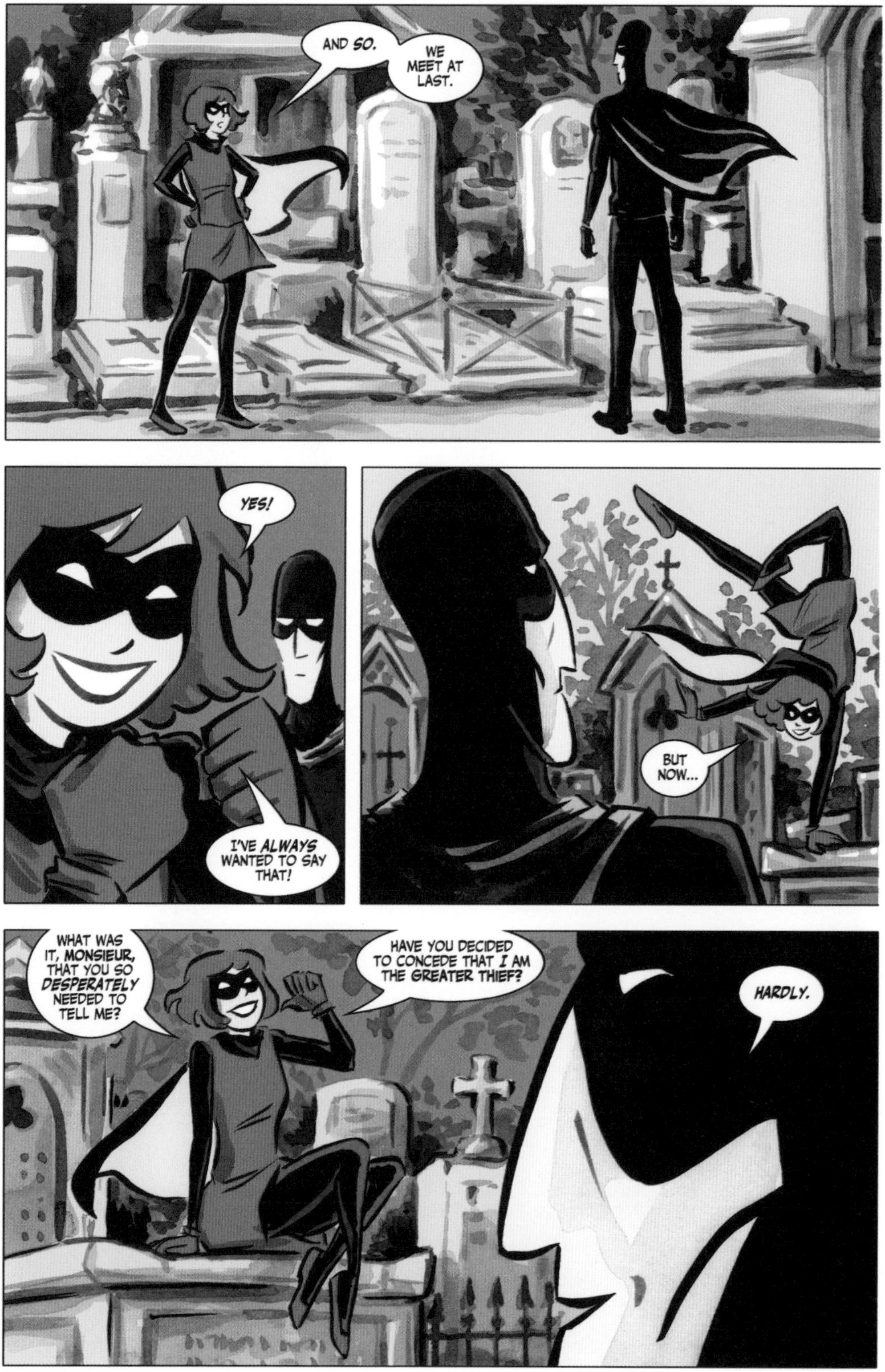
AND SO.
WE MEET AT LAST.
YES!
I'VE ALWAYS WANTED TO SAY THAT!
BUT NOW...
WHAT WAS IT, MONSIEUR, THAT YOU SO DESPERATELY NEEDED TO TELL ME?
HAVE YOU DECIDED TO CONCEDE THAT I AM THE GREATER THIEF?
HARDLY.

Bandette isn't necessarily a realistic superhero. Armed with the stolen skills of multiple martial artists, plus a can of (very nicely labeled) knockout gas, she seeks to disarm crooks effectively and quickly. Her counterpart is the equally dashing, though somewhat more sedately dressed, gentleman thief Monsieur (who by day is a rare-book and coin dealer).

Though he's Bandette's rival in the "morally good criminal" business, Monsieur also seeks to protect the young thief when Bandette's enemies decide she needs to be destroyed. Absinthe, the leader of the mysterious underground cabal called FINIS, sends his deadliest assassin, the golden-haired Matadori, to claim Bandette's head. Of course she and Matadori spend more time trading quips and compliments than blows and brutality, and thus Absinthe must raise the stakes after Matadori fails in her mission. At the same time, Bandette and Monsieur compete to find evidence against Absinthe, and to steal his greatest treasures, in order to humiliate him and get him locked him away for good.

Never fear; Bandette may be young but her methods are foolproof. From robbing mansions to saving lives, she does it all with grace and charm . . . and a certain amount of roguish flirtation. Even better, this comic gets away from the idea that superheroes have to be dark, brooding loners in order to be enjoyable or worthy of thought. *Bandette* is a truly beautiful comic-book success that also happens to be immensely readable by audiences of all ages.

In addition to being a fantastic comic, *Bandette* is also the harbinger of a new era of comics distribution. Distributed in digital issues first through Comixology by Monkeybrain, the issues were then collected in regular trades by Dark Horse.

ESSENTIAL READING: *Bandette Vol. 1: Presto!* (Dark Horse Comics, 2013) collects the first five issues.

BETH ROSS	Disrespected fast-food worker turned president of the United States	66 We let regular people die in order to dump more money on celebrities and billionaires. 99
		Created by: Mark Russell, Ben Caldwell, and Mark Morales
		First appearance: *Prez* #1 (DC Comics, 2015)

Before you say, "Wasn't *Prez* actually published in the 1970s?" . . . the answer is yeah, DC did produce a short-lived series about the "first teen president of the U.S.A." But today we have a new Prez, and her name is Beth Ross.

The gist is the same: a kid president somehow gets elected and embarks on a series of bizarre and vaguely political adventures. The connecting thread between the 1970s version and the current comic is that the first Prez becomes the vice president in the new series (though in this universe, he lost his presidential race as a teen). So Past Prez functions as Beth Ross's mentor and guide through the unique American political climate of 2036.

Let's get down to the business of this hip, new Prez. Winning small notoriety as a result of a viral video of her hair getting trapped in a corn dog fryer (and earning the moniker "Corn Dog Girl" as a result), Beth is quickly embroiled

in a presidential election. Various factions threaten to vote for her if they don't receive the luxuries they demand from the "legitimate" presidential nominees. This backfires, and purely by accident (the House of Representatives is not so bright) Beth ends up elected president.

This could have been a disaster if any other incidental celebrity had been voted in. But luckily, Beth Ross is a girl imbued with a strong work ethic and moral compass, imparted upon her by her father (who dies tragically of a curable disease shortly before she's elected). Her first act is to fill her cabinet with actual smart people, renowned in their respective fields but with absolutely no experience in politics. Next, she undertakes a formal apology tour to various nations on behalf of everything America has done to them.

Prez is cheeky, though the satire is a bit too wincingly cute and surface level. (It's funny to have America apologize because of the atrocities they've done! A robot is transgender and it's funny because it's a robot! Army militants visually disguise targets as turkeys to make them easier to kill!) The art is exceedingly well matched to the story, with an adorable and hyperexpressive aesthetic that lends itself to a manic, dystopian America ruled by people with a three-second attention span and prone to fits of childlike urges. Beth Ross is one of only a handful of global citizens who seem to have their heads on straight, despite the selfish madness that pervades their world.

The dystopian society of *Prez* is ruled by social media. Presidents appear on popular streaming video stars' webcasts. People in a financial crisis can earn money for medical cures and immigration fees through humiliating game shows that involve physical torture. If they fail at that, they can always go on welfare—as long as they don't mind becoming walking billboards for various corporations who sponsor the benefits system. Pharmaceutical developers manufacture cures and hold them hostage against promises of more power granted by governmental agencies. The heads of the world's largest corporations meet in shadow committees with their faces cybernetically distorted by corporate logos.

It's a clever conceit. Yet it's nice that *Prez* also lets us believe that in this dystopia, a morally straight person like Beth is able not only to become the most powerful head of state, but to excel at the job as well.

ESSENTIAL READING: Meet Beth Ross in *Prez*, vol. 1 (DC Comics, 2016).

BLAZE	Sweet-natured wannabe turned lead singer	66 *This is crazy dream-come-true stuff.* 99
		Created by: Kelly Thompson, Sophie Campbell, and M. Victoria Robado
		First appearance: *Jem and the Holograms* #3 (IDW Publishing, 2015)

Blaze is one of the first new characters introduced in the *Jem and the Holograms* comics series by IDW Publishing, based on the popular 1980s animated television show by Hasbro. The premise of the comic is the same as the cartoon: Jerrica Benton is the daughter of an inventor and lead singer of a struggling rock band. She discovers Synergy, an artificial intelligence built by her father, that helps her transform into the far more glamorous and vivacious singer Jem. Meanwhile her bandmates continue to be called by their real names (unfair). Together, the group pushes its way into the music biz, pitting themselves against their cutthroat and ruthless rivals the Misfits, led by the supremely cranky green-haired singer Pizzazz.

Blaze, aka Leah Dwyer, shows up when the Misfits' number one groupie Clash phones to ask for a favor. Because Blaze works for a catering company, she's enlisted to help Clash sabotage Jem's charity fundraiser (though Blaze thinks she's just helping out a friend with some much-needed work). At first, upon hearing about her friend's scheme, Blaze is horrified. But she quickly recovers and asks for a favor in return—meeting the Misfits. Hey if you've already done the crime, you may as well get something out of it.

Later in the series, after Pizzazz is in a car accident, Blaze replaces her as the Misfits' lead singer. Clash—Blaze's sometimes-friend, sometimes-rival—is insanely miffed not to have gotten the gig. Still, Clash is there for her when Blaze confesses her deep fear that the all-girl group will turn against her if they find out she's a transgender woman. Clash convinces Blaze to come out to them. Upon hearing the news the group proceeds to just yawn and ask if she's punctual. (Real-world lesson: no one should feel pressured by friends to come out.)

The comic really looks like a much more polished version of the (admittedly not-so-great) television program it was based on: bright, intense, fun, and

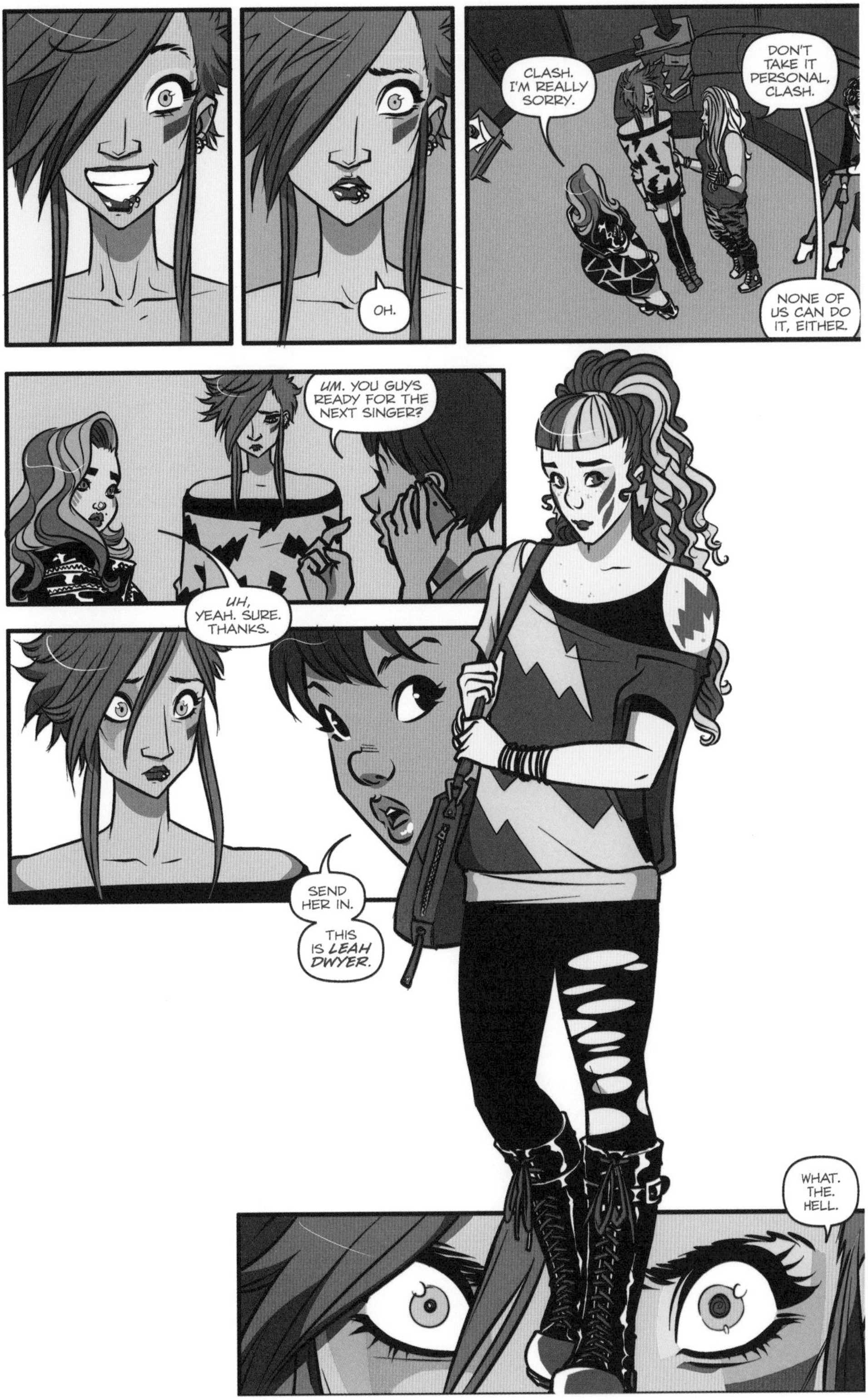
OH.
CLASH. I'M REALLY SORRY.
DON'T TAKE IT PERSONAL, CLASH.
NONE OF US CAN DO IT, EITHER.
UM. YOU GUYS READY FOR THE NEXT SINGER?
UH, YEAH. SURE. THANKS.
SEND HER IN.
THIS IS LEAH DWYER.
WHAT. THE. HELL.

candy colored, with vibrant hues mixing on each page thanks to color artist M. Victoria Robado. The characters, in appearance and personality, are all different. Sophie Campbell's drawing skill imbues them with distinct personal styles: punky, rockabilly, soft, glittery. Their behaviors range from sullen and shy to sporty, ambitious, and quiet. The dynamic feels more complex and authentic than the average team ensemble book.

With so few transgender characters in comics, Blaze is a noteworthy addition. And a character whose adventures focus on having fun and adventures (and singing!) is definitely worth seeking in the comics aisle.

Now if only Blaze would ditch the Misfits and join the Holograms instead…

ESSENTIAL READING: Check out *Jem and the Holograms, Volume 3: Dark Jem* (IDW, 2016), where you'll see much more of Blaze than in previous volumes.

BOLD RILEY	A beautiful princess who sets off on a whirlwind adventure of love and heroics	**66**She sported with the girls until hardly a single heart had been left unbroken within the city walls.**99**
		Created by: Leia Weathington
		First appearance: *The Legend of Bold Riley* (Northwest Press, 2012)

In the fictional region of Prakkalore, India, a royal family is blessed with three beautiful children, the youngest of whom is the princess Rilavashana SanParite.

Growing up, Rilavashana's favorite royal tutor taught her history and expanded her knowledge of the world outside her palace and town, dubbing her Riley because of his unfamiliarity with her language. At the age of sixteen, Riley grows restless, as many a young adventurer does in classic stories. She begins spending all her time engaging in risky activities, especially hunting dangerous game and breaking the hearts of the most beautiful women in the city. Riley's rakish attitude soon starts to embarrass her family, who encourage the princess to pursue her interests beyond the city walls. And so Bold Riley sets off, riding on a spirited horse and carrying a sword by her side.

Using her wits, Riley manages to survive her first adventure, tricking a group of demons determined to eat a flock of sheep and casually decapitating them all. In gratitude, the shepherd of the flock reveals himself to be a deity in disguise, granting Riley well-wishes and warm clothes for her journey. (What, cheap guy, no magic sword?)

Riley travels on and discovers various abandoned women in states of unhappiness; their husband (who is the same man) has become hard and cold. Luckily Riley has the cure for the coldness left behind by this Romeo. It's sex,

of course. Riley is a generous hero after all, but she also has a duty to pursue knowledge, and so she discovers the cause of the man's betrayals and eventually kills him. (It's okay, he was possessed.) Bold Riley returns to his wives to pass on the news . . . and sleep with them again. What? They're sad! Various other adventures pit Riley against supernatural evils, as well as beautiful and seductive women (some kind, some cannibals). Through each she triumphs and rides off on the wind, an adventurer whose feet are restless, her soul satisfied only by more travels.

The Legend of Bold Riley is a classic story of adventure and heroism, starring a young woman who uses her skills against the horrors and demons in her land. On the surface, it would be easy to dismiss the story as an attempt to tell a traditional male adventurer's tale in the guise of a female hero. But Riley often uses her sense of compassion to make her way through the world. She might go to bed with a bunch of women—of both this world and the supernatural—but she always checks in on them and their feelings afterward, not callously discarding them after they've served their purpose. These little distinctions speak to a depth of storytelling that isn't often seen in comics. The mix of swords and sorcery with compassion and tenderness makes Bold Riley a complex hero, and one who should be celebrated.

Published through Northwest Press, a small LGBT comics publisher, *The Legend of Bold Riley* didn't reach as wide an audience as it deserved. Like other small-press projects, the art duties are shared among a few artists. As a result, the story is broken into a series of small adventures, each with a different illustrator. This system works in a book where the adventures change from one issue to the next, and with a solid writer to bridge the gap, the whole thing feels mostly cohesive. Bold Riley is a heroine we need, and I hope we continue to see more of her travels in the years to come.

ESSENTIAL READING: Pick up *The Legend of Bold Riley* (Northwest Press, 2012), which contains all of her adventures to date.

CALLIE	A dreamy-eyed high school set designer learning about crushes and friendship	**"Things get a little crazy sometimes, but we keep it together."**
		Created by: Raina Telgemeier
		First appearance: *Drama* (Scholastic/Graphix, 2012)

In the young-adult graphic novel *Drama*, the spotlight is not on the stage, but on the stage crew. And specifically on the behind-the-curtain trials and tribulations of a middle school drama-class production of *Moon over Mississippi*. The star of the story is Callie, an energetic purple-haired girl eager to jump into opportunities—be they kissing her crush within minutes of finding out he's newly single or jumping on board to organize set design for the play.

But this is middle school, and of course nothing goes according to plan. Callie's crush gets back together with his ex, leaving her upset and confused. Adding fuel to the fire, her ideas for set design are scrapped as too unrealistic and expensive. Well, she is a dreamer!

Callie is also relentlessly hopeful, versatile in the face of change, and incredibly ambitious. *Drama* is likely one of the most cheerful and pleasant graphic novels I've ever read, showcasing the pleasure of new friendships. Callie's friendships are profoundly important to her. Her defining relationships in the story are with aspiring actor Justin, as they bond over their common crush, and Justin's brother Jesse, who quickly becomes Callie's new crush. The positive portrayal of a variety of straight and gay romances as natural (if nonetheless complicated!) earned *Drama* a Stonewall Award honor in 2013.

Drama's praise is well deserved. It's a simple story of a relatable experience (the all-too-familiar love triangle), with a twist ending, starring an engaging protagonist who perseveres against all difficulties, even when everything completely falls apart. Trust me, it's impossible to just read a few pages without sitting down and absorbing the whole story. Because you just need to know what happens to Callie and her friends!

Raina Telgemeier is the undisputed master of comics. Each of her books starts—and stays—on the *New York Times* best-seller list, taking up the majority of the spots for paperback graphic novels. Her comic-book adaptations of the classic teen drama series *The Baby-Sitters Club*, and her autobiographical memoirs *Smile* and *Sisters*, have cemented her reputation as the most important voice in modern comics, bridging the divide between YA literature and graphic novels. Raina shows that sometimes comics *are* for kids. And that makes them no less deserving of attention, praise, or honors.

ESSENTIAL READING: *Drama* (Scholastic, 2012).

DEATHFACE GINNY	Death's daughter in a mythical Old West, on a mission of revenge	66My name is Ginny. I am by rights and rearing the reaper of vengeance.99
		Created by: Kelly Sue Deconnick and Emma Ríos
		First appearance: *Pretty Deadly* #1 (Image Comics, 2013)

"Attend the song of Deathface Ginny, and how she came to be . . . " And what a ballad it is! Deathface Ginny, antihero of the fantasy Western series *Pretty Deadly*, is the literal daughter of Death, who fell in love with a mortal woman. A sort of folk hero, Ginny is said to have been raised by Death as a tool of vengeance for those wronged by "men who have sinned." But her personal mission revolves around hunting down her late mother's abusive husband, "the Mason Man." It was his tortuous imprisonment of Ginny's mother that drew Death to her in the first place.

Standing against Ginny is Death's other agent, Big Alice, a beautiful woman made of butterflies(!). And mixed into it all is a mysterious little girl who might be the savior of humankind, the destroyer of Death, or both.

Deathface Ginny is enigmatic, frightening, and utterly powerful. When she enters a scene, you can practically hear the sound leave the room, allowing you to focus on her cold eyes and scarred skin. Despite supernatural origins, she is a straightforward deadly enemy, who prefers to let her rifle or knife do the talking in matters of revenge. We know little about Ginny as a character, just the broad strokes of her life story. We don't know what books she likes to read, if she has thoughts on how to cook steak, what her favorite flowers are, or if she has any allergies.

And that's good. The less we know about Deathface Ginny, the more frightening she is. She's a perfect monster, but one who has no malice.

As a comics genre, Westerns have a bad rep. Mostly because, like romance comics, they've tended to be fairly formulaic and included, well, let's say *problematic* representations of some racial and gender identities. The stories tend to

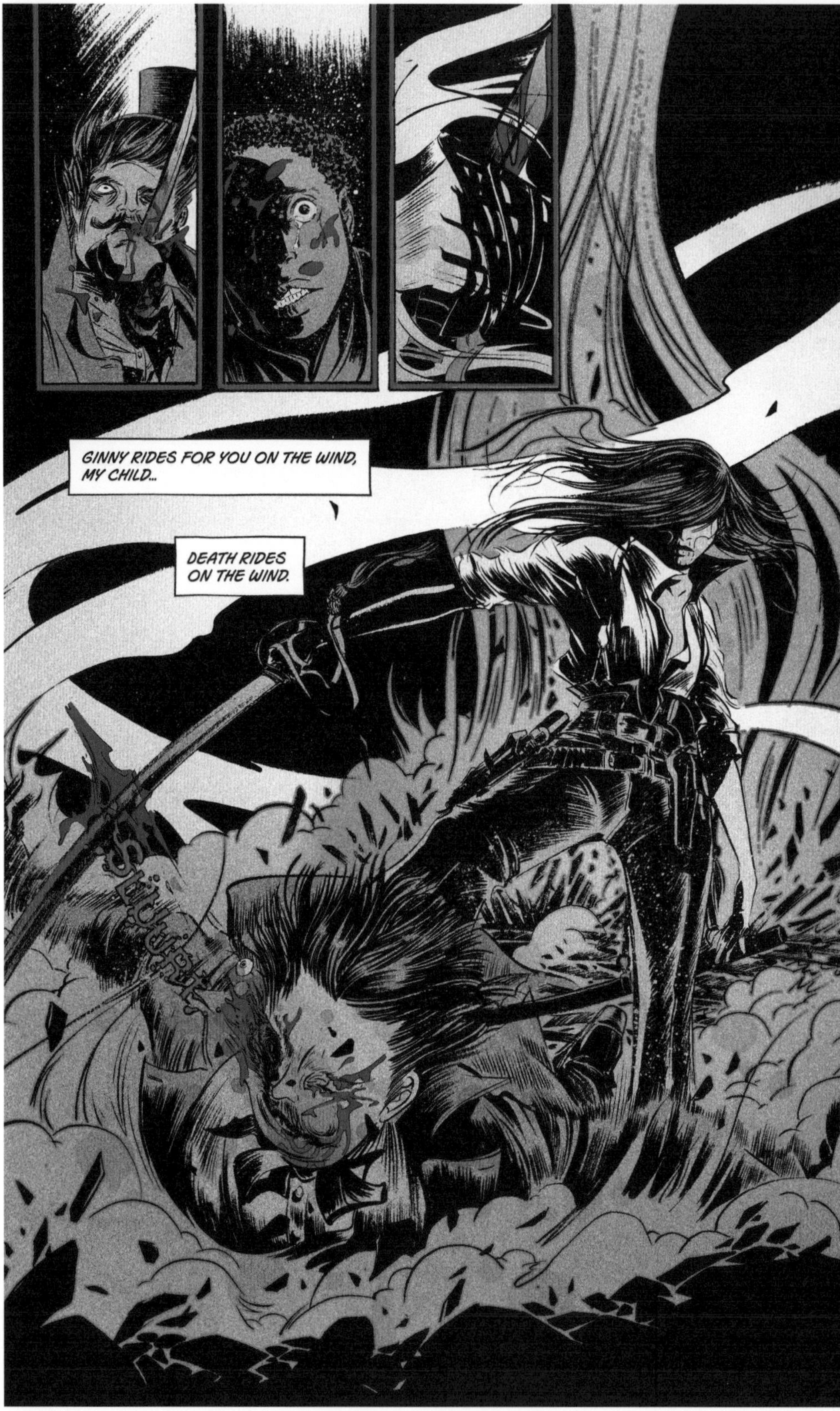
GINNY RIDES FOR YOU ON THE WIND, MY CHILD...
DEATH RIDES ON THE WIND.

be fairly colonialist and full of puffed-up male machismo. *Pretty Deadly* stands in opposition to those tropes, offering a revolving cast of female characters, all of whom are strong and, more important, distinct from one another. The comic hasn't yet branched off into indigenous representations, disappointingly. But the roles of black Americans in the Old West are well explored through several secondary characters who take the lead in the second arc of the series. In addition, *Pretty Deadly* successfully reinvents the Western by combining it with a genre that's particularly popular these days: supernatural fantasy. The result is a compelling story with a rich cast of characters, and despite being a story about Death and mortals, all the characters are surprisingly nuanced and not cookie-cutter evil in the least.

And the art! Lush and atmospheric, the imagery is paired with dialogue that's dreamy and expertly paced. *Pretty Deadly* is a gorgeous comic with mythic depths, and you probably should read it right now. You don't want Deathface Ginny wondering why you haven't.

ESSENTIAL READING: *Pretty Deadly, Volume 1: The Shrike* (Image Comics, 2014).

GWEN DYLAN	Sure she's a zombie, but she only eats brains *for good*	"Am I already shambling towards Brainless Zombie Town?"
		Created by: Chris Roberson, Mike Allred, and Laura Allred
		First appearance: *iZombie* #1 (DC Comics/Vertigo, 2010)

Gwen is your average modern girl. She hangs out at the local coffee shop. Her best friends are a stylish model with agoraphobia and a nerdy guy obsessed with D&D. She works hard at her night job and dreads the thought of possibly going back to school to finish earning her degree.

Yes, yes, she's also a zombie who eats brains. And, okay, her friends turn out to be a 1960s-era ghost and a shapeshifting were-terrier.

By its title, *iZombie* may sound like a "hipper than you can handle it" comic, but I swear Apple products don't come up once. In fact, Gwen is pretty much a Luddite, with no concept of how to use most types of technology. She's also a down-on-her-luck character. She's burdened with the self-chosen moral responsibility of solving the unresolved deaths of the corpses whose brains she must dig up and devour in order to maintain her own intelligence. (Uh, forgot to mention: her night job is digging graves at a cemetery.)

In many ways, especially at the beginning, the comic functions as a typical television "monster of the week" series, à la *Buffy the Vampire Slayer*, with touches of the vampire-ghost-werewolf roommate drama *Being Human* woven in. But beyond the monsters and the adventures, *iZombie* showcases one simple fact, time and time again: when you believe that you're unique and you stay isolated, you'll never have a chance to find others like you. As Gwen starts to leave her crypt and coffeehouse more often, she discovers that there *are* other creatures like her. Some call themselves "revenants," "mummies," or simply "smart zombies." But, of course, not all have the same moral sense as Gwen does.

In short order, Gwen finds herself in a Romeo-and-Juliet-style romance with the handsome and capable monster hunter Horatio, who eventually discovers her secret. Oh, and Horatio's ex-girlfriend, the love of his life? Was killed by a zombie. Like all good lovers, the pair manages to get through this bump in their relationship and work together to prevent the upcoming apocalypse. But Gwen is always front and center, the heroine of her own story. She's not infallible, but her worries and failures make her a character of some depth, spurring the series along at a rapid pace that's always enjoyable.

Filled with pop culture references, *iZombie* is a fun and clever take on the traditional supernatural mystery comic. Its epic mythology is revealed slowly as the series progresses, so the reader never feels burdened by the weight of too much happening at once. Even when multiple superteams of bionic zombies, poltergeists, and Frankensteins (I know, Frankenstein was the doctor's name; fine, they're golems) are introduced, the series keeps its pace without being rushed.

As for the art? Mike Allred and Laura Allred—probably best known for the *Madman* series—are, as always, a fantastic team. And guest artists on standalone stories, such as J. Bone and Gilbert Hernandez, add to *iZombie*'s appeal. The colors and designs are retro inspired, best exemplified by Gwen's best friend, the ghost Ellie, with her perfectly coiffed hair and rotating selection of minidresses. The visual style of the series perfectly matches the lighthearted tone of the melodrama.

ESSENTIAL READING: *iZombie Omnibus* (DC Comics, 2015) is a massive collection with all the stories you might want to read.

KATH, RAVEN, AND ANGIE

Three mobster queens taking their rightful place at the top of the food chain	*"I don't need you to f***in' save me."*
	Created by: Ollie Masters, Ming Doyle, and Jordie Bellaire
	First appearance: *The Kitchen* #1 (DC Comics/Vertigo, 2015)

The three women who make up the protagonists of *The Kitchen* are equally distinct, yet their story is impossible to tell by focusing on just one of them. Each is a gangster's wife in the Hell's Kitchen neighborhood of 1970s New York City. When their husbands are sent to jail, the women see the industry their men built begins to crumble, and so they step in to make things right. That involves a lot of shooting and kicking people. This is a crime drama, not a redemption story.

Kath and Raven are sisters who grew up poor and Irish. Kath is aggressively practical; when her husband is arrested, she instantly springs into action to collect on his debts owed by the lowlifes that work for him. She insists that her fellow mob wives begin collecting as well, to preserve the crime legacy until their

husbands return. That's not enough for Kath, though, and she decides to follow in her crime-boss father's footsteps and run the business with Raven. She's the boss of her crew, until her soft side lets her become too attached to a young prostitute, jeopardizing the business. Meanwhile, Raven quickly grows from following Kath's lead to running the organization, making hidden deals with other mob bosses without informing her partners.

Angie is the wildcard, transforming from mild mannered to vicious in a manner of moments. She's creative in her ways, too, picking up torture methods quickly from Kath and Raven's psychotic brother Tommy.

Then their boys get out early, eager to pick the business back up, but with one problem . . . the girls got used to driving things and have no use for them. They're making deals, racking up body counts, and becoming the toughest mob bosses the city has ever seen.

This series is gorgeous. Not only are the covers by

Becky Cloonan super iconic, but the masterful rough and tough art of these beautiful women by Ming Doyle makes for an amazingly visual crime noir. The fashions and aesthetics of the era are vividly rendered, and the colors by Jordie Bellaire are intense when needed, but also capture all the muted, earthy tones of seventies style.

The Kitchen is a gritty, pulpy crime drama with violence, betrayal, and gorgeous clothes, full of girls being awful humans. What's not to love?

ESSENTIAL READING: *The Kitchen* (Vertigo, 2015) is a self-contained series, so if you pick up the trade collection you'll have the full story.

KEEGAN	A tough and cool runaway with the knowledge of an ancient volcano goddess	66 *Chaos and order moves through our blood, flowing like lava, through our veins.* 99
		Created by: Johnnie Christmas and Tamra Bonvillain
		First appearance: *Island* #7 (Image Comics, 2016)

Keegan is the descendant of mystical Fire Goddesses, a tough no-nonsense woman who takes what she wants and is just looking to survive.

In the world of "Firebug," a serialized story appearing in the Image Comics anthology *Island*, the planet's fate is determined by a line of volcano goddesses who have, over time, retreated farther and farther into their mountain. In the present day, there are only two groups left that believe in them: the Cult of the Goddess and the Third Wave. The Cult is a group of powerful women who worship the concept of the goddess as the force of creation; they have presence in the police force, granting them powerful status. By contrast, the Third Wave is an anarchist splinter group that believes the goddess exists in a physical form and is being held captive by the Cult.

And Keegan? She's both a runaway from the Cult and the most recent Fire Goddess descendant. She comes to the Third Wave with the news that she knows where the goddess is. Keegan quickly becomes involved in a love triangle between Third Wave leader Aria and Aria's boyfriend Griffin, a pink-haired punk with an unexpected romantic side that leads him to be a compulsive flower thief.

Keegan is a very cool and commanding presence, rocking oversized aviator sunglasses and an attitude against Aria. For her part, Aria tolerates Keegan—despite her stealing Aria's boyfriend—because of the knowledge that Keegan has (though no one knows Keegan's parentage until later).

The group discovers that the Fire Goddess is very much alive, though far from being a goddess of wisdom, she is impetuous, demanding, and quick to

anger. She lives a life full of luxury (and wine) and has no care for the lives of her would-be rescuers, instantly decimating the first Third Wavers she meets when they fail to reveal where her daughter is (and for not fetching her wine and snacks quickly enough). When a panicked Griffin reflexively shoots and kills the goddess, the legacy of her divine powers are bestowed upon Keegan.

The first chapter of the story tells you just enough to give a sense of Keegan's world. The characters are well drawn and unique, and the artwork is phenomenal. Johnnie Christmas's inks of beautiful women have style and form, but the women's fashions are modern, and their weight lies on their bones as it would in real life. In this story, you see women who don't look like pinup models, though they're beautiful; they are women who choose fashion and clothing for themselves, be it for practicality, beauty, or fun. And not enough good can be said about Tamra Bonvillain's colors. The vividness of the volcano goddesses and their power gives the comic an intense warmth that can almost be felt radiating off the page.

ESSENTIAL READING: The "Firebug" stories appear serially in issues of *Island*, starting with no. 7 (Image Comics, 2016).

MAIKA HALFWOLF	A mysterious magical woman with a thirst for blood and vengeance	❝That which frightens my enemies is my friend.❞
		Created by: Marjorie Liu and Sana Takeda
		First appearance: *Monstress* #1 (Image Comics, 2015)

Monstress is a series that follows Maika Halfwolf, a 17-year-old former slave seeking answers to why her people are being imprisoned and tortured . . . and how she came to have powers that drive her with an insatiable hunger for living flesh.

Maika is a member of the magical creature-human hybrid society called the Arcanics, though she mostly passes as human. Even though a truce has been declared between them and humans, Arcanics are considered fair game for torture and murder by a ruling caste of warrior witch nuns. Infiltrating the stronghold where terrible experiments are taking place on her people, Maika kills Yvette, a

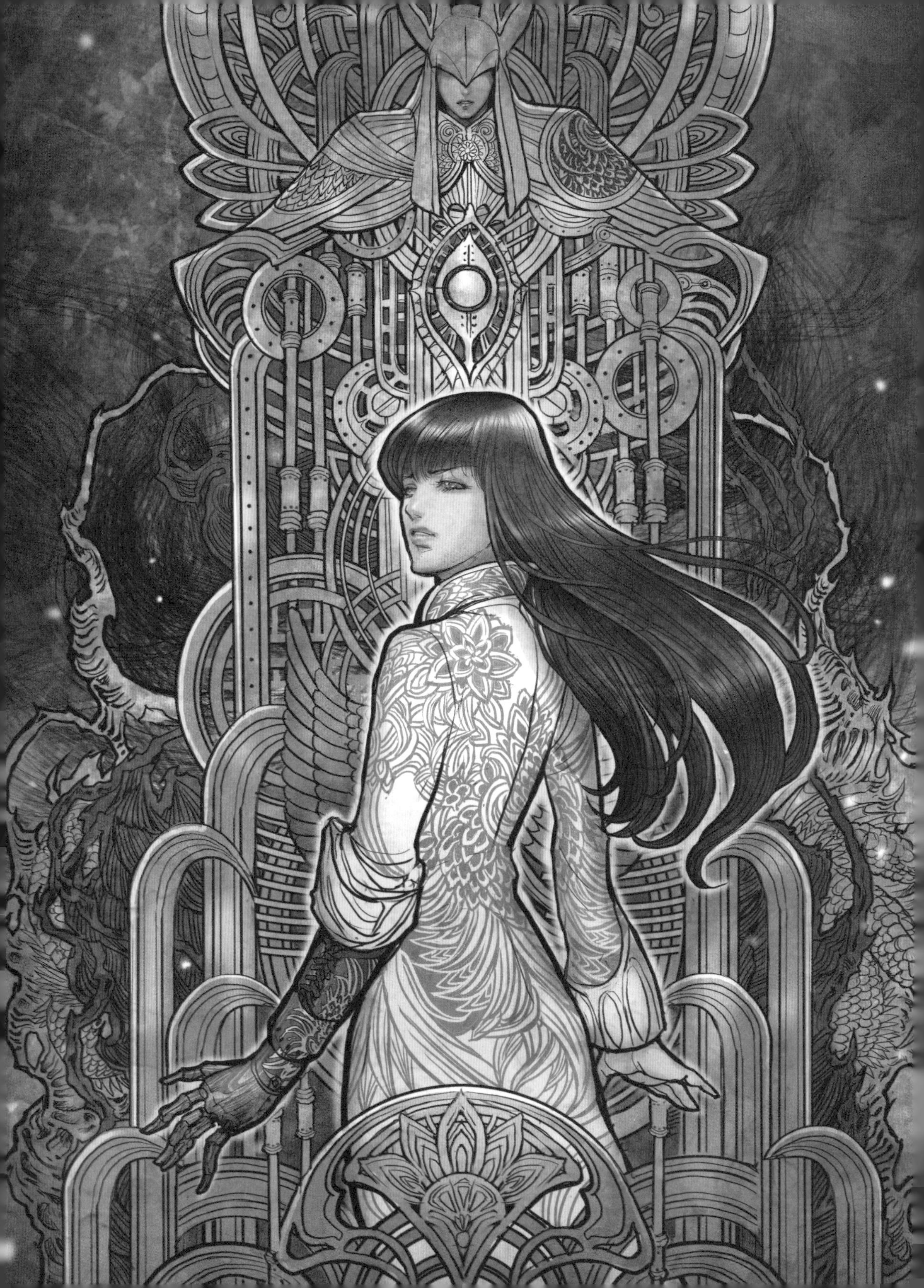

mysterious woman who seems to know more about Maika's history and heritage than Maika does; on her way out, Maika steals a mystical artifact.

She also liberates the prisoners and takes two along: an adorable fox-looking little girl named Kippa and an unnamed little boy. They're shortly joined by Ren, a cat with two tails who seems to have an uncanny knowledge of the history of the world they live in. Together the group journeys back to the homeland of the Arcanics, and while traveling they discover the full extent of Maika's terrible powers, rooted in an otherworldly evil known as Monstrum.

Monstress shows its characters no mercy. The ruling humans are vicious and brutal, exterminating their own people to publicly portray the Arcanic as bloodthirsty and savage. It's the humans, however, who are attempting to distill medicines called Lilium from the blood, organs, and flesh of captured Arcanics.

Though it sounds like a fairly standard adventure-fantasy novel, *Monstress* is much more epic in scope than most comics. It crosses genres fluidly and is more of a horror comic than you might expect. I mean, yeah, there are unicorns, but they disembowel and kill people with their horns. And sure, there are adorable talking cats, who slit the throats of their enemies with their claws. Moreover, *Monstress* is frightening in its depictions of that which is usually considered taboo even in horror stories: the maiming and torture of children. And for good reason; that's a hard subject to depict without seeming to be exploitative and vulgar for the sake of shock.

But *Monstress* goes there, showcasing characters who are captured and experimented on as children and showing the real damage they've suffered. That these characters are only partly human doesn't make it any easier to watch their pain, as Sana Takeda draws them with both human vulnerability and animal innocence. The little boy that joins their journey early on, for example, is never given a name because he barely lasts one issue. After he has his hands amputated by the cruel experimenters, his luck doesn't get much better when he joins forces with Maika, who in a fit of sudden bloodlust seemingly devours him.

Despite the savagery of the comic, the art is soft and beautiful. Takeda handles both the line art, which is intrinsically detailed, and the muted, painted watercolors. It's a surprisingly whimsical look for a story that is truly terrifying.

ESSENTIAL READING: The first trade collection will introduce you to this world, so pick up *Monstress* vol. 1 (Image Comics, 2016).

PENNY ROLLE	Incarcerated prisoner who won't stand down to anyone	"Why do folks gotta say what I am, mother? Ain't it enough to know who I am?"
		Created by: Kelly Sue DeConnick and Valentine De Landro
		First appearance: *Bitch Planet* #1 (Image Comics, 2014)

I could write about any of the cast of *Bitch Planet*, because by and large they're all interesting, complex, female characters, whether they're the villains or the heroes. The heroes in this instance are a group of mostly black women on a prison planet. The setting is a dystopian future world, where infractions against form and proper behavior are met with strict disciplinary measures. The hero of the series is a fighter and professional athlete named Kamau Kogo, but all of the female inmates have strong roles, and each gets her own spotlight issues.

We're introduced to Penny Rolle as comic relief. Her first appearance has her refusing to wear a too-small jumpsuit, claiming it would only fit one breast at most, and clocking a guard who tries to restrain her. We learn in her solo story, a few issues later (drawn by Robert Wilson IV), that she was just 22 years old at the time of her incarceration.

Raised by her grandmother, Penny was a happy, playful child, despite her mother being a reactionary rebel who wasn't content to play the good compliant wife. At age 8, Penny is taken to be a ward of the state and allowed only infrequent visits to her grandma, who is mocked for her large size by the kids at Penny's school. Penny isn't exactly weak, and she stands up for her grandma—sometimes via physical altercations. This isn't pleasing to the head of the school, who lectures and disciplines Penny for her infractions. But Penny's anger is only suppressed, not eliminated. Eventually she loses control after hearing a series of self-hating remarks by women about their weight and racist rants about Penny's size from some white dudes.

Arrested and delivered to Bitch Planet, Penny is sent to therapy to visualize her ideal sense of self so that treatment can help her reach something approximating this ideal. The guards are given a rude surprise when her self-image ends up being exactly who she is now.

Bitch Planet isn't afraid to shy away from either nonglamorous female nudity or themes of extreme violence and pain. It's a book that examines the humanity in the backstories of each of the inmates, most of whom are victims of an oppressive and stringent system. The gist of the plot is that the inmates are chosen to put together a sports team—for an indeterminate sport somewhat similar to rugby—to battle against professional athletes. The match is intended to be a ratings winner, but the girls have other ideas. With most of the ruling class in attendance, they plan to win the competition and sabotage the ship it's held on.

But the ruling class has other plans, too. They're hoping to send a message of their own—by killing the prisoners while they're competing, to encourage obedience and pliancy among women. As the drama unfolds, Penny works primarily as the muscle of the group, protecting smaller girls from being crushed in the melee so they can run the ball over to the end goal (or something like that . . . the sports references weren't jiving too well for me).

A character who doesn't look like most women in media, and who's comfortable in her own skin, is an important and effective symbol. And Penny is a character worth exploring even beyond what her appearance represents. She's a hero who manages to find joy and humor in situations that are nothing short of intolerable.

ESSENTIAL READING: *Bitch Planet Volume 1: Extraordinary Machine* (Image Comics, 2015) takes you into the world of Bitch Planet and Penny Rolle's past.

MS. MARVEL (KAMALA KHAN)

Young teenager torn between obeying her parents and being a superhero

"When you decide not to be afraid, you can find friends in super unexpected places."

Created by: G. Willow Wilson, Adrian Alphona, and Ian Herring

First appearance: *Ms. Marvel* #1 (Marvel Comics, 2014)

Most legacy characters (i.e., new characters who take the name of a previous superhero) tend to be fairly unremarkable and quick to vanish. One exception has been the new Ms. Marvel. Kamala Khan took this superhero moniker after Carol Danvers (see page 124) became a legacy character herself. Carol took the name Captain Marvel from her predecessors Mar-Vell (I know, I know, that name kills me too) and Monica Rambeau. It's okay, though; Carol eventually gives Kamala the thumbs-up to call herself Ms. Marvel.

The new Ms. Marvel got lots of attention from the news media—by which I mean the real-world news media, not the *Daily Bugle*—because she's a Muslim Pakistani American written by a Muslim woman. Her book is also one of the best-drawn and best-colored comics on the market. Illustrator Adrian Alphona provides detailed line work and incredibly expressive characters that pair well with colorist Ian Herring's subtle hues. It's no wonder that *Ms. Marvel* is frequently a best-selling title.

Along those lines, it's interesting to note that *Ms. Marvel* tends not to be the top seller of single issues. But the first trade collection of her stories turned out to be the best-selling trade in comics the month it debuted. And so far, each subsequent volume has broken the top 5 in sales the month it premiered. People are buying her books in droves, but readers are not necessarily the comic-book-store crowd. *Ms. Marvel* is a signifier, like the books of Raina Telgemeier (see page 218), of a new trend of marketplace success for comics sold in bookstores and other sales outlets outside the comic-book store.

So who is this new Ms. Marvel? Kamala Khan is a normal bubbly teenager obsessed with the Avengers, to the point that she writes fanfiction (nothing smutty) about them having adventures and being friends. Frustrated with her parents' strict rules, and feeling outcast at her mostly white school, one day Kamala sneaks out of her house to go to a mixed-gender party. But she finds something even more mysterious than the opposite sex—she somehow gets enveloped in a transformative fog, and after a hallucination of Captain Marvel singing to her in Urdu, she wakes up with superpowers. Suddenly Kamala can become whoever she wants to be, manipulating her body's form at will. She becomes blonde and popular, taking on a form somewhere between Carol Danvers and Zoe the mean rich girl from school. Eventually, Kamala is convinced by her friend to be herself. And to start fighting crime. She does a great job at it, combining her natural compassion with a drive to being the best superhero there is. She even gets to meet her heroes and squee over them!

Kamala has superpowers, but she also has super heart, and her adventures are always tempered by her sense of morality and justice. She's an iconic superhero in the old school way; balancing her duties as a daughter and teenage student are equally important to her as saving the world.

Ms. Marvel is a fangirl turned superheroine. She showcases the power of fans who want to see themselves represented on the page. If Kamala Khan signifies the future of the superhero genre in particular, and the comics medium as a whole, then I think we can all look forward enthusiastically to the future.

And who knows, maybe one day we'll see Kamala move on and take up the Captain Marvel name herself.

OH IT'S YOU AGAIN

YOU SAUCY NUISANCE

INDEX

A

A-1 Comics, 53
Aardvark-Vanaheim, 101
Abel, Jessica, 157, 183
Able, Jack, 54
abortion, 143
Abortion Eve, 101
Absinthe, 212
Ackerman, Forrest J., 92
Action Comics, 13, 70, 71
actresses, 28–29, 39–40, 81
Adams, Ann, 64
Addams, Wednesday, 185
Adolescent Radioactive Black Belt Hamsters, 127
advice columns, 109–10
AIDS, 140
Alascia, Vince, 90
Alias, 191, 194–95
aliens, 14–17, 27, 44, 77, 83–84, 92–95, 113–16, 116–17, 123, 124, 125, 148, 150, 202–3, 230, 231
Allen, Brooke A., 209
Allen, Gale, 31–32
Allred, Laura, 221, 222
Allred, Mike, 221, 222
All Star Comics, 46
Alpha Flight, 124
Alphona, Adrian, 202, 230, 231
Amazing-Man Comics, 14
American Comics Group, 59
American Woman, 158–59
Amethyst: Princess of Gemworld, 157
Amphibianwoman, 120
anarchists, 161–62, 224
Anderson, Murphy, 26
Angel, 135
Angie, 223–24
Annabelle, 184–85
Antarctic Press, 158
Antje, 139
Ant-Man, 75, 194
Apex Novelties, 75
Aquaman, 74
Arcanics, 225, 227
Archie Comics, 33, 34, 51, 58, 61, 81, 82, 164, 100
Aria, 224
Artbabe, 157
Ashtoreth, 132
Asian comics, 100, 116–18, 139
Astro Boy, 132
Atwood, Margaret, 119, 172
Aurora, Bambi, 94
Austin, Terry, 135
Ava's Demon, 209
The Avengers, 100, 124, 176, 194, 231
Avery, Tex, 132
A Wrinkle in Time, 84

B

Baby-Sitters Club, 208, 219
Ball, Bunny, 59, 81–83
Bandette, 210–12
Barbarella, 77–79

Baron, Mike, 139
Barreaux, Adolphe, 17
Basset, Bogart, 132
Batgirl, 75, 96–97
Batman, 15, 26, 74
The Battle for Independents, 178
Batwoman, 96
Beast, 52, 135
Beaton, Kate, 198
Beatty, Terry, 143, 166
Beauty and the Beast, 165, 184
Bechdel, Alison, 129, 183, 233
Bechdel Test, 30, 129
Beck, Joel, 75
Being Human, 222
Bell, Julie, 157
Bellaire, Jordie, 223
Bell Features, 44
Bell Syndicate, 37
Bendis, Brian Michael, 191
Benton, Jerrica, 214
Benulis, Bill, 54
Berger, Karen, 157
Bernbaum, Sheila Fay (Sunflower), 147–49
Bertinelli, Helena, 97
Berube, Elizabeth Safian, 74, 101
Betty, 82, 100
Big Alice, 219
Big Ethel, 61
The Big Machine, 145
Bikini Luv, 79–81
Binder, Otto, 70
Bitchy Bitch, 9, 160–61
Bitch Planet, 156, 228
Black Cat, 28–30
black comics, 13, 19, 20–21, 100, 101, 102–3, 109–10, 118–119, 132–33, 170–72, 219–221, 228
Black Fury, 37, 39
Black Lightning, 119
Black Phantom, 52–53
Black Widow, 35
Blade, 182
Blaire, Allison (Dazzler), 129, 135–37
Blaisdel, Tex, 76
Blake, Betty, 13
Blaze, 214–16
Blondie, 13
Blue Bolt, 27
Blue Circle Comics, 30–31, 36
Bogart, Humphrey, 132
Boiler, David, 166
Bolle, Frank, 52
Bone, 166, 197
Bone, J., 222
Bonvillain, Tamra, 224
Bowie, David, 138
Bradbury, Jack, 59
Bragg, Stan, 76
Breeden, Jennie, 183
Bridwell, Ed Nelson, 76
Brigman, June, 129, 157
Brimstone, 131
Broadway Babes, 59

Brown, Torchy, 13, 20–21
Buell, Marjorie Henderson, 22
Buffy the Vampire Slayer, 164, 222
Bugs Bunny, 132
Bunny, 81
Buscema, John, 123
Butch, Bitchy, 121, 160–61
Byrne, John, 130, 135

C

Cage, Luke, 119, 134, 176, 194, 195
Cain, Cassandra, 97
Caldwell, Ben, 212
California Comics, 118
Callie, 218–19
Campbell, April, 129
Campbell, Sophia, 214, 216
Canada, 27, 44–45, 119–21, 185–86, 198–99, 204–205
Candy, Nick, 39
Captain America, 133, 194
Captain Flash, 67, 68
Captain Huey, 133
Captain Marvel, 27, 123, 124, 230, 231
Captain Saracen, 32
Caraway, Hattie, 232
Career Girl Romances, 90
Carroll, Emily, 209
Carter, Linda, 86
cartoons, 23, 47, 63, 68, 71, 79, 182, 214
Casper the Friendly Ghost, 68–69
Castle, Frank, 143
Castle Waiting, 157, 164–66
The Cat, 74
Cathy, 161
Catwoman, 94
censorship, *see* Comics Code Authority
Century, Penny, 141
Chandler, Laura, 105–107, 185
Charlton Comics, 51, 79, 85, 86, 89, 90, 106
Charmaigne, 109
Chascarillo, Maggie, 141–43
Chastel, Désirée (DiDi), 185–86
Chesty, Chester, 112
Chicanos, 188
children's comics, 15, 22–23, 68–69, 95, 107–109, 173–74
Chili, 82
Chin, Foo Swee, 184, 185
Chito, 52
Christmas, Johnnie, 224, 225
Chubby, 34
Cinderella, 184
Circus Girl, 27, 44
Claremont, Chris, 135
Clark, Dr. Brian, 62–63
Clark, Lewis, 133
Clash, 214
Classics Illustrated, 51
The Claw, 67–68

Cleopatra, 121–22
Clint the Hamster Triumphant, 127
Cloonan, Becky, 209, 224
Colan, Gene, 123
Colletta, Vince, 62, 85, 89
Collins, Katherine, 101
Collins, Max Allan, 143
Comeau, Joey, 209
comedy comics, 27, 55, 74, 75, 77, 79–81, 100, 118–19, 132–33, 149–51, 175–76, 183, 185–86
The Comic Buyer's Guide, 128
Comico, 139
comics, history of, 8–9; independent, 83, 101, 107, 108, 128–29, 172, 183
Comics Code Authority, 50–51, 64, 75, 76, 86, 101, 121
comic strips, 12, 20, 44, 86, 102–103, 185, 198
ComiXology, 208, 212
Commandette, 44
communists, 81
Compos, Maritza, 183
Conan the Barbarian, 129
Connell, Del, 110
Conner, Amanda, 34
Conway, Carla, 123
Conway, Gerry, 123
Coover, Colleen, 195, 196, 210
Corsetto, Danielle, 190
cosplay, 13, 94, 129
Cothran, John David, 121
counterculture comix, 75, 101, 104, 113, 119, 169, 183
Courtney Crumrin, 184
Crane, Betsy, 85–86
Crespi, Susan, 157
Cridland, Charles, 27
crime fighters, 43, 96–97, 130–31, 132–33, 230–31. See also detectives
Crime Smashers, 19, 55, 56
Crumb, Robert, 75
Crypt-Keeper, 63
Cult of the Goddess, 224
Culture Publications, 15, 17, 19
Cundy, Simone, 174–75
Cutey Bunny, 132–33
Cutie Honey, 132
Cyblade/Shi, 178
cyborgs, 163
Czajkowski, Michelle, 209

D

Daffy Damsels, 59
Daffy Dotty, 59
Dagan, 116
D'Agostino, Jon, 79
Danvers, Carol (Ms. Marvel), 100, 123–24, 194, 230, 231
Daredevil, 134
Dark Horse Comics, 170, 173, 186, 212

The Dark Knight Returns, 172
Dark Mansion of Forbidden Love, 105, 106, 107
Darkseid, 131
Dark Shadows, 106
Daw, Diana, 13
Dawn, 94
Dazzler, 129, 135–37
DC Comics, 12, 19, 27, 44, 47, 51, 64, 70, 74, 75, 76, 86, 96, 97, 100–101, 105, 106, 109, 116, 119, 129, 130, 156–57, 161–62, 163, 174, 182, 209, 212, 221, 223
Deadpool, 176
Dean, Karolina, 202
Deathface Ginny, 219–221
DeCarlo, Dan, 57, 58
DeConnick, Kelly Sue, 79, 219, 228
de Guzman, Maria (The Jaguar), 163–64
De Landro, Valentine, 228
Delay, Harold, 36–37
Dell, Watt, 15–17
Dell Comics, 27, 51, 102, 103
DeMatteis, J. M., 147
Denham, Brian, 158
Dennis the Menace, 22
Detective Amos, 134
Detective Comics, Inc., *see* DC Comics
detectives, 12, 17–19, 31, 44–45, 54–56, 76–77, 90–92, 94, 100, 123–24, 133–35, 143–45, 176, 178–79, 188–95, 230–31
Diamond Comic Distributors, 208
DiDi, 185–86
Dingle, Pat, 27
Dirge, Roman, 184
Dirty Plotte, 157
A Distant Soil, 129
Ditko, Steve, 175
Divas, Dames & Daredevils, 15, 36, 37
DiZuniga, Tony, 105
Dizzy Dames, 59, 61
Doctor Doom, 135, 176
dolls, 184–85
dominatrix, 47
Dominguez, Ray, 141
Donenfield, Harry, 19
Doran, Colleen, 129
Dorscheid, Les, 139
Doucet, Julie, 157
Douglas, Myrtle, 13
Dowling, Lea, 129
Down, Lucius, 197
Doyle, Cynthia, 86
Doyle, Ming, 209, 223, 224
Draculina, 94
Dragonella, 83–84
dragons, 197
Drake, Marla (Black Fury), 37, 39
Drama, 208, 218
Drawn & Quarterly, 157

Dr. Cruel, 139
Dr. Pangea, 200–201
Dr. Ruiz, 163
Duffy, Jo, 101
Dumb Bunny, 77
Dwyer, Leah (Blaze), 214–16
Dykes to Watch Out For, 129
Dylan, Gwen, 221–22
Dynamite Damsels, 101, 104, 105
dystopias, 9, 159, 170–72, 212–15

E

Eastman, Kevin, 128
East Village Other, 75
EC Comics, 50, 51, 63–64, 83, 122, 185
Eclipse Comics, 138, 143, 145
Eisman, Hy, 81
Eisner, Will, 132
Eisner Award, 164, 166
Elfquest, 101, 107, 157, 166
Empowered, 186–88
The Enchantress, 135
Englehart, Steve, 109, 110
Enigma, 157
Envy, 205
Epic Comics, 147, 157
Eros Comix, 195
Esmerelda, 82
Eve, 64
Evilisha, 76
Evily, 94
Ewins, Brett, 145

F

Faerie Star, 121
fairy-tale comics, 164–66
fan culture, 9, 13, 75, 94, 129, 182–83, 209
Fantagraphic Books, 129, 141, 157, 160
FAN-tastic, 132
Fantastic Four, 202
fantasy comics, 9, 36–37, 83–84, 107–9, 121–23, 147–49, 197–98, 219–21, 225–27
Fantasy Quarterly, 107
Fantomah, 14, 35
Farrar, Rita (Señorita Rio), 39–40
fashion, 20, 34, 37, 82, 88, 102–103, 138–39
Fashion in Action, 138–39
Fawcett Comics, 27, 51
Fegredo, Duncan, 174–75
Feldstein, Al, 63
Fell, Elitta, 157
Feller, Lucy, 31
The Feminine Mystique, 232
feminist comix, 9, 23, 100, 101, 104–5, 116–18, 120–21, 123–24, 160–61, 187, 194, 230–31
Fiction House, 26, 27, 31, 39, 40, 54, 64
Fight Comics, 39, 40

film, 47, 75, 77, 94, 103, 182–83, 205
Finder, 157
FINIS, 212
Firebug, 224
First Love Illustrated, 51
Fite, Linda, 74
Flag, Rick, 130
Flagg, Starr, 40–42
Flamebird, 96
The Flash, 71
Flowers, Ramona, 204–205
Flyin' Jenny, 13
Foglio, Kaja, 209
Foglio, Phil, 209
Fonda, Jane, 77
The Forbidden Tales of Dark Mansion,
  106
Ford, Gail, 55–56
Forest, Jean-Claude, 77
Fortune, Shirley, 27
Foster, Cleve, 103
Foster, Friday, 102–103
Foster, Hal, 84
Fox, 50
Fox, Gardner, 40–42, 52, 96
Fox, Ginger, 139–41
Foxx, Freda (Superbitch), 118–19
Fradon, Ramona, 74
Franson, Leanne Rae, 169
Friedlander, Barbara, 101
Friedrich, Gary, 90
Friends of Lulu, 23
FSc, 184, 185
*The Further Fattening Adventures of
  Pudge, Girl Blimp*, 101

G

Gabriele, Al, 28
Gaiman, Neil, 64, 65, 157, 185
Gaines, William, 63
Galactus, 135, 176
Gambrell, Dorothy, 183
Garrity, Shaenon K., 183
Gaydos, Michael, 191, 194–95
Gerrard, Bart, 119
Gibbons, Dave, 170, 172
Giddings, Noelle, 157
G.I. Jane, 54–55
Gill, Joe, 89
The Girl, 161–62
Girl, 174, 175
Girl Friday, 55–56
Girl Genius, 209
The Girl Patrol, 31–32
The Girl Squadron, 31–32
Girls with Slingshots, 190–91
Giunta, John, 14–15
Give Me Liberty, 170
Glass, Hopey, 141
Gloeckner, Phoebe, 183
Glomb, 83–84
Gloria, 34
goddesses, 132, 159, 195–96, 224–25
Go-Go, 79

Golden Age Treasury, 68
Gold Key, 88, 110
Goofy Gertie, 59
Gordon, Barbara (Batgirl), 75, 96–97
Gothic Love, 106
Gran'ma Ben, 197
Grant, Helen, 62–63, 86
graphic novels, 9, 157, 182–83, 208,
  218–19
Graphic Policy, 209
Graphic Story Monthly, 160
Grayson, Devin, 157
Great Comics, 34, 35
Great Lakes Avengers, 176
Greene, Sid, 96
van Greenpockets, Arnold, 82
Gregory, Roberta, 104, 121, 129,
  157, 160
Grier, Pam, 103
Griffin, 224–25
Grove Press, 77
Guerra, Pia, 209
Guttman, Gabe, 86

H

Haberlin, Brian, 178
Hale, Hilaria, 57
Hale, Nancy, 109
Halfwolf, Maika, 225–27
Hamster Vice, 128
Hark! A Vagrant, 198
Harmon, Ira, 118
Harvestar, Rose, 197–98
Harvey, Alfred, 28–29
Harvey, Warren, 81
Harvey Comics, 28, 51, 54, 68,
  81, 82
Haunted Love, 106
Haunt of Fear, 63
Hawkman, 26
Heer, Jeet, 75
Hellcat, 194
Henderson, Erica, 176
The Heretics, 145
Hernandez, Gilbert, 222
Hernandez, Jaime, 141
Heroes, Inc., 83, 84
Herring, Ian, 230, 231
Hicks, Faith Erin, 183
Hilkert, John G., 44
Hilliard, Diana, 62
Hillman, David, 166
Hillman Productions, 43
Hilty, Joan, 157
Hippolyte, 47
Hi-School Romances, 51
Hollingsworth, Matt, 194
Holmes, Sherlock, 132
homelessness, 200–201
homophobia, 116, 168, 172
homosexuality, 50, 106, 108, 143,
  168, 209
The Hood, 15
Hope, Sandra, 157

Horatio, 222
Horne, Emily, 209
Horne, Rick, 29
horror comics, 44, 63–64, 92–95,
  106, 122, 173–74, 184–85, 209,
  225, 227
Hot Stuff, 68
Howard, Tini, 179
Howard the Duck, 176
The Hulk, 135
hypnotic powers, 17

I

icons
  Batgirl, 75, 96–97
  Ramona Flowers, 204–205
  Little Lulu, 12, 22–23, 51
  Ms. Marvel, 100, 123–24, 194,
    230–31
  Silk Spectre, 152–53
  Supergirl, 70–71, 75, 100
  Witchblade, 94, 178–79
  Wonder Woman, 14, 27, 46–47,
    75, 157
IDW Publications, 188, 214
Image Comics, 156, 178, 219, 224,
  225, 228
immortality, 14–15, 17, 148
Impact Comics, 164
Indians, 64, 67
indigenous cultures, 64–67
Inferior Five, 77
Inspector Belgique, 210
Inspector Lestrade, 132
Inspector Madson, 55–56
interracial relationships, 110
invisibility, 47, 75, 92, 202
Invisible Woman, 75
Iron Circus Comics, 209
Iron Fist, 100, 101
Iron Man, 176
Isis, 100
Island, 224
It Ain't Me Babe, 101
iZombie, 221

J

Jackson, Janie (Tomboy), 67–68
Jacobson, Luke, 134
Jaffee, Al, 76
The Jaguar, 163–64
Jain, 164–66
Jalisco, Alejandrina Yolanda, 188–90
Jane 6EM35 (Magician from Mars),
  14–15
Janus, 196
Javins, Marie, 157
Jem and the Holograms, 214
Jink, 166–68
The Johnny Nemo Magazine, 145
Joke Comics, 44
Jones, Jessica, 176, 191–95
Josie and the Pussycats, 100

Jughead Jones, 61
Jumbo Comics, 26
jungle girl comics, 13, 27, 40,
  149–51, 163–64
Junkyarders, 145
Justice League, 130
juvenile delinquency, 50

K

Kahn, Jenette, 100
Kalish, Carol, 128–29
Kane, Betty (Batgirl), 96
Kane, Kathy (Batwoman), 75, 96–97
Karn, Murray, 44
Karoleen, 117
Kath, 223–24
Kearney, Megan, 184
Keegan, 224–25
Keene, Katy, 33–34, 82
Keene, Sis, 33
Kelly, K. O., 33
Kelly, Walt, 132
Kent, Clark, *see* Superman
Khan, Kamala (Ms. Marvel), 100,
  123–24, 194, 230–31
Kickstarter, 209
Kildale, Malcolm, 14–15
Kill Your Boyfriend, 161
King Features, 20
Kippa, 227
Kirby, Jack, 43
The Kitchen, 209, 223–24
Kitt, Eartha, 103
Kleenex, 23
Knight, Eric, 158–59
Knight, Frances, 138
Knight, Misty, 100, 101, 119
Knives Chau, 205
Knothead Nancy, 59
Knothead Nellie, 59
Kogo, Kamau, 228
Kotto, Yaphet, 103
Krypto the Superdog, 71
Kurtzman, Harvey, 132
Kwitney, Alisa, 157

L

Lady Death, 95
Lady Satan, 35
Lagacé, Gisèle, 183, 185, 209
Laird, Peter, 128
Lane, Lois, 8, 51, 71
Lane, Susan, 74
Lang, Scott (Ant-Man), 194
Lark, Linda, 86
Larson, Hope, 209
Last Gasp, 113
Latinas, 39–40, 188–90
Lawrence, Jim, 102, 103
Lee, Linda (Supergirl), 70–71, 75,
  100
Lee, Stan, 76
Leetah, 107–9
Legends, 130

L'Engle, Madeleine, 84
Lennox, Annie, 138
Lenore, 184, 185
lesbians, 26, 104–5, 160–61, 202
Leslie, Eugene, 55
Lev Gleason Publications, 51
libraries, 145, 147, 164–65, 205, 209
Lightning Lords, 117
Liliane, 169–170
Li'l Jinx, 100
Li'l Vampi, 95
Little Annie Fanny, 86
Little Lulu, 12, 22–23, 51
Liu, Marjorie, 209, 225
Locas, 141
Longarón, Jorge, 102, 103
Longshot, 135
Looney Lucy, 59
Loubert, Deni, 101
Love & Rockets, 128, 141, 157
Lucy the Real Gone Gal, 58–59
Lumsdon, David, 185, 209
L.U.S.T. (Legion of Undesirable
    Super Types), 87
Luthor, Lex, 71

M

MA3, 185, 209
Mack, David, 194
Madame Strange, 34–36
Mad Dog, 133
MAD magazine, 71, 77, 81, 112, 132
Madman, 222
Madonna, 138
Magazine Enterprises, 40, 52
magic, 13, 14–15, 27, 44–45, 47,
    94, 112, 120, 132, 145, 159, 165,
    173–74, 178–79, 197–98, 225–27
Magician from Mars, 14–15
Mailer, Norris Church, 134
Male Annual, 86
Ma'nan, 149
manga, 94, 108, 132–33, 157, 178,
    182
Manhunt, 40
Man Huntin' Minnie, 59–61
Manning, Jack, 110
Mantis, 100
Margot, 17
Marie, Hannah, 173
Marine, Maureen, 9, 36–37
marketing, 101, 128–29, 137, 208,
    231
Marrs, Lee, 16, 113
Mars, Johnny, 139
Marston, William, 46
Martians, 14–15, 113–16
Martin, Ann M., 208
Martin, Laura, 157
Maruca, Brian, 200
Marvel Comics, 12, 37, 51, 62, 63,
    74, 75, 76, 82, 86, 100–101, 106,
    108, 119, 123–24, 129, 133, 134,
    135, 137, 147, 156–57, 175–76,

182, 191–95, 202, 209, 230
Marvel Girl, 75
Mar-Vell, 230
Marvel Super-Heroes, 123
Marzan, Jose, Jr., 163
Masters, Ollie, 223
Matadori, 212
The Matrix, 182
Matsumoto, Daffy, 141
Maxilla Maw, 158
Mayo, Ralph, 64
McCarthy, Carrie, 129
McFarlane, Todd, 156
McJack, Jamie, 190–91
McNeil, Carla Speed, 157
Medley, Linda, 157, 164–66
Ménage à 3 (MA3), 185, 209
merchandising, 23, 47
mermaids, 36–37, 198–99
Meskin, Mort, 43, 67
Mesmer, Hugo, 17
Mesmer, Olga, 12, 15–17
Messner-Loebs, William, 163
Meugniot, Will, 121, 149
Meyer, Helen, 51
Michelinie, David, 116
Miller, Frank, 170, 172
Millie the Model, 82
Milligan, Peter, 145, 147, 157,
    174–75
Mills, Tarpé, 37, 39
Minoru, Nico, 202
The Misfits, 83–84
Misfits, 214
misogyny, 104, 112
Miss America, 27
Miss Fury, 14, 20, 37–39, 163
Miss Pepper, 59
Miss Vanderlip, 134
Miyazawa, Takeshi, 202
Mizumo, Junko, 184
mobsters, 143, 223–24
models, 33–34, 59, 76–77, 81–83,
    102–3, 131, 134, 221
The Modniks, 88
MODOK, 124
Mojoverse, 137
Monkeybrain Comics, 210, 212
Monsieur, 212
Monstrum, 227
Montress, 209, 225, 227
Mooney, Jim, 86
Moon Press Productions, 121
Moonshadow, 147–49
Moonwatcher, 117
Moppet, Lulu, 12, 22–23
moral code, 13
Morales, Mark, 212
Mordden, Ethan, 105
Morojo, 13
Moronica, 59
Morrison, Grant, 157, 161, 162
mothers, 107, 109, 137, 140, 169,
    191

Ms. magazine, 233
Ms. Marvel, 100, 123–24, 194,
    230–31
Ms. Tree, 133, 143–45
Muerta mob, 143
Mufatti, Steve, 68
Mulvihill, Patricia, 157
Munsey, Tracy, 157
Murdock, Matt, 134
Murray, Will, 175
Muslims, 230–31
mutants, 14–15, 83–84, 100, 129,
    135–37, 176, 202
Muth, Jon J., 147
My Date, 43
Mygorgs, 116–17
My Secret Life, 89
Mystra, 83–84

N

Naifeh, Ted, 184
Nanny Goat Productions, 104
National Comics Publications, *see*
    DC Comics
National Organization for Women,
    232
Native Americans, 64–67
Naughty Bits, 129, 160
Nazis, 28–29, 31, 36–37, 39–40,
    47, 91
Neil the Horse, 101
Nelson, Fred, 31
Nelvana of the Northern Lights,
    27, 44
Neptina, 13
Netflix, 191, 194
New Avengers, 191
Newell, Mindy, 157
New Funnies, 51
New Mutants, 129
Newton, Wayne, 139
New York Times, 218, 233
Nibbil and Annie, 195–96
Nightmares & Fairytales, 184
Night Nurse, 100, 101
Ninjette, 187
Nitrozac, 183
Nodell, Jacque, 110
noir comics, 188–90, 223–24
North, Dakota, 133–35
North, Jack, 31–32
North, Ryan, 176
Northwest Press, 209, 216, 217
Nudine, 83, 84
nudity, 13, 19, 77, 83, 118, 121–22,
    228
nuns, 165, 225
nurse comics, 54, 62–63, 74, 75,
    85–86, 89–90, 100
nymphomaniacs, 83
Nyoka the Jungle Girl, 27
NYT Syndicate, 102

O

O'Connell, Mitch, 139
O'Day, Angel, 76–77
Odyssey, 198
O'Hare, Kelly (Cutey Bunny),
    132–33
Oksner, Bob, 76
The Old Witch, 63–64, 185
Olio Press, 164
Olsen, Jimmy, 70
Oksner, Bob, 30
O'Malley, Bryan Lee, 204–205
Oni Press, 204
Ormes, Jackie, 13, 20
orphans, 71, 90–91, 105–107, 148,
    200–201
Ortiz, Speedy, 141
Ostrander, John, 130, 166
outlaws, 32, 52–53

P

Pacific Comics, 129, 149
Painkiller Jane, 94–95
Pakistanis, 231
Pantha, 94
paper dolls, 20–21, 34
Parallax, 75
Parker, Pat, 54
Passion, Ivan, 87
Peanuts, 19
Penn, Laura, 109
Penn, Sean, 138
Peril, Pauline, 110–12
Peter, Harry, 46
Peterson, Page, 109–10
Pezzini, Sara (Witchblade), 94,
    178–79
Phantom Lady, 44, 94
The Phantom Menace, 182
Phelps, Frieda, 104–105
photographers, 30–31, 102–103
Pilgrim, Scott, 204
Pindar, 165
Pini, Richard, 101, 108
Pini, Wendy, 101, 108, 166
pinup queens, 33–34
Pipsqueak Papers, 84
Pittsburgh Courier, 20
Pizzazz, 214
Planet Comics, 31, 32
Plastino, Al, 70
Playboy, 86
Pocket Comics, 28–29
Pogo, 132
Polka Dot Pirate, 44
Pollack, Rachel, 157
Polly of the Plains, 13
poltergeists, 222
polyamorous relationships, 191
Poole, Gary, 88
pornography, 143, 195
Porter, Gail, 30–31
Power Man, 101, 194
Power Pack, 129

Powers, Austin, 88
Powers, Elissa Megan (Empowered), 186–88
pregnancy, 153, 164–66, 194
Prescott, Rodney, 17
Pretty Deadly, 156, 219
Prez, 212–14
Prince Daru, 31–32
Prince Hal, 84
princesses, 9, 14, 27, 36–37, 46–47, 58–59, 75, 132–33, 157, 159, 164–66, 197–98, 200, 216–17
Prince Valiant, 84
Prisley, Elvis, 81
prisoners, 228–29
private eyes, *see* detectives
Private Super-Detective, 56
Prize Comics, 109
Prof, 149
prostitution, 143, 199, 223
Pudge, Girl Blimp, 9, 113–16
pulp magazines, 12, 17
The Pulse, 191, 195
Purgatori, 95
Purple Man, 194
Pussycat, 86–87

Q

Quagmire, Joshua, 132
Quasar, 135
Queen of Venus, 32

R

Race, Rand, 141
racism, 20, 35–36, 116, 118, 188, 190, 228
Ra-Harahkte, 132
Rambeau, Monica, 230
Ramrod, Stevey, 133
Rangers, 54
Rankin, Hugh, 17
rape, 20, 117, 174, 179
Raven, 223–24
Raye, Jetta, 57–58
ray guns, 32
Reagan, Ronald, 131, 132
The Rebels, 166
rebels, 9
Red Mask, 52–53
Red Sonja, 100
Reed, Phyllis, 74
Reese, Ralph, 83
Reinman, Paul, 123
Reject, 88
Ren, 227
Renée, Lily, 26, 40, 58
Renegade Press, 133
reporters, 27, 29, 35, 39, 40, 42, 44–45, 68, 82, 92, 100, 110–12, 123–24, 138, 141, 157, 176, 188, 191–95, 209, 214, 216–17, 219, 221, 228–29, 230–31
romance comics, 51, 57–58, 59–61, 62–63, 74, 75, 85–86, 90–92, 100,

101, 105–107, 109–10, 149–51, 157, 185, 190–91, 195
Rose, 197
Ross, Beth, 212–14
Roxanne, 139
Roy, Adrienne, 157
Rugg, Jim, 200
Runaways, 202
Rural Home Publishing, 30, 36
Russell, Mark, 212

S

Sabrina the Teenage Witch, 100, 122
Saga, 209
Sally the Sleuth, 12, 17–19, 56, 178
Salmons, Tony, 133
Sanchez, Jessie (Street Angel), 200–201
The Sandman, 157
Sandman series, 65
SanParite, Rilavashana (Bold Riley), 216–17
Satrapi, Marjane, 183
Saturday Evening Post, 22
Saucy Mermaid, 198–99
Scarlet Witch, 176
Scary Godmother, 173–74
Scheele, Christie, 133
Scholastic/Graphix, 218
science fiction comics, 13, 14–15, 57–58, 83–84, 100, 116–18, 147–51
S.C.O.R.E., 87
'Scot, 88–89
Scout, 138
Screwball Sal, 59
Secret Hearts, 109
Secrets of Sinister House, 106
Seeley, Tim, 179
Señorita Rio, 39–40
Severin, Marie, 51, 123
sex comics, 77–79, 94, 108, 113–16, 118–19, 132–33, 158–59, 166–68, 178–79, 185–86, 195–96, 198–99
sexuality, 13, 50–51, 168, 169
Shade, Sindi, 9, 145–47
The Shadow, 27
Shag, 83–84
shape shifters, 43, 92–95, 166–68, 202, 221, 231
Shaw, Justine, 183
Sheena, Queen of the Jungle, 13, 26
She-Hulk, 100
S.H.I.E.L.D., 137
Shouri, 209
Showcase, 76
Silk Spectre, 152–53
Silver Surfer, 108
Silvestri, Marc, 178
Sim, Dave, 101
Simeon, Sam, 76
Simon, Joe, 43
Simonson, Louise, 129

The Sinister House of Secret Love, 106
Sinn, Tiffany, 90–92
Sinnott, Joe, 85, 89, 123
Sirius Entertainment, 173
Sistah Spooky, 187
sisters, 52–53, 89–90, 94, 175, 197–98, 223–24
Sisters, 208, 219
Skrulls, 202
Skullhead, 53
Slater, Doris, 27
Slave Labor Graphics, 184, 185, 200
slaves, 116–18, 225
Sleeping Beauty, 164–65
Small Favors, 195
Smile, 208, 219
Smith, Jeff, 166, 197
Smith, Robert, 116
Smith, Sue and Sally, 86, 89–90
Snyder, John K., III, 138
Snyder, Marcia, 26
A Softer World, 209
soldiers, 31–32, 54–55, 100, 123–24, 194, 230–31
Solis, Vivian "Frogmouth," 141
Southern Cross, 209
Space Gophers, 133
Speed Comics, 29
Spicy Detective Stories, 17, 19
Spicy Mystery Stories, 15, 17
Spicy Tales, 56
Spider-Girl, 194
Spider-Man, 134, 156
Spider-Woman, 100
Spidey Super Stories, 101
spies, 34–36, 39–42, 47, 86–87, 91–92, 149–51
The Spirit, 132
Squirrel Girl, 175–77
Stag Annual, 86
Standard Comics, 57
Stanhall Comics, 55
Stanley, K. Sandra, 183
Staples, Fiona, 209
Starfire, 100, 116–18
Starjammers, 124
Starlight, 9, 64–67
Starr, Brenda, 20, 103
stereotyping, 35
Sterling, 67
Stevenson, Noelle, 209
Stockton, Richard, 158
Stonewall Award, 218
Storm, 100
Strain, Christina, 202
Strauss, Victoria (American Woman), 158–59
Streaky, 71
Street Angel, 200–201
Strong, Ajax, 81
St. John, 51, 58
stuntwomen, 28–29
subversion, 9
Suicide Squad, 131

Sunflower, 147–49
Super Ann, 13
Superbitch, 118–19
Super-Detective, 55
Superdyke, 104
Supergirl, 70–71, 75, 100
Superham, 120
Super-Heroes, 175
Superhomeys, 187
Superman, 12, 13, 15, 26, 44, 51, 74
Survival-Woman, 119–121
Sutton, Tom, 92
Swan, Curt, 70
Swift, Rex, 91
Synergy, 214

T

T&A Comics, 53
Takeda, Sana, 209, 225, 227
Tales from the Crypt, 63
Tamaki, Jillian, 209
Tamaki, Mariko, 209
Tartar, 112
Task Force X, 130
The Teenage Mutant Ninja Turtles, 128
Teen Secret Diary, 85
telepathy, 83–84, 90, 159, 168, 170, 172, 202
television, 71, 75, 97, 178, 182–83, 214
Telgemeier, Raina, 208, 209, 218, 231
Tellington, Hazel, 190
Temofonte, Saida, 157
Tezuka, Osamu, 132
theater, 233
thieves, 210–12
Third Wave, 224–25
This magazine, 119
Thomas, Jean, 101
Thomas, Roy, 32, 123
Thomases, Martha, 133, 134–35
Thompson, Jill, 157, 173
Thompson, Kelly, 214
Thompson, Maggie, 23, 30
Through the Woods, 209
Thugboy, 187
Thump, 117
Thunderbolts, 124
Tiger Girl, 40
Tijuana bibles, 13
timeline, 232–33
Timely Comics, 37
time travel, 121–22
Tim Holt, 52
Tits & Clits, 101
Tobin, Paul, 210
Tom and Jerry, 51
Tomboy, 67–68
Tracy, Dick, 13
trade collections, 157
transgender characters, 161, 209, 213, 214–16
treasure hunters, 166–68

Tree, Michael (Ms. Tree), 133, 143–45
Trillo, Carlos, 188
Trojan, 19, 55
Trotman, Spike, 209
troublemakers, 22–23
Tuner, Linda (Black Cat), 28–30
Turner, Michael, 178–79
twins, 89–90, 94, 175

U

Ultra Violet, 43
underground comics, *see* counterculture comix
unicorns, 227
Unit One, 84

V

Valentina, 117
Valentino, Serena, 184
Vampirella, 44, 92–95
vampires, 63, 94
Vanity, 149–151
Van Ronson, Randy, 33
Vaughan, Brian K., 202, 209
Vault-Keeper, 63
The Vault of Horror, 63
Venusians, 15–17
Veronica, 82, 100
Vertigo, 157, 162, 174, 221, 223
Vess, Charles, 197
vigilantes, 34–36, 39–40, 67–68, 130
violence, 50–51
Violence Against Women Act, 233
Viscardi, Nick, 39
V Magazine, 77
von Kampf, Baroness Erica, 37
Vosburg, Mike, 116, 117

W

Waid, Mark, 164
waitresses, 185–86
Walker, Patsy (Hellcat), 194
Waller, Amanda, 130–31
Walt Disney's Comics and Stories, 51
Walters, Jane (G.I. Jane), 54–55
war comics, 27, 54, 55, 74
Warp Graphics, 166
Warren, Adam, 186–88
Warren Comics, 94
Warren Publishing, 92
warriors, 9, 46–47, 64–67, 116–18, 197–98, 202–203
Washington, Martha, 170–72
Wasp, 75
Watchmen, 172
Watters, Shannon, 209
Watts, Irene N., 183
Weakheart, 112
webcomics, 182, 183, 208–209
    Annabelle, 184
    DiDi, 185–86
    Liliane, 169
    Jamie McJack, 190

The Saucy Mermaid, 198
Wein, Glynis, 129, 135
Wein, Len, 130
Weltjens, Jochen, 158
Wendy the Good Little Witch, 68–69, 82
Werewolf by Night, 101
werewolves, 30–31, 63, 94, 101
Wertham, Fredric, 50
West Coast Avengers, 176
Western comics, 8, 29, 52–53, 66, 74, 219–21
Wheeler-Nicholson, Major Malcolm, 19
White, Lloyd, 88
Whitney, Ogden, 40–42
wholesale distribution, 27
Whyte, Ron, 83
Wilbur Comics, 33, 34
Williams, David Antoine, 163
Williams, Vanessa, 143
Williams, Wheels, 88
Wilson, Billy "Cube," 88
Wilson, G. Willow, 230
Wilson, Robert, IV, 228
The Wing, 27, 44–45
Wimmen's Comix, 101, 113
Winstead, Mary Elizabeth, 205
Winter, Chuck, 34
Witchblade, 94, 178–79
Woggon, Bill, 33, 34
Wohl, David, 178
Wojtkowski, Charles, 90
Womanwoman, 120–21
Women's Army Auxiliary Corps (WAC), 54–55
women's history, 232–33
Women's Space Battalion, 31–32
Wonder Woman, 14, 27, 46–47, 75, 157
Wood, Tatjana, 74
Wood, Wally, 83, 84, 86
Woolfolk, Dorothy, 105, 106
World War II, 26, 27, 35, 40, 51

X

Xavin, 202–203
X-Babies, 137
X-Factor, 129
X-Men, 100, 124, 135, 179
X-ray vision, 17

Y

Yale, Kim, 157
Yeung, Craig, 202
Young Love, 109
Young Romance, 51, 74, 109
Y: The Last Man, 209

Z

Zdarsky, Chip, 176
Zeit-Geist, Phoebe, 87
Zelda the Witch, 121–23
Zip-a-Tone, 132

Ziuko, Tom, 130
zombies, 65, 221–22
Zudella, Achmed, 34, 35

Front cover: Pauline Peril by Jack Manning, © 1970 by Gold Key Comics; Sue and Sally Smith by Joe Sinnott and Vince Colletta, © 1962 by Charlton Comics; Bitchy Butch by Roberta Gregory, © 1990 by Roberta Gregory; Torchy Brown by Jackie Ormes, © 1950 by the Smith-Mann Syndicate; Ms. Tree by Terry Beatty, © 1981 by Max Collins and Terry Beatty; Wonder Woman by H. G. Peter, © 1941 by DC Comics; Martha Washington by Dave Gibbons and Robin Smith, © 1990 by Frank Miller and Dave Gibbons; Ramona Flowers by Bryan Lee O'Malley, © 2004 by Bryan Lee O'Malley; Barbarella by Jean-Claude Forest, © 1962 by Jean-Claude Forest; Street Angel by Jim Rugg, © 2004 by Jim Rugg; Maggie Chascarillo by Jaime Hernandez, © 1982 by Jaime Hernandez; Angel O'Day by Bob Oksner, © 1969 by DC Comics; Friday Foster by Jorge Longaron, © 1970 by New York Times Syndicate; Jamie McJack by Danielle Corsetto, © 2004 by Danielle Corsetto; Cutey Bunny by Joshua Quagmire, © 1982 by Joshua Quagmire; Bold Riley by Leia Weathington, © 2012 by Leia Weathington; Jetta Raye by Dan DeCarlo, © 1953 by Standard Comics **Back cover:** Magician from Mars by John Giunta and Malcolm Kildale, © 1939 by Centaur Publishing; Wendy the Good Little Witch by Warren Kremer, © 1961 by Harvey Comics; Empowered by Adam Warren, © 2007 by Adam Warren; Ultra Violet © 1947 by Hillman Productions; Deathface Ginny by Emma Rios and Jordie Bellaire, © 2013 by Milkfed Criminal Masterminds, Inc. and Emma Rios; Pussycat by Bill Everett, © 1965 Marvel Comics; Ms. Tree by Terry Beatty, © 1981 by Max Collins and Terry Beatty; Superbitch by Ira Harmon, © 1977 by Ira Harmon; Starlight by Ralph Mayo, © 1950 by Fiction House; Little Lulu, © 1960 by Western Publishing; The Jaguar by Rod Whigham, Pam Eklund, Tom Ziuko, © 1991 by Archie Publications Inc; Squirrel Girl by Paul Pelletier, Rick Magyar, and Wil Quintana. © 1992 by Marvel Comics; Angel O'Day by Bob Oksner, © 1969 by DC Comics; Jink by Wendy Pini, © 1994 by Warp Graphics Inc.; Lucy the Real Gone Gal, © 1953 by St. John Publications; DiDi by Gisèle Lagacé & M. Victoria Robado, © 2008 by Gisèle Lagacé and David Lumsdon; G.I. Jane by Bill Benulis, © 1952 by Fiction House; Nibbil by Colleen Coover, © 2000 by Colleen Coover

2: Ramona Flowers by Bryan Lee O'Malley, © 2004 by Bryan Lee O'Malley; **6:** Sindi Shade by Brett Ewins, © 1985 by Peter Milligan and Brett Ewins; **8:** Sally the Sleuth © 1950 by Trojan Magazines; **12:** Sally the Sleuth by Adolphe Barreaux, © 1934 by Culture Publications; **14:** Magician from Mars by John Giunta and Malcolm Kildale, © 1939 by Centaur Publishing; **16:** Olga Mesmer by Watt Dell, © 1937 by Culture Publications; **18:** Sally the Sleuth, © 1950 by Trojan Magazines; **20–21:** Torchy Brown by Jackie Ormes, © 1950 by the Smith-Mann Syndicate; **22:** Little Lulu, © 1960 by Western Publishing; **26:** The Wing by Jerry Lazare, © 1942 by Bell Features; **28:** Black Cat by Joe Simon, © 1946 by Harvey Comics; **29:** Black Cat, © 1946 by Harvey Comics; **30:** Gail Porter by Bob Oksner, © 1944 by Rural Home Publishing; **32:** Gale Allen by George Carl Wilhelms, © 1940 by Fiction House; **33:** Katy Keene by Bill Woggon, © 1945 by Archie Comics; **35:** Madame Strange by Charles A. Winter, © 1941 by Great Publications; **36:** Maureen Marine by Harold Delay, © 1944 by Rural Home Publishing; **38:** Miss Fury by Jack Kirby, © 1942 by Bell Syndicate; **40:** Señorita Rio by Nick Cardi, © 1942 by Fiction House; **41:** Starr Flagg by Ogden Whitley, © 1953 by Magazine Enterprises; **42:** Starr Flagg by Bob Powell, © 1953 by Magazine Enterprises **43:** Ultra Violet © 1947 by Hillman Productions;

45: The Wing by Jerry Lazare, © 1942 by Bell Features; **46:** Wonder Woman by H. G. Peter, © 1941 by DC Comics; **50:** Wendy the Good Little Witch by Warren Kremer, © 1961 by Harvey Comics; **52:** Black Phantom by Frank Bolle, © 1956 Magazine Enterprises; **54:** G.I. Jane by Bill Benulis, © 1952 by Fiction House; **56:** Gail Ford by Pierre Charpentier, © 1950 by Fiction House; **57:** Jetta Raye by Dan DeCarlo, © 1953 by Standard Comics; **58:** Lucy the Real Gone Gal, © 1953 by St. John Publications; **60:** Man-Huntin' Minnie by Jack Bradbury, © 1952 by American Comics Group; **62:** Nurse Helen Grant by Vince Colletta, ©1957 by Marvel Comics; **65 66:** Starlight by Ralph Mayo, © 1950 by Fiction House; **67:** Tomboy by Edvard Moritz, © 1954 by Sterling; **69:** Wendy the Good Little Witch by Steve Muffatti, © 1961 by Harvey Comics; **70:** Supergirl by Curt Swan and Sheldon Moldoff, © 1966 by DC Comics; **74:** Barbarella by Jean-Claude Forest, © 1962 by Jean-Claude Forest; **76:** Angel O'Day by Bob Oksner, © 1969 by DC Comics; **78:** Barbarella by Jean-Claude Forest, © 1962 by Jean-Claude Forest; **80:** Bikini Luv by Jon D'Agostino and Jim Aparo, © 1966 by Charlton Comics; **82:** Bunny Ball by Hy Eisman, © 1966 by Harvey Comics; **83:** Mystra by Wally Wood, © 1969 by Wally Wood; **84:** Dragonella by Wally Wood, © 1969 by Wally Wood; **85:** Nurse Betsy Crane by Dick Giordano, © 1961 by Charlton Comics; **87:** Pussycat by Bill Everett, © 1965 Marvel Comics; **88:** 'Scot by Lloyd White, © 1967 by Gold Key Comics; **89:** Sue and Sally Smith by Joe Sinnott and Vince Colletta, © 1962 by Charlton Comics; **91:** Tiffany Sinn by Charles Nicholas and Vince Alascia, © 1966 by Charlton Comics; **93, 95:** Vampirella by Tom Sutton, © 1969 by Dynamite Entertainment **94:** Vampirella by Mike Royer, © 1969 by Dynamite Entertainment; **96:** Batgirl by Carmine Infantino, © 1967 by DC Comics; **100:** Pudge, Girl Blimp by Lee Marrs, © 1973 by Lee Marrs; **102:** Friday Foster by Jorge Longaron, © 1970 by New York Times Syndicate; **104:** Frieda Phelps by Roberta Gregory, © 1976 by Roberta Gregory; **106:** Laura Chandler by Tony diZuniga, © 1971 by DC Comics; **108:** Leetah by Wendy Pini, © 1978 by Warp Graphics, Inc; **109:** Page Peterson by Steve Englehart and Vince Colletta, © 1971 by DC Comics; **111–2:** Pauline Peril by Jack Manning, © 1970 by Gold Key Comics; **114–5:** Pudge by Lee Marrs, © 1973 by Lee Marrs; **117:** Starfire by Ernie Chan and Vince Colletta, © 1976 by DC Comics; **118:** Superbitch by Ira Harmon, © 1977 by Ira Harmon; **120:** Survival Woman by Margaret Atwood, © 1975 by Margaret Atwood; **123:** Zelda the Witch by Will Meugniot, © 1977 by Will Meugniot; **124:** Ms. Marvel by Winslow Mortimer and Mike Esposito, © 1977 by Marvel Comics; **128:** Maggie Chascarillo by Jaime Hernandez, © 1982 by Jaime Hernandez; **130–31:** Amanda Waller by John Byrne, Karl Kesel, and Tom Zuko, © 1986 by John Byrne; **132:** Cutey Bunny by Joshua Quagmire, © 1982 by Joshua Quagmire; **134:** Dakota North by Tony Salmons and Max Scheele, © 1986 by Marvel Comics; **136:** Dazzler by John Romita Jr., Alfredo Alcala, and Glynis Wein, © 1980 by Marvel Comics; **137:** Dazzler by Bob Larkin, © 1981 by Marvel Comics; **138:** Fashion In Action by John K. Snyder III, © 1985 by John K. Snyder III; **140:** Ginger Fox by Mitch O'Connell and Les Dorscheid, © 1986 by Mike Baron and Mitch O'Connell; **141–2:** Maggie Chascarillo by Jaime Hernandez, © 1982 by Jaime Hernandez; **144:** Ms. Tree by Terry Beatty, © 1981 by Max Collins and Terry Beatty; **145–46:** Sindi Shade by Brett Ewins, © 1985 by Peter Milligan and Brett Ewins; **148:** Sunflower by Jon J. Muth, © 1985 by J.M. DeMatteis and Jon. J. Muth;

150-151: Vanity by Will Meugniot and Jo Meugniot, © 1984 by Will Meugniot; **152:** Silk Spectre by Dave Gibbons and John Higgins, © 1986 by DC Comics; **156:** Martha Washington by Dave Gibbons and Robin Smith, © 1990 by Frank Miller and Dave Gibbons; **158:** American Woman by Brian Denham and Jochen Weltjens, © 1998 by Brian Denham; **160:** Bitchy Butch by Roberta Gregory, © 1990 by Roberta Gregory; **161:** The Girl by Phillip Bond, D'Israaeli, and Daniel Vovvo, © 1995 by DC Comics; **163:** The Jaguar by Rod Whigham, Pam Eklund, Tom Ziuko, © 1991 by Archie Publications Inc; **165–66:** Jain by Linda Medley, © 1997 by Linda Medley; **167:** Jink by Wendy Pini, © 1994 by Warp Graphics Inc.; **169:** Liliane by Leanne Rae Franson, © 1992 by Leanne Rae Franson; **171:** Martha Washington by Dave Gibbons and Robin Smith, © 1990 by Frank Miller and Dave Gibbons; **173:** Scary Godmother by Jill Thompson, © 1997 by Jill Thompson; **175:** Simone Cundy by Duncan Fegredo and Nathan Eyring, © 1996 by DC Comics; **177:** Squirrel Girl by Paul Pelletier, Rick Magyar, and Wil Quintana. © 1992 by Marvel Comics; **178:** Witchblade by Marc Silvestri, Batt, and Ashby Manson, © 1995 by Marc Silvestri; **182:** Street Angel by Jim Rugg, © 2004 by Jim Rugg ; **184:** Annabelle by FSc, © 2002 by Serena Valentino; **186:** Didi by Gisèle Lagacé & M. Victoria Robado, © 2008 by Gisèle Lagacé and David Lumsdon; **187:** Empowered by Adam Warren, © 2007 by Adam Warren; **189:** Alejandrina Yolanda Jalisco by Eduardo Risso, © 2005 by Carlos Trillo and Eduardo Risso; **191:** Jamie McJack by Danielle Corsetto, © 2004 by Danielle Corsetto; **192–93:** Jessica Jones by Michael Gaydos and Matt Hollingsworth, © 2001 by Marvel Comics; **195–96:** Nibbil by Colleen Coover, © 2000 by Coleen Coover; **197:** Rose Harvestar by Charles Vess, © 2000 by Jeff Smith; **199:** Saucy Mermaid by Kate Beaton, © 2009 by Kate Beaton; **200–1:** Street Angel by Jim Rugg, © 2004 by Jim Rugg; **203:** Xavin by Takeshi Miyazawa, Craig Yeung and Christina Strain, © 2005 by Marvel Comics; **204:** Ramona Flowers by Bryan Lee O'Malley, © 2004 by Bryan Lee O'Malley; **208:** Bold Riley by Leia Weathington, © 2012 by Leia Weathington; **210–11:** Bandette by Colleen Coover, © 2012 by Paul Tobin and Colleen Coover; **213:** Beth Ross by Ben Caldwell, © 2015 by DC Comics; **215:** Blaze by Sophie Campbell and M. Victoria Robado, © 2015 by Hasbro; **217:** Bold Riley by Leia Weathington, © 2012 by Leia Weathington; **218:** Callie by Raina Telgemeier and Gurihiru, © 2012 by Raina Telgemeier; **220:** Deathface Ginny by Emma Rios and Jordie Bellaire, © 2013 by Milkfed Criminal Masterminds, Inc. and Emma Rios; **222:** Gwen Dylan by Mike Allred and Laura Allred, © 2010 by Monkeybrain, Inc. and Michael Allred; **224:** Kath, Raven, and Angie by Becky Cloonan, © 2015 by Ollie Masters and Ming Doyle; **225:** Keegan by Johnnie Christmas and Tamra Bonvillain, © 2016 by Johnnie Christmas; **226:** Maika Halfwolf by Sana Takeda, © 2015 Marjorie Liu and Sana Takeda; **228:** Penny Rolle by Robert Wilson IV and Chris Peter, © 2014 by Milkfed Criminal Masterminds, Inc.; **229:** Penny Rolle by **230:** Ms. Marvel by Adrian Alphona and Ian Herring, © 2014 by Marvel Comics; **232:** Blaze by Sophie Campbell and M. Victoria Robado, © 2015 by IDW Publishing; **238:** Martha Washington by Dave Gibbons and Robin Smith, © 1990 by Frank Miller and Dave Gibbons; **240:** Starfire by Ernie Chan and Vince Colletta, © 1976 by DC Comics; Dragonella and St. George by Wally Wood, © 1969 by Wally Wood;

ACKNOWLEDGMENTS

The author wishes to thank Steve Manale, Roberta Gregory, Spike Trotman, Trina Robbins, Mariko Tamaki, Jacque Nodell, Calum Johnston, Ryan North, Dani Vulnavia, Molly Jane Kremer, John K Snyder III, Shaenon Garrity, Dave Karlen, Rico Renzi, Sista To Funky, Shary Flenniken, Diana Tamblyn, Colleen Doran, Amy Ziegfeld, Comicchron & John Jackson Miller, Brian Cronin, Irene Vartanoff, T Campbell, Gisèle Lagacé, Katie Schenkel, Tim Hanley, Maggie Thompson, Neil Mechem, Ivan Salazar, Megan Kearney, Will Murray, all the editors at Grand Comics Database (comics.org), Tini Howard, Maritza Campos, and all other comics fans and researchers who've enthusiastically helped her on this journey.